ZOMBIE TALES

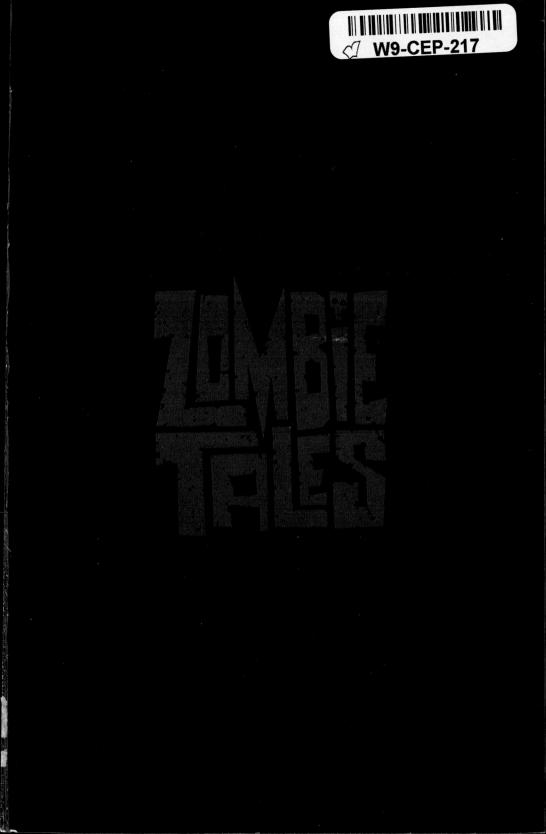

ROSS RICHIE & ANDREW COSBY - FOUNDERS
ADAM FORTIER - VP NEW BUSINESS
MARSHALL DILLON - MANAGING EDITOR
ED DUKESHIRE - ART DIRECTOR
CODY DEMATTEIS - PUBLISHING COORDINATOR
ORIGINAL EDITOR for ZOMBIE TALES: THE DEAD - MARSHALL DILLON
ASSEMBLED BY JOYCE EL HAYEK AND MARSHALL DILLON

ZOMBIE TALES   vol I   June 2007
Published by BOOM! Studios.

Zombie Tales

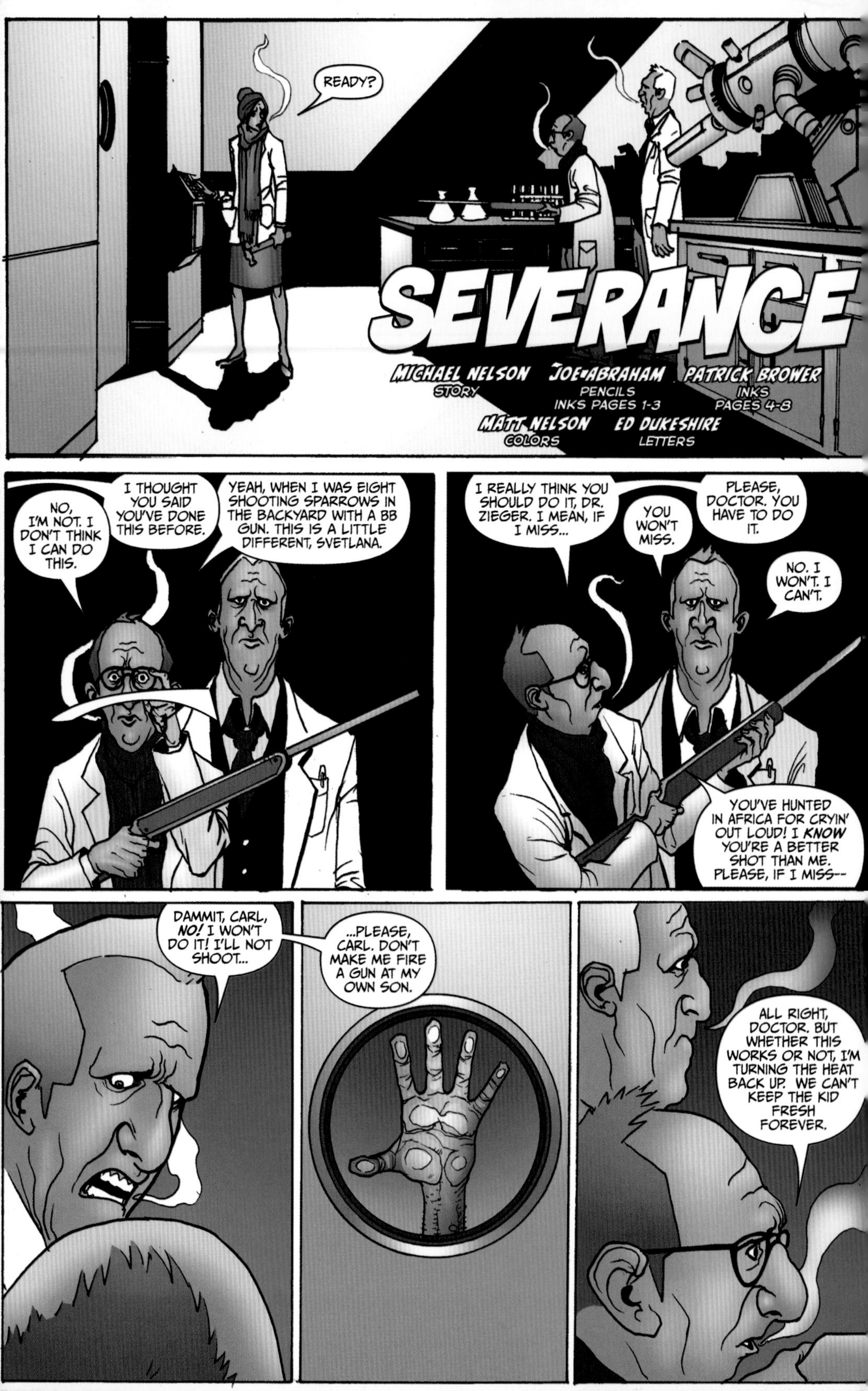
READY?
SEVERANCE
MICHAEL NELSON STORY
JOE ABRAHAM PENCILS INKS PAGES 1-3
PATRICK BROWER INKS PAGES 4-8
MATT NELSON COLORS
ED DUKESHIRE LETTERS
I THOUGHT YOU SAID YOU'VE DONE THIS BEFORE.
NO, I'M NOT. I DON'T THINK I CAN DO THIS.
YEAH, WHEN I WAS EIGHT SHOOTING SPARROWS IN THE BACKYARD WITH A BB GUN. THIS IS A LITTLE DIFFERENT, SVETLANA.
I REALLY THINK YOU SHOULD DO IT, DR. ZIEGER. I MEAN, IF I MISS...
PLEASE, DOCTOR. YOU HAVE TO DO IT.
YOU WON'T MISS.
NO. I WON'T. I CAN'T.
YOU'VE HUNTED IN AFRICA FOR CRYIN' OUT LOUD! I KNOW YOU'RE A BETTER SHOT THAN ME. PLEASE, IF I MISS--
DAMMIT, CARL, NO! I WON'T DO IT! I'LL NOT SHOOT...
...PLEASE, CARL. DON'T MAKE ME FIRE A GUN AT MY OWN SON.
ALL RIGHT, DOCTOR. BUT WHETHER THIS WORKS OR NOT, I'M TURNING THE HEAT BACK UP. WE CAN'T KEEP THE KID FRESH FOREVER.

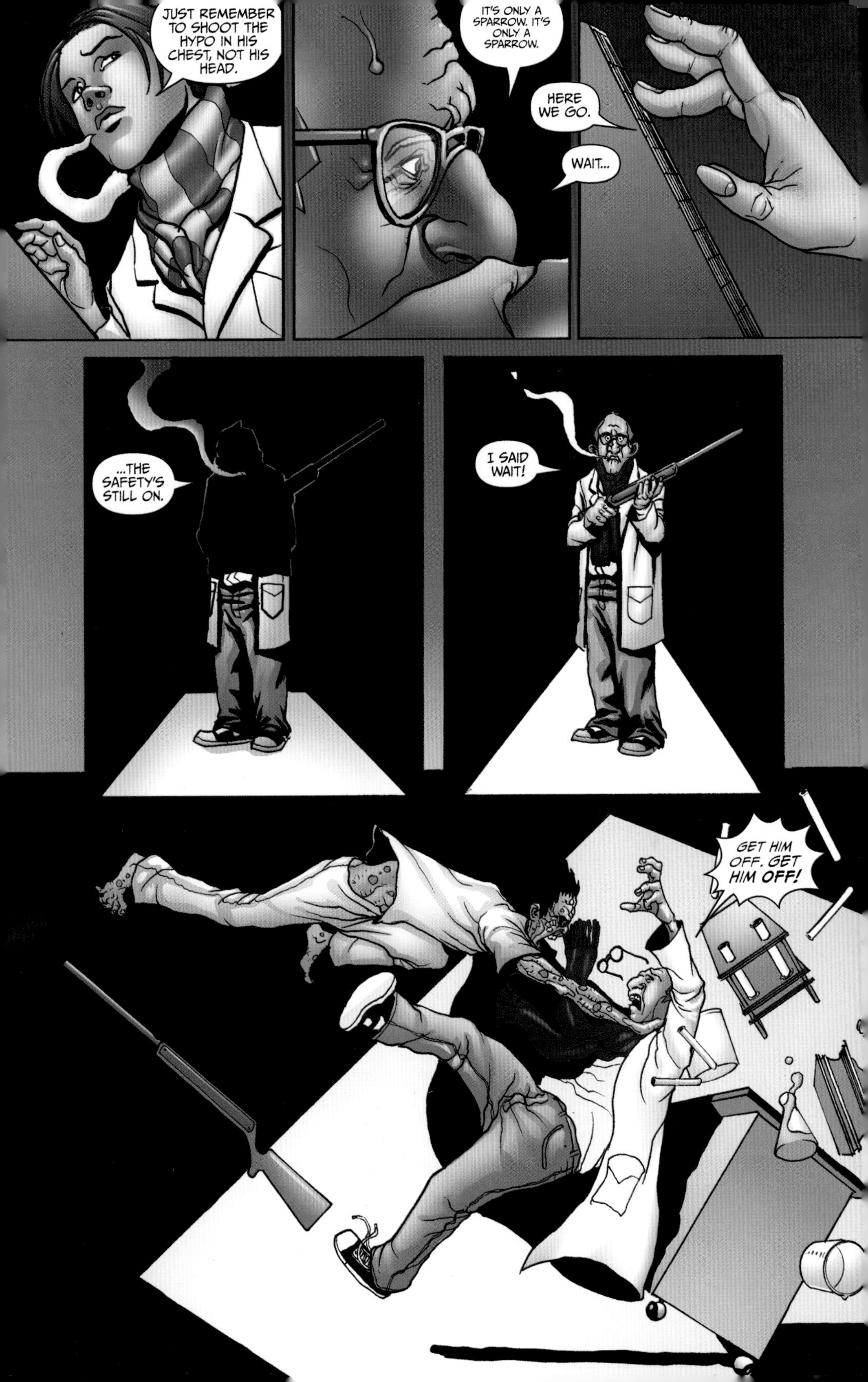
JUST REMEMBER TO SHOOT THE HYPO IN HIS CHEST, NOT HIS HEAD.
IT'S ONLY A SPARROW. IT'S ONLY A SPARROW.
HERE WE GO.
WAIT...
...THE SAFETY'S STILL ON.
I SAID WAIT!
GET HIM OFF. GET HIM OFF!

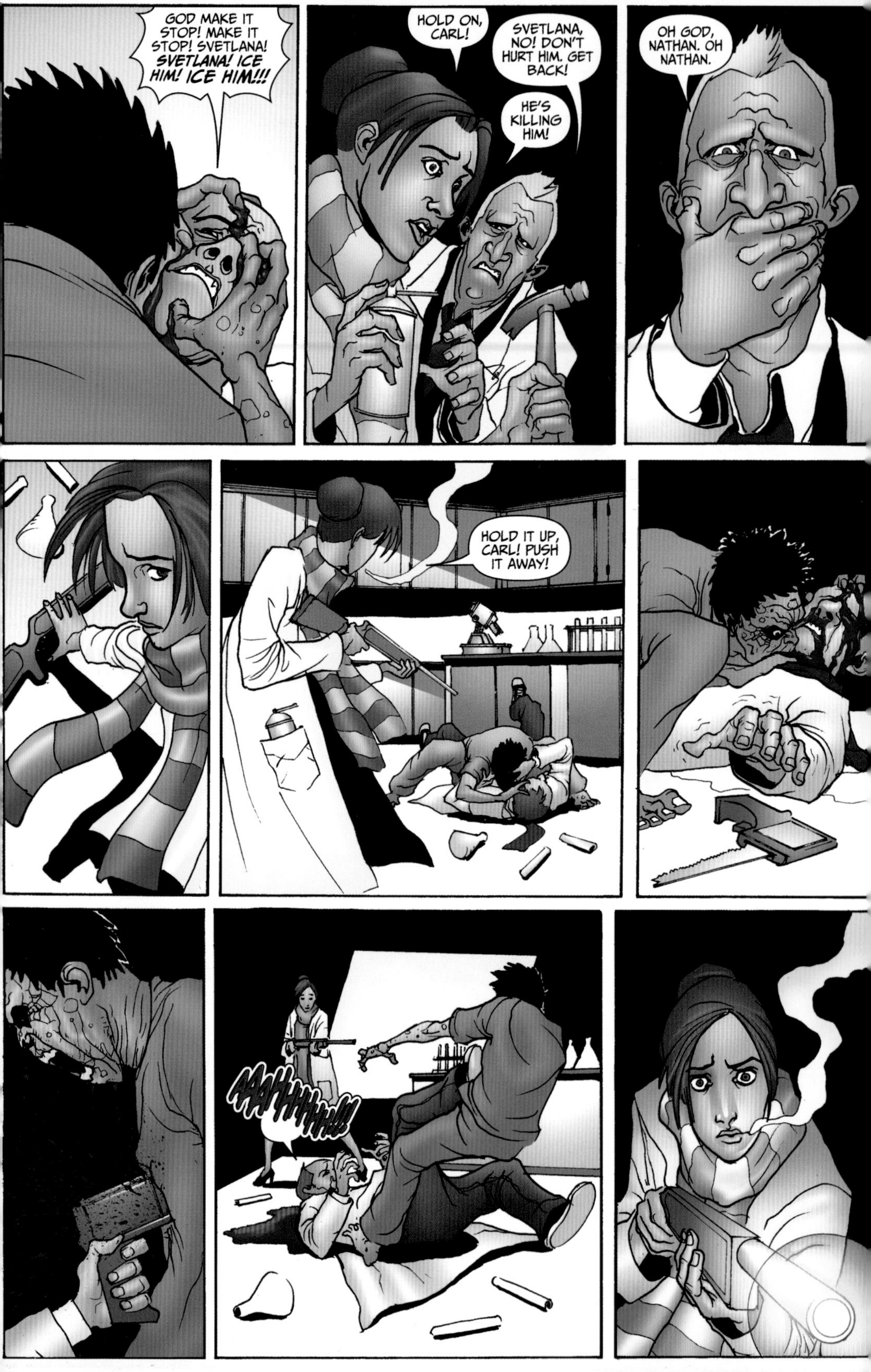
GOD MAKE IT STOP! MAKE IT STOP! SVETLANA! SVETLANA! ICE HIM! ICE HIM!!!
HOLD ON, CARL!
SVETLANA, NO! DON'T HURT HIM. GET BACK!
HE'S KILLING HIM!
OH GOD, NATHAN. OH NATHAN.
HOLD IT UP, CARL! PUSH IT AWAY!
AAAHHHHHH!!!

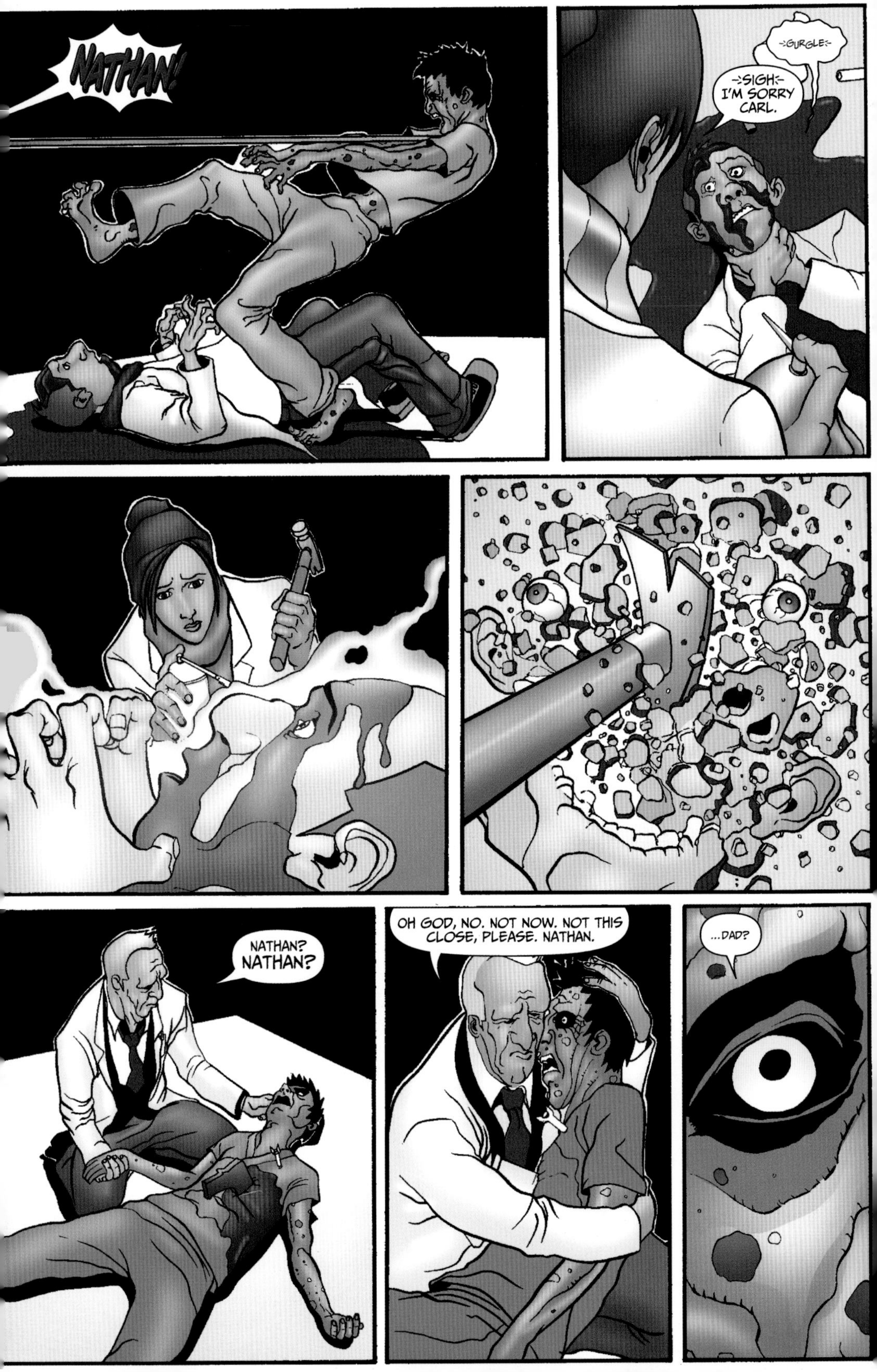
NATHAN!
-GURGLE-
-SIGH- I'M SORRY CARL.
NATHAN? NATHAN?
OH GOD, NO. NOT NOW. NOT THIS CLOSE, PLEASE. NATHAN.
...DAD?

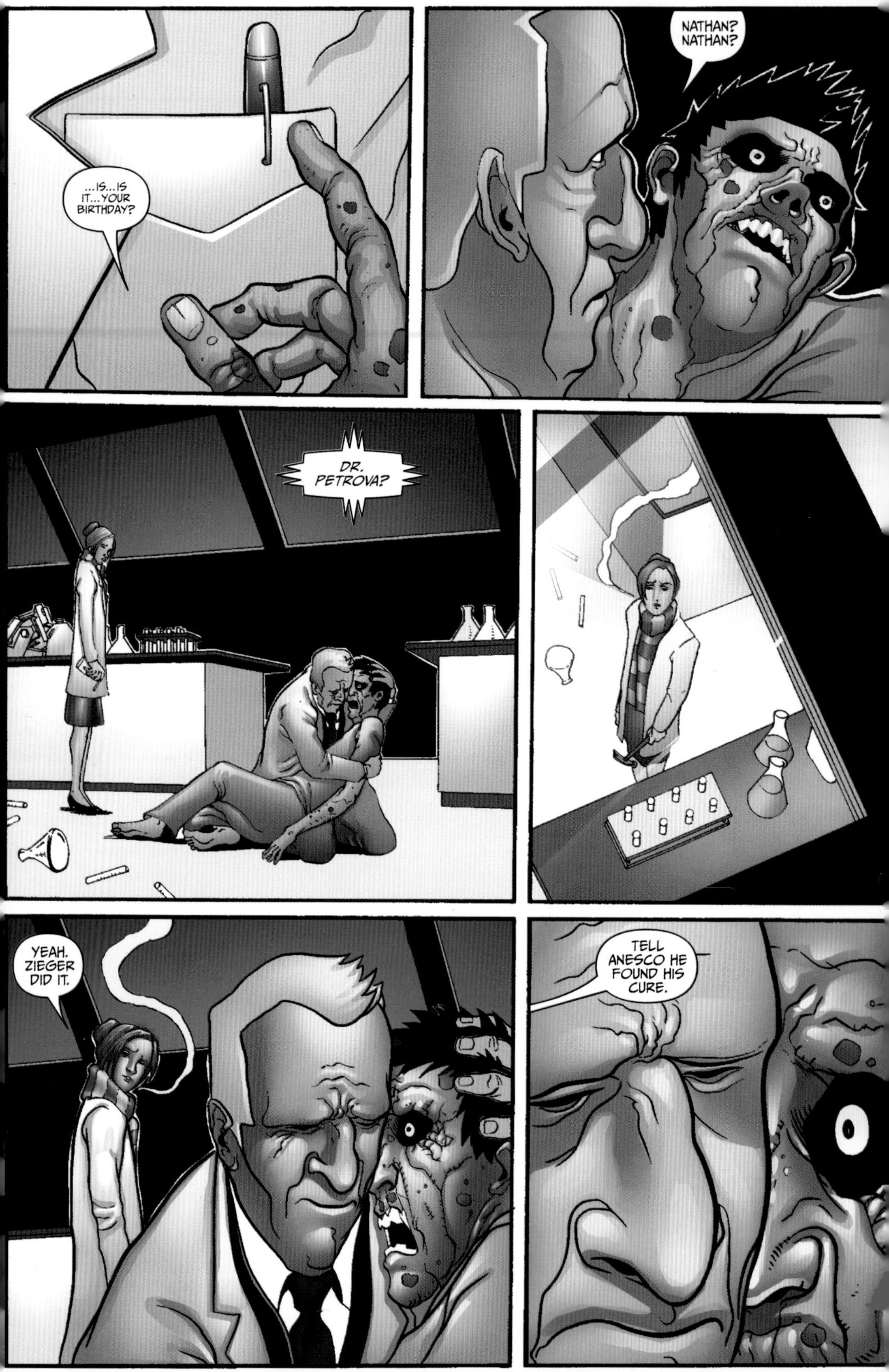
...IS...IS IT...YOUR BIRTHDAY?
NATHAN? NATHAN?
DR. PETROVA?
YEAH. ZIEGER DID IT.
TELL ANESCO HE FOUND HIS CURE.

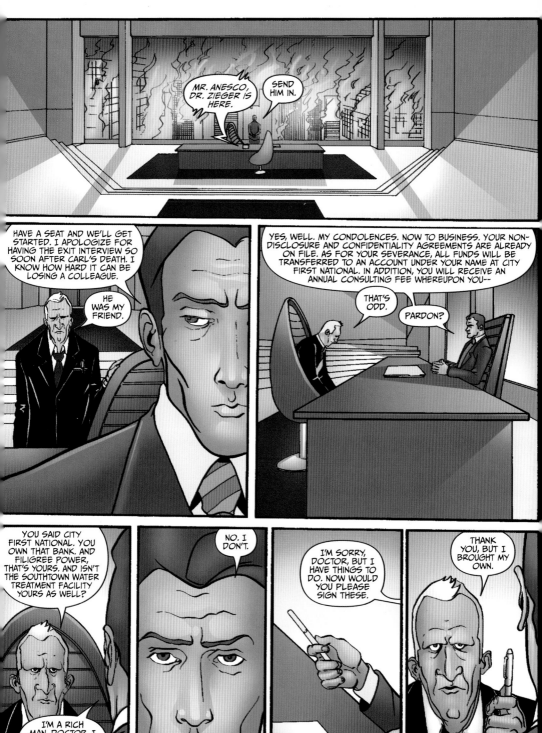

MR. ANESCO, DR. ZIEGER IS HERE.

SEND HIM IN.

HAVE A SEAT AND WE'LL GET STARTED. I APOLOGIZE FOR HAVING THE EXIT INTERVIEW SO SOON AFTER CARL'S DEATH. I KNOW HOW HARD IT CAN BE LOSING A COLLEAGUE.

HE WAS MY FRIEND.

YES, WELL. MY CONDOLENCES. NOW TO BUSINESS. YOUR NON-DISCLOSURE AND CONFIDENTIALITY AGREEMENTS ARE ALREADY ON FILE. AS FOR YOUR SEVERANCE, ALL FUNDS WILL BE TRANSFERRED TO AN ACCOUNT UNDER YOUR NAME AT CITY FIRST NATIONAL. IN ADDITION, YOU WILL RECEIVE AN ANNUAL CONSULTING FEE WHEREUPON YOU--

THAT'S ODD.

PARDON?

YOU SAID CITY FIRST NATIONAL. YOU OWN THAT BANK. AND FILIGREE POWER, THAT'S YOURS. AND ISN'T THE SOUTHTOWN WATER TREATMENT FACILITY YOURS AS WELL?

I'M A RICH MAN, DOCTOR. I OWN BUSINESSES ALL OVER THE CITY. WHAT'S YOUR POINT?

JUST THAT THE CITY IS BURNING DOWN AROUND US AND THE ONLY FUNCTIONING REMNANTS OF CIVILIZATION HAPPEN TO BELONG TO YOU. RATHER ODD, DON'T YOU THINK?

NO. I DON'T.

I'M SORRY, DOCTOR, BUT I HAVE THINGS TO DO. NOW WOULD YOU PLEASE SIGN THESE.

THANK YOU, BUT I BROUGHT MY OWN.

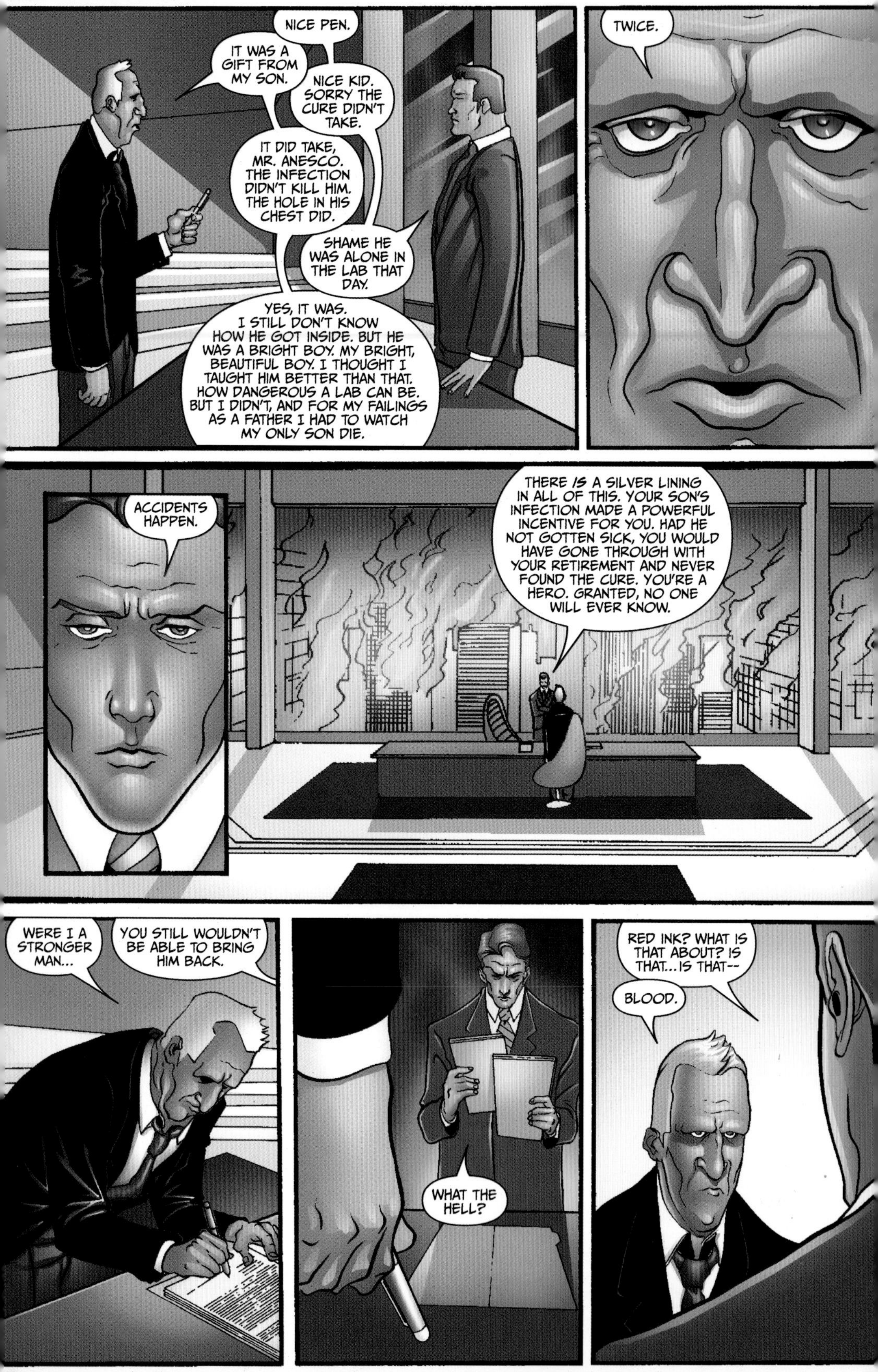
NICE PEN.
IT WAS A GIFT FROM MY SON.
NICE KID. SORRY THE CURE DIDN'T TAKE.
IT DID TAKE, MR. ANESCO. THE INFECTION DIDN'T KILL HIM. THE HOLE IN HIS CHEST DID.
SHAME HE WAS ALONE IN THE LAB THAT DAY.
YES, IT WAS. I STILL DON'T KNOW HOW HE GOT INSIDE. BUT HE WAS A BRIGHT BOY. MY BRIGHT, BEAUTIFUL BOY. I THOUGHT I TAUGHT HIM BETTER THAN THAT. HOW DANGEROUS A LAB CAN BE. BUT I DIDN'T, AND FOR MY FAILINGS AS A FATHER I HAD TO WATCH MY ONLY SON DIE.
TWICE.
ACCIDENTS HAPPEN.
THERE *IS* A SILVER LINING IN ALL OF THIS. YOUR SON'S INFECTION MADE A POWERFUL INCENTIVE FOR YOU. HAD HE NOT GOTTEN SICK, YOU WOULD HAVE GONE THROUGH WITH YOUR RETIREMENT AND NEVER FOUND THE CURE. YOU'RE A HERO. GRANTED, NO ONE WILL EVER KNOW.
WERE I A STRONGER MAN...
YOU STILL WOULDN'T BE ABLE TO BRING HIM BACK.
WHAT THE HELL?
RED INK? WHAT IS THAT ABOUT? IS THAT... IS THAT--
BLOOD.

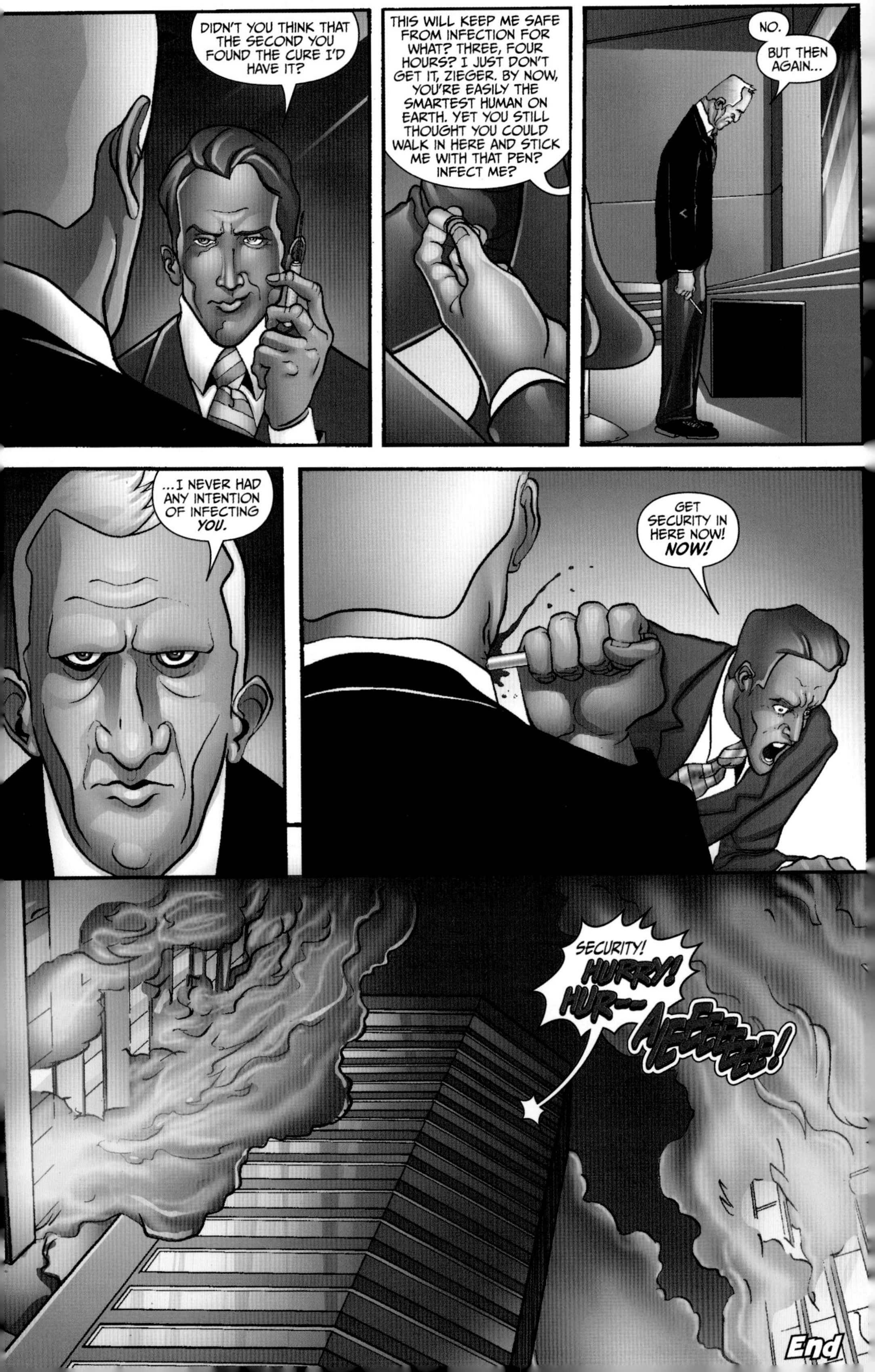
DIDN'T YOU THINK THAT THE SECOND YOU FOUND THE CURE I'D HAVE IT?
THIS WILL KEEP ME SAFE FROM INFECTION FOR WHAT? THREE, FOUR HOURS? I JUST DON'T GET IT, ZIEGER. BY NOW, YOU'RE EASILY THE SMARTEST HUMAN ON EARTH. YET YOU STILL THOUGHT YOU COULD WALK IN HERE AND STICK ME WITH THAT PEN? INFECT ME?
NO.
BUT THEN AGAIN...
...I NEVER HAD ANY INTENTION OF INFECTING *YOU.*
GET SECURITY IN HERE NOW! ***NOW!***
SECURITY! HURRY! HUR--
AIEEEEEEEE!
End

DADDY SMELLS DIFFERENT

MY NAME IS ZACH! I'M THIS MANY!
STORY: JOHN ROGERS
ART: ANDY KUHN

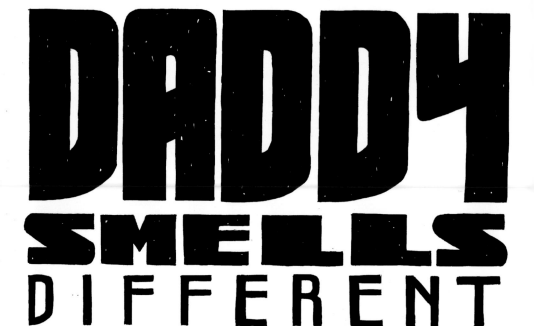

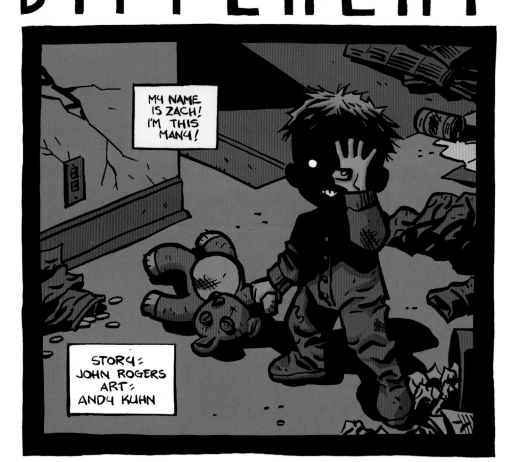

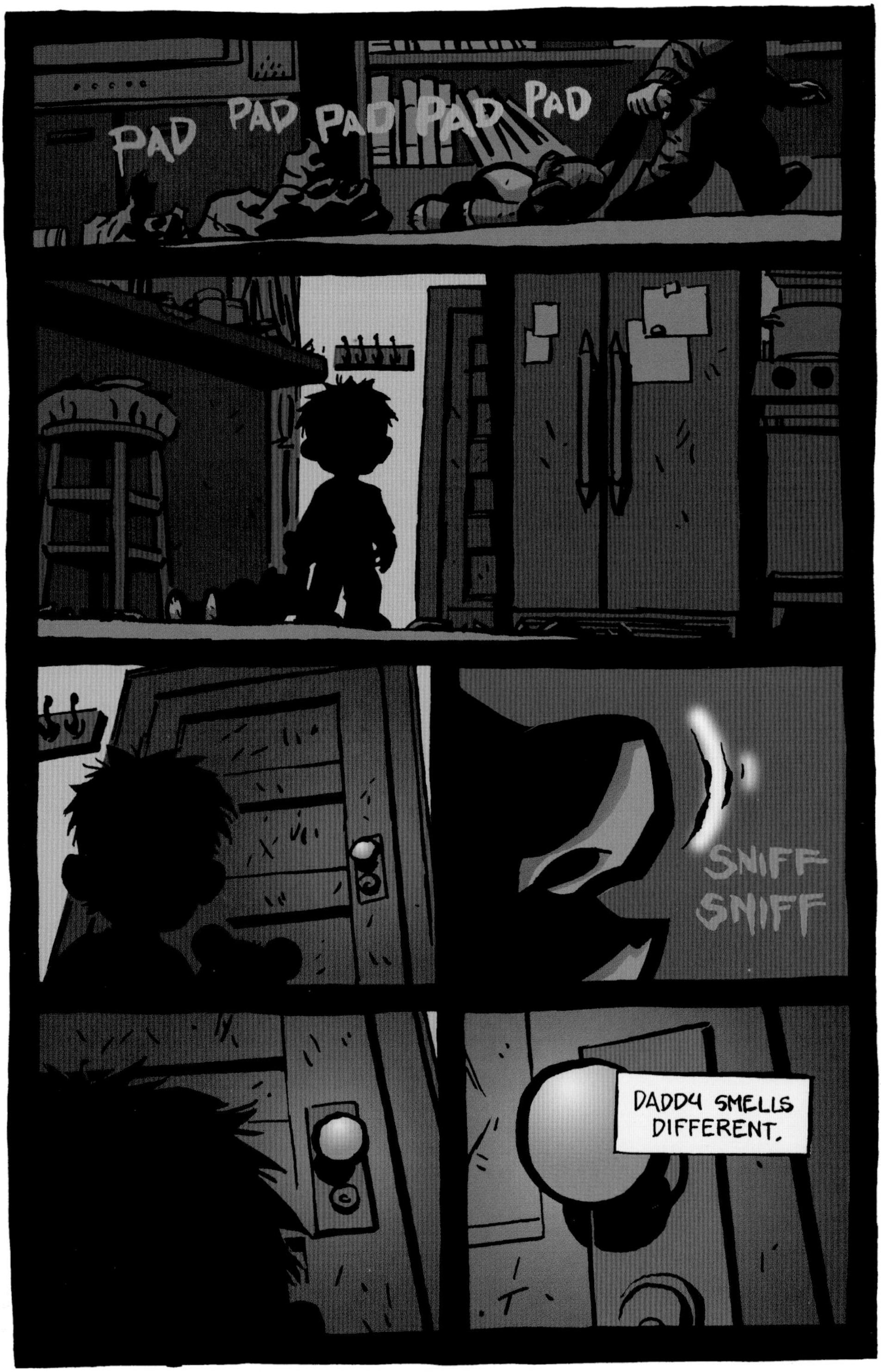
PAD PAD PAD PAD PAD
SNIFF SNIFF
DADDY SMELLS DIFFERENT.

BEFORE

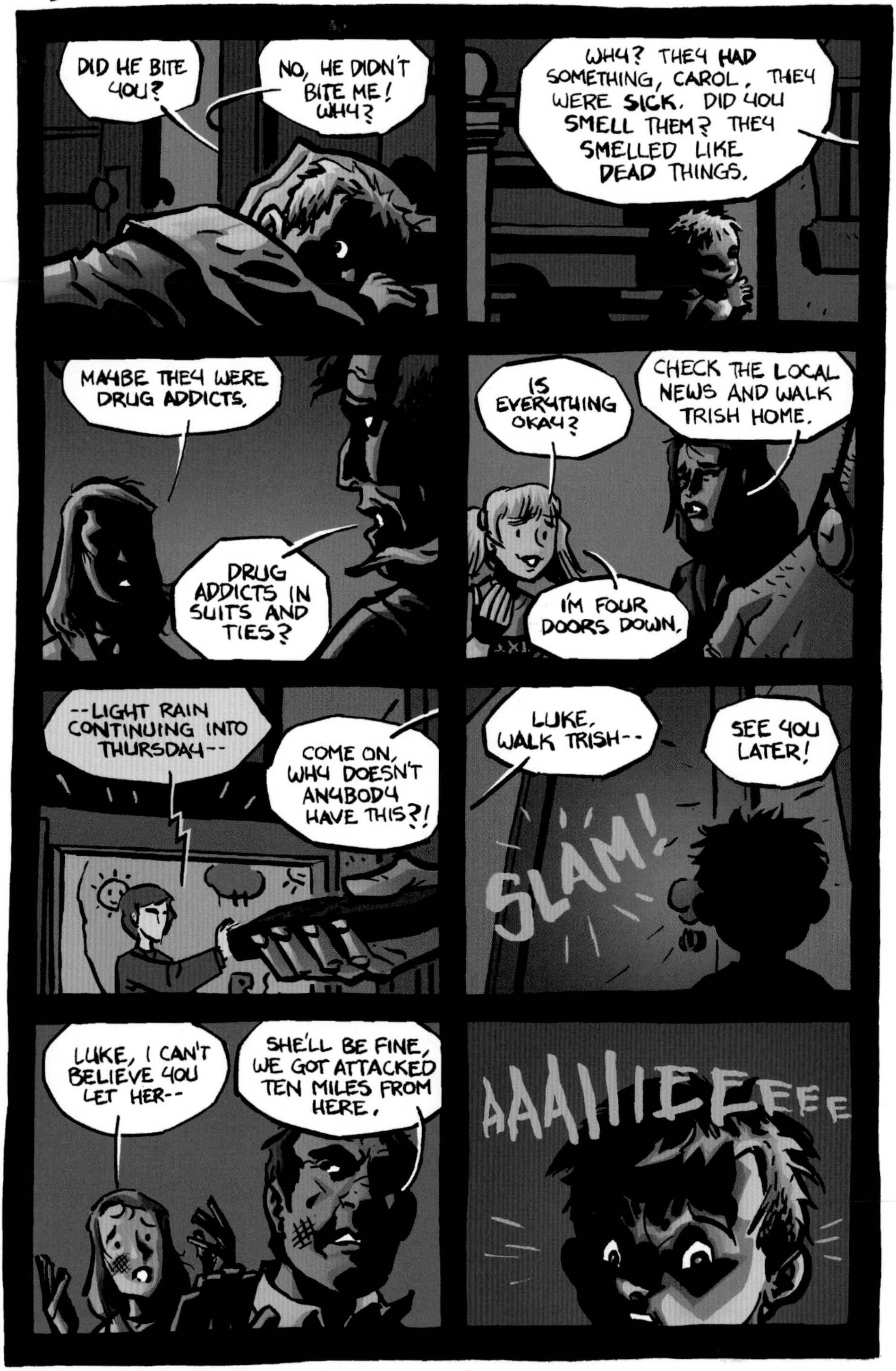
DID HE BITE YOU?
NO, HE DIDN'T BITE ME! WHY?
WHY? THEY HAD SOMETHING, CAROL, THEY WERE SICK. DID YOU SMELL THEM? THEY SMELLED LIKE DEAD THINGS.
MAYBE THEY WERE DRUG ADDICTS.
DRUG ADDICTS IN SUITS AND TIES?
IS EVERYTHING OKAY?
CHECK THE LOCAL NEWS AND WALK TRISH HOME.
I'M FOUR DOORS DOWN.
--LIGHT RAIN CONTINUING INTO THURSDAY--
COME ON, WHY DOESN'T ANYBODY HAVE THIS?!
LUKE, WALK TRISH--
SEE YOU LATER!
SLAM!
LUKE, I CAN'T BELIEVE YOU LET HER--
SHE'LL BE FINE, WE GOT ATTACKED TEN MILES FROM HERE.
AAAIIIEEEEEE

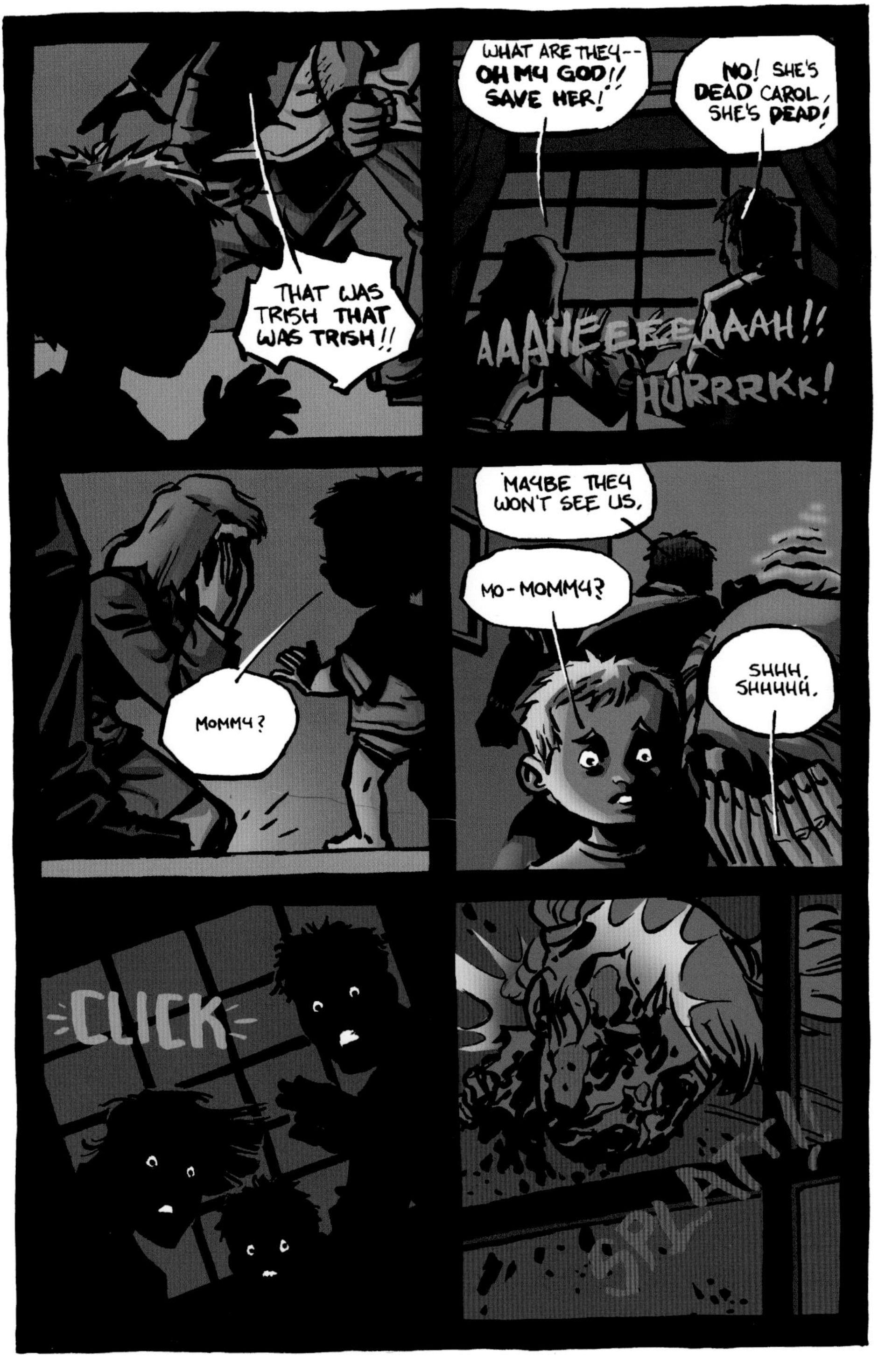
THAT WAS TRISH THAT WAS TRISH!!
WHAT ARE THEY-- OH MY GOD!! SAVE HER!
NO! SHE'S DEAD CAROL, SHE'S DEAD!
AAAHEEEEAAAH!!
HURRRKK!
MOMMY?
MAYBE THEY WON'T SEE US.
MO-MOMMY?
SHHH, SHHHHH.
CLICK

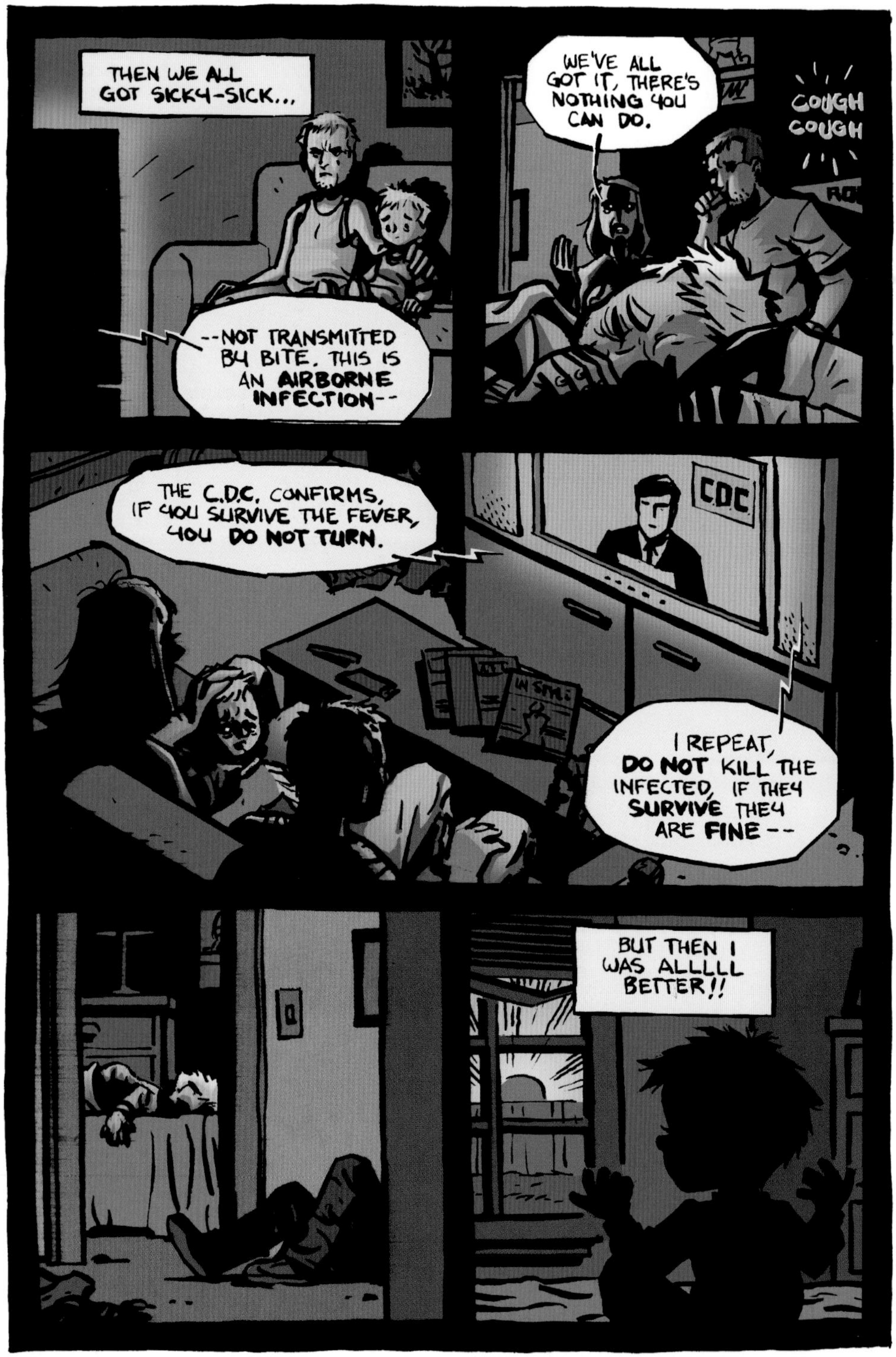
THEN WE ALL GOT SICKY-SICK...
--NOT TRANSMITTED BY BITE. THIS IS AN AIRBORNE INFECTION--
WE'VE ALL GOT IT, THERE'S NOTHING YOU CAN DO.
COUGH COUGH
THE C.D.C. CONFIRMS, IF YOU SURVIVE THE FEVER, YOU DO NOT TURN.
CDC
I REPEAT, DO NOT KILL THE INFECTED, IF THEY SURVIVE THEY ARE FINE--
BUT THEN I WAS ALLLLL BETTER!!

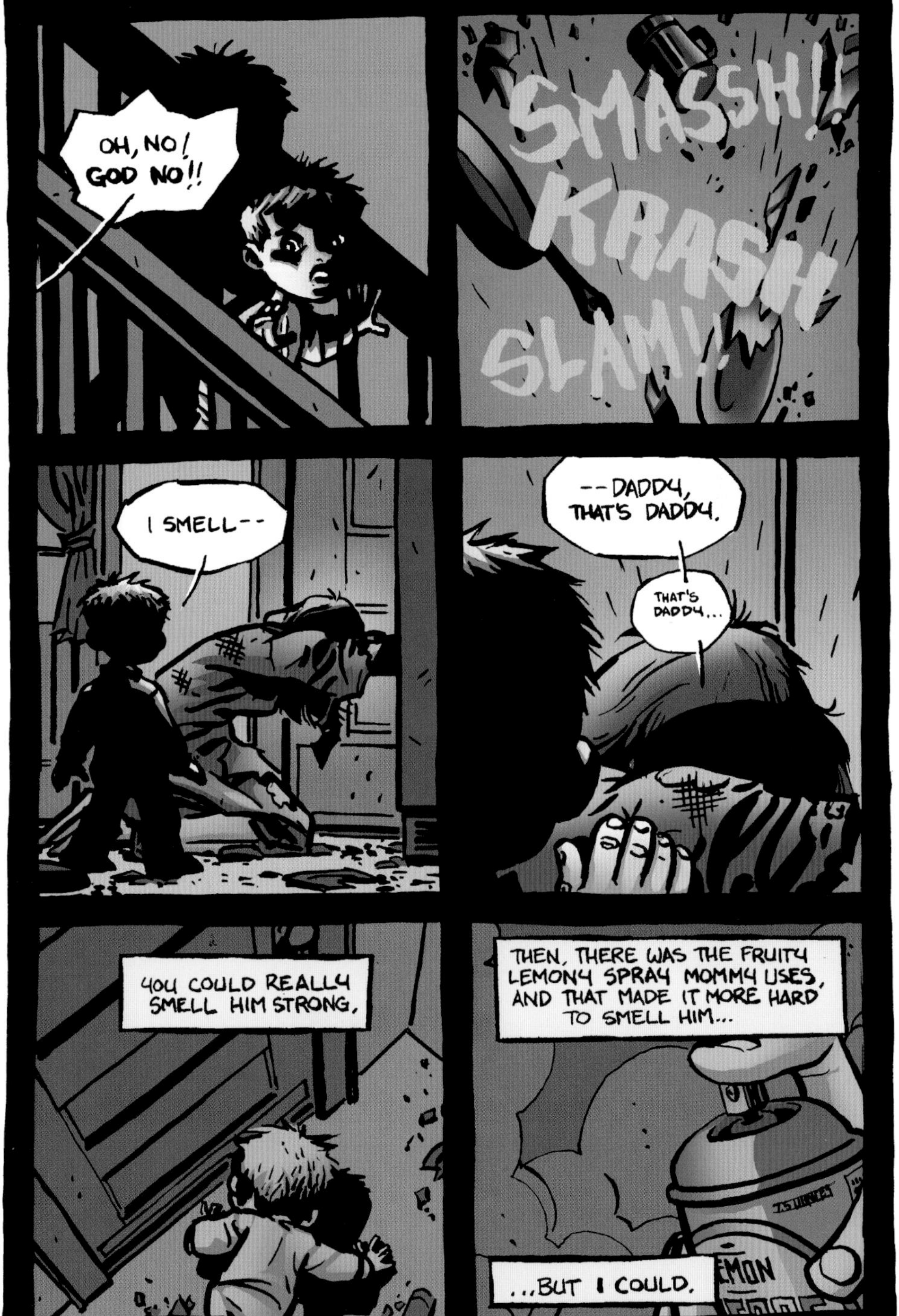
OH, NO! GOD NO!!
SMASSH!!
KRASH
SLAM!!
I SMELL--
--DADDY, THAT'S DADDY.
THAT'S DADDY...
YOU COULD REALLY SMELL HIM STRONG.
THEN, THERE WAS THE FRUITY LEMONY SPRAY MOMMY USES, AND THAT MADE IT MORE HARD TO SMELL HIM...
...BUT I COULD.

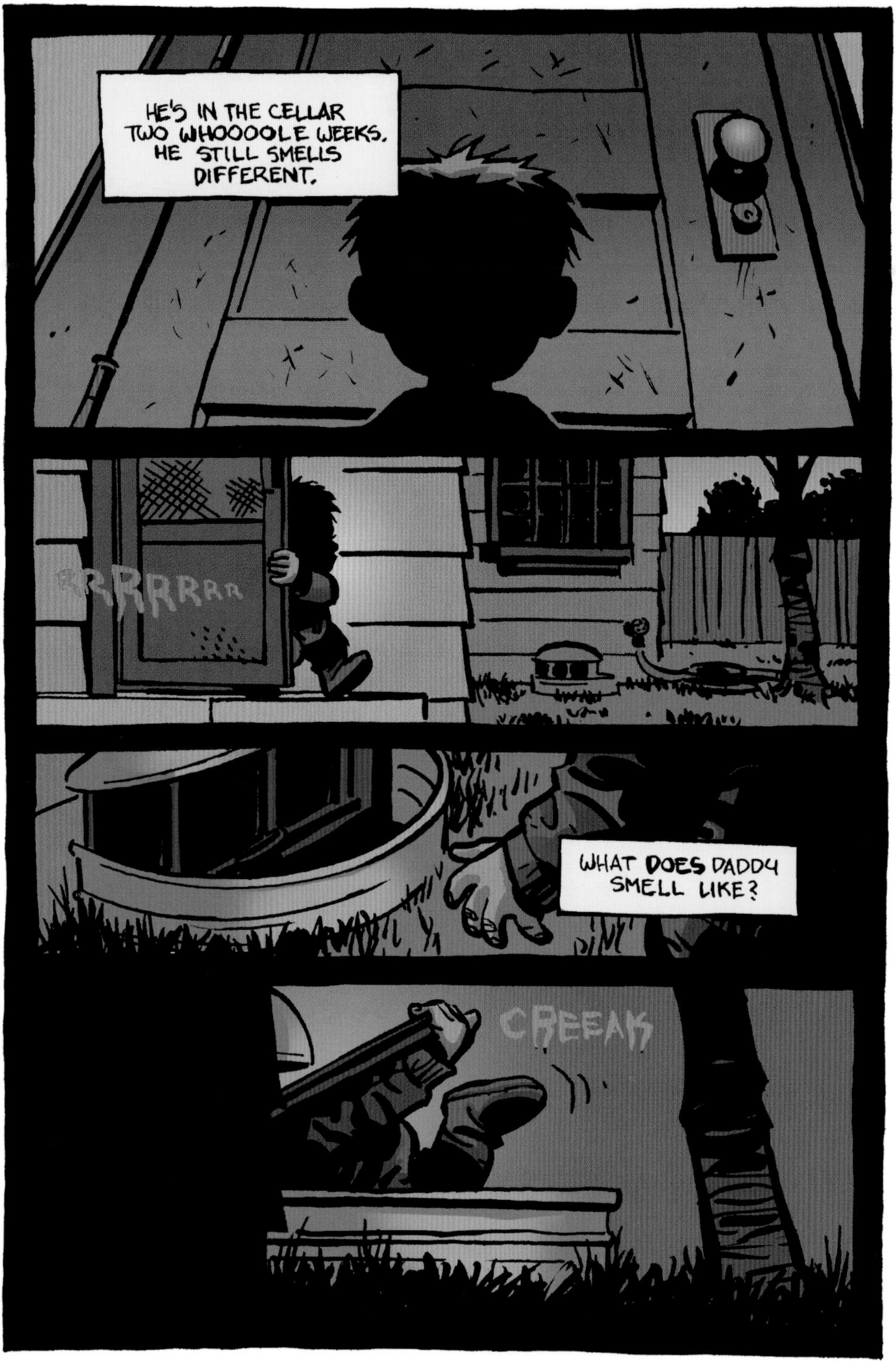
HE'S IN THE CELLAR TWO WHOOOOLE WEEKS. HE STILL SMELLS DIFFERENT.
RRRRRRRR
WHAT **DOES** DADDY SMELL LIKE?
CREEAK

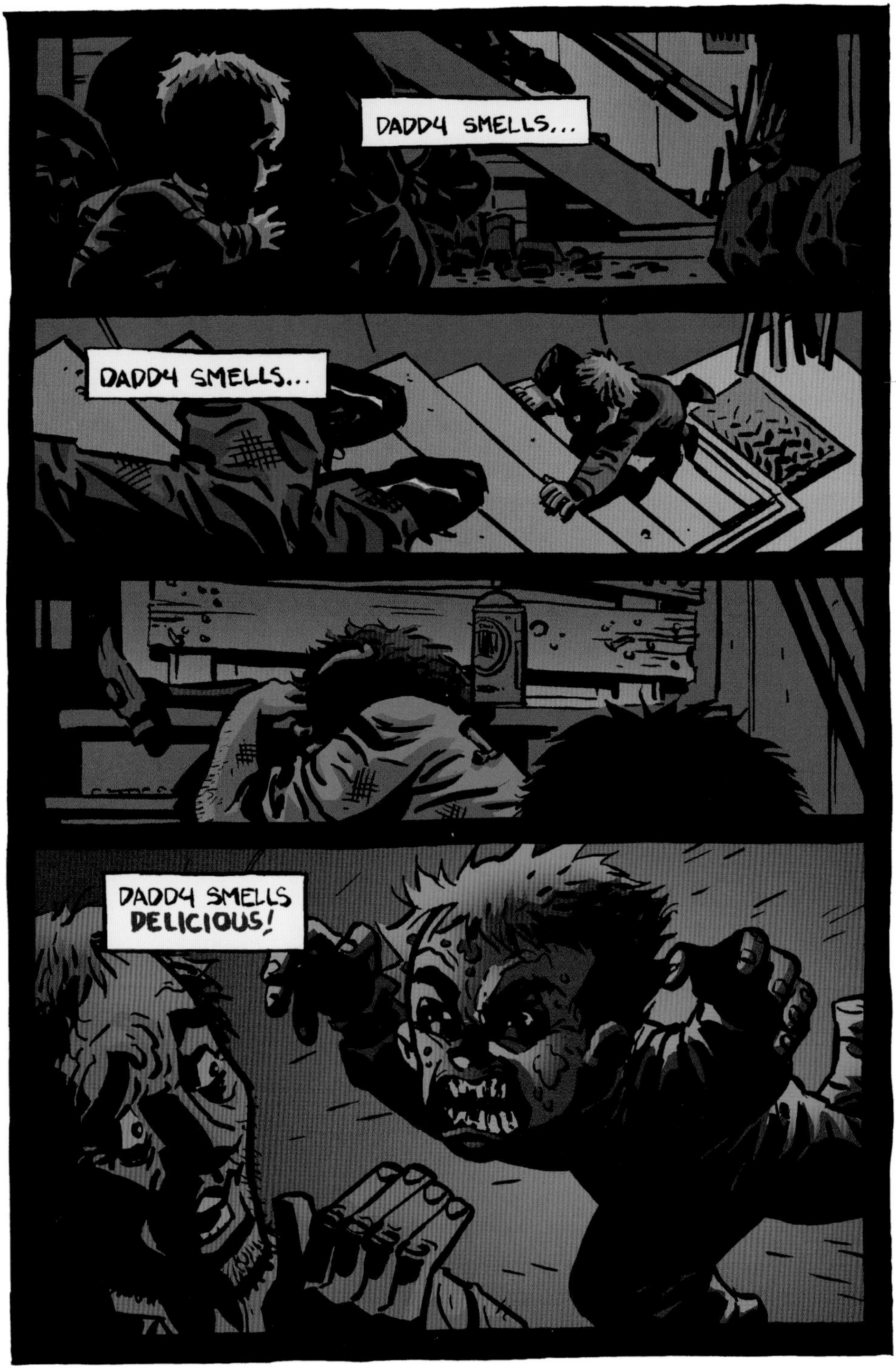
DADDY SMELLS...
DADDY SMELLS...
DADDY SMELLS DELICIOUS!

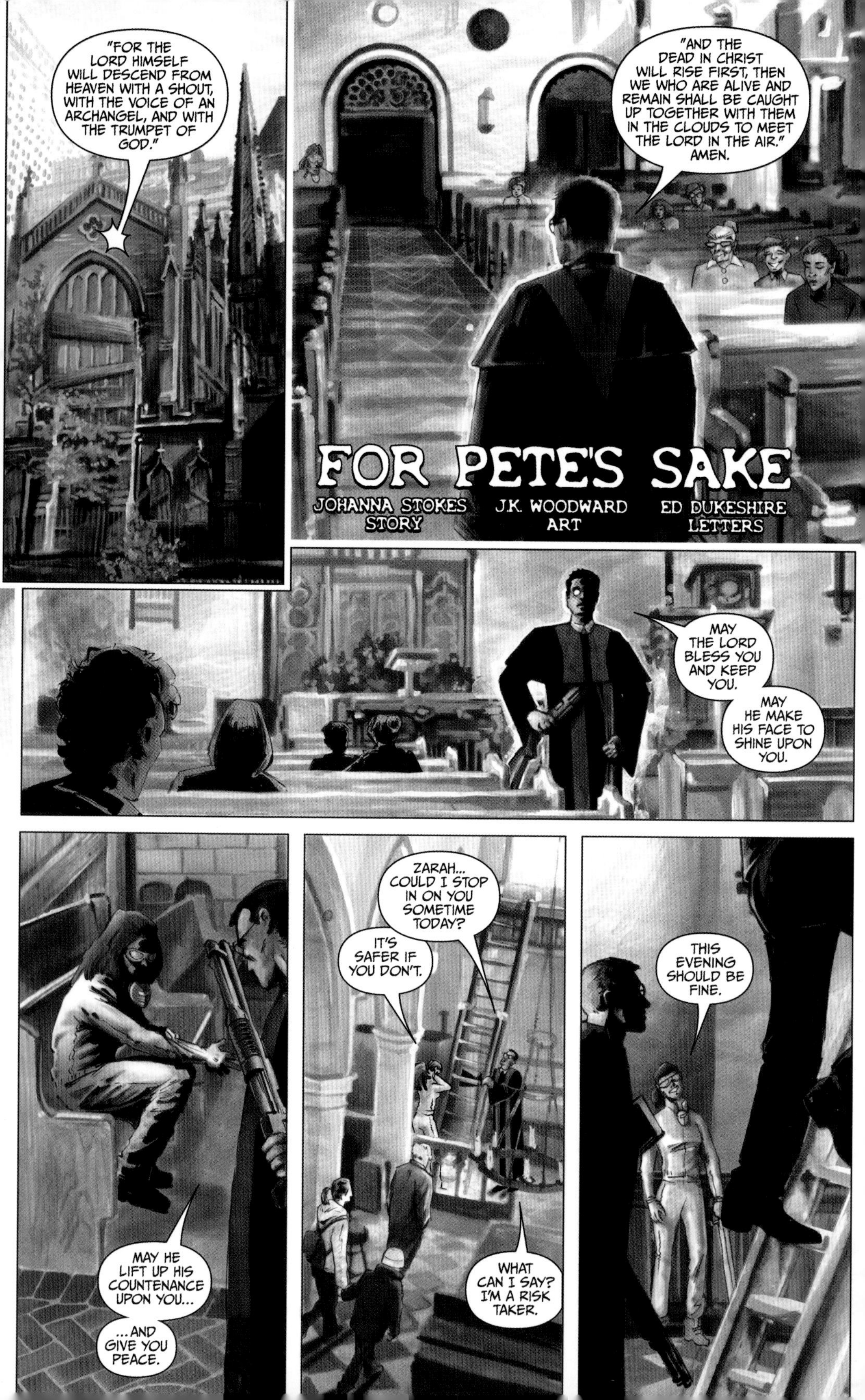
"FOR THE LORD HIMSELF WILL DESCEND FROM HEAVEN WITH A SHOUT, WITH THE VOICE OF AN ARCHANGEL, AND WITH THE TRUMPET OF GOD."
"AND THE DEAD IN CHRIST WILL RISE FIRST, THEN WE WHO ARE ALIVE AND REMAIN SHALL BE CAUGHT UP TOGETHER WITH THEM IN THE CLOUDS TO MEET THE LORD IN THE AIR." AMEN.
FOR PETE'S SAKE
JOHANNA STOKES STORY
J.K. WOODWARD ART
ED DUKESHIRE LETTERS
MAY THE LORD BLESS YOU AND KEEP YOU.
MAY HE MAKE HIS FACE TO SHINE UPON YOU.
MAY HE LIFT UP HIS COUNTENANCE UPON YOU...
...AND GIVE YOU PEACE.
ZARAH... COULD I STOP IN ON YOU SOMETIME TODAY?
IT'S SAFER IF YOU DON'T.
WHAT CAN I SAY? I'M A RISK TAKER.
THIS EVENING SHOULD BE FINE.

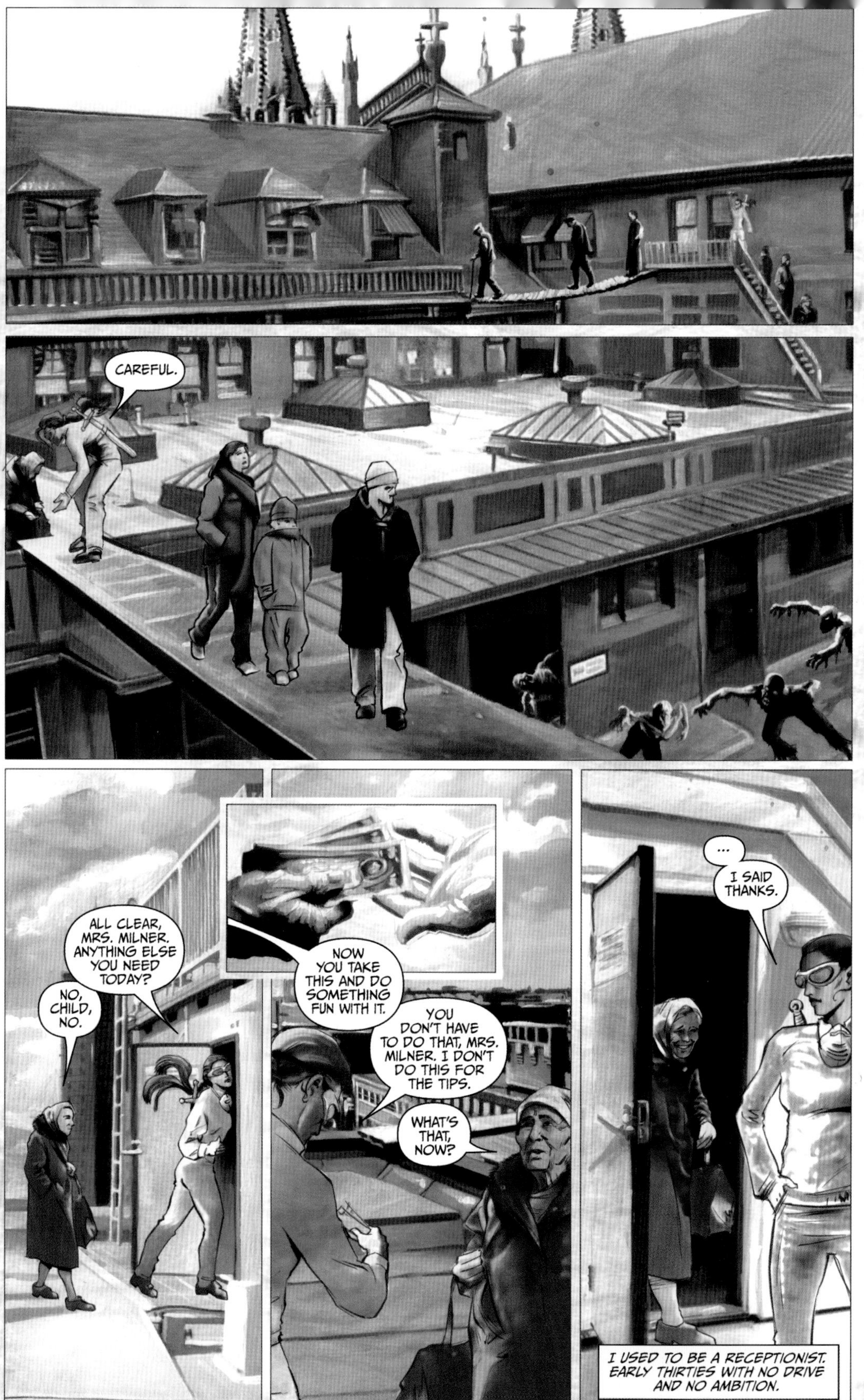
CAREFUL.
ALL CLEAR, MRS. MILNER. ANYTHING ELSE YOU NEED TODAY?
NO, CHILD, NO.
NOW YOU TAKE THIS AND DO SOMETHING FUN WITH IT.
YOU DON'T HAVE TO DO THAT, MRS. MILNER. I DON'T DO THIS FOR THE TIPS.
WHAT'S THAT, NOW?
...
I SAID THANKS.
I USED TO BE A RECEPTIONIST. EARLY THIRTIES WITH NO DRIVE AND NO AMBITION.

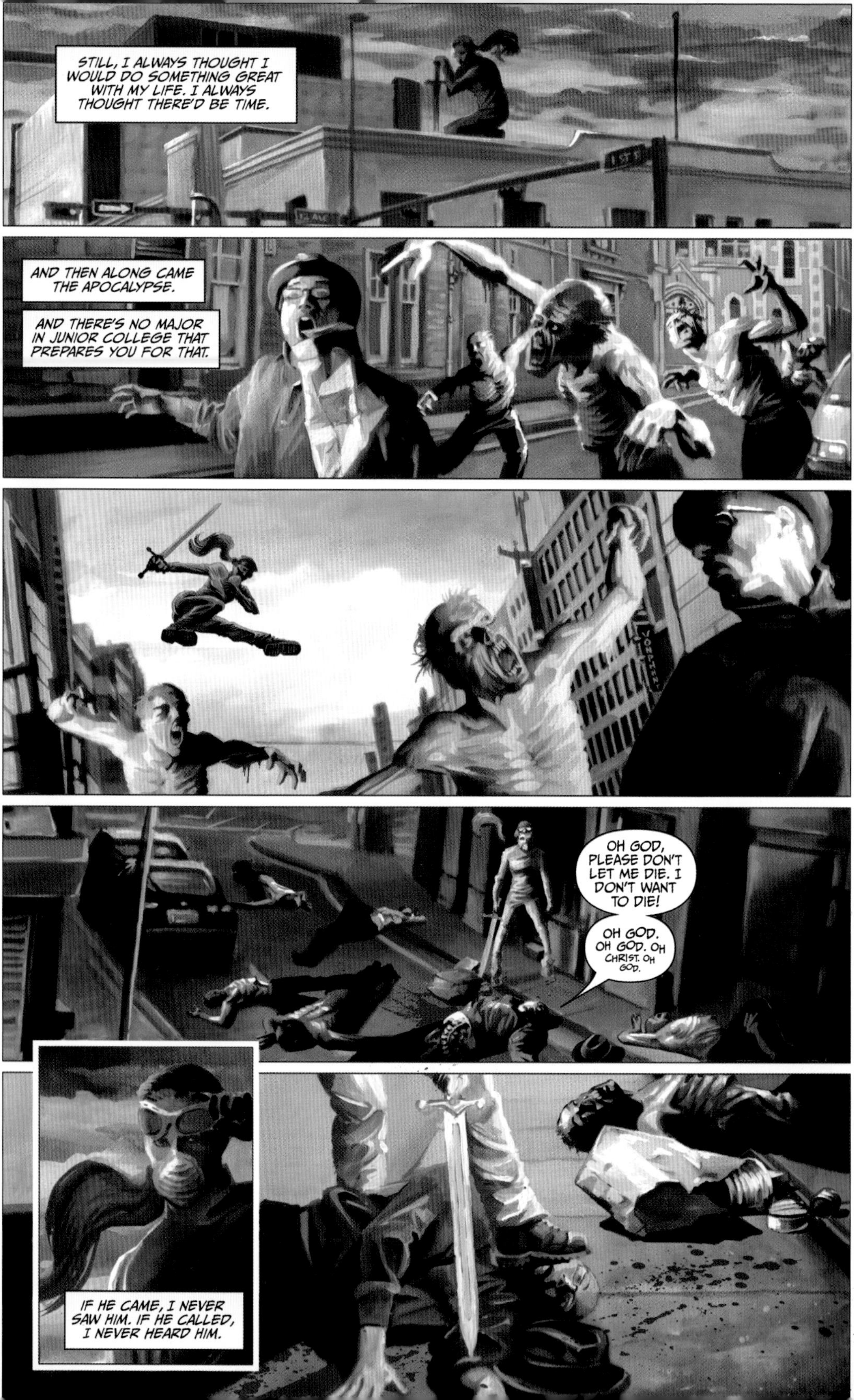
STILL, I ALWAYS THOUGHT I WOULD DO SOMETHING GREAT WITH MY LIFE. I ALWAYS THOUGHT THERE'D BE TIME.
1 ST
AND THEN ALONG CAME THE APOCALYPSE.
AND THERE'S NO MAJOR IN JUNIOR COLLEGE THAT PREPARES YOU FOR THAT.
OH GOD, PLEASE DON'T LET ME DIE. I DON'T WANT TO DIE!
OH GOD. OH GOD. OH CHRIST. OH GOD.
IF HE CAME, I NEVER SAW HIM. IF HE CALLED, I NEVER HEARD HIM.

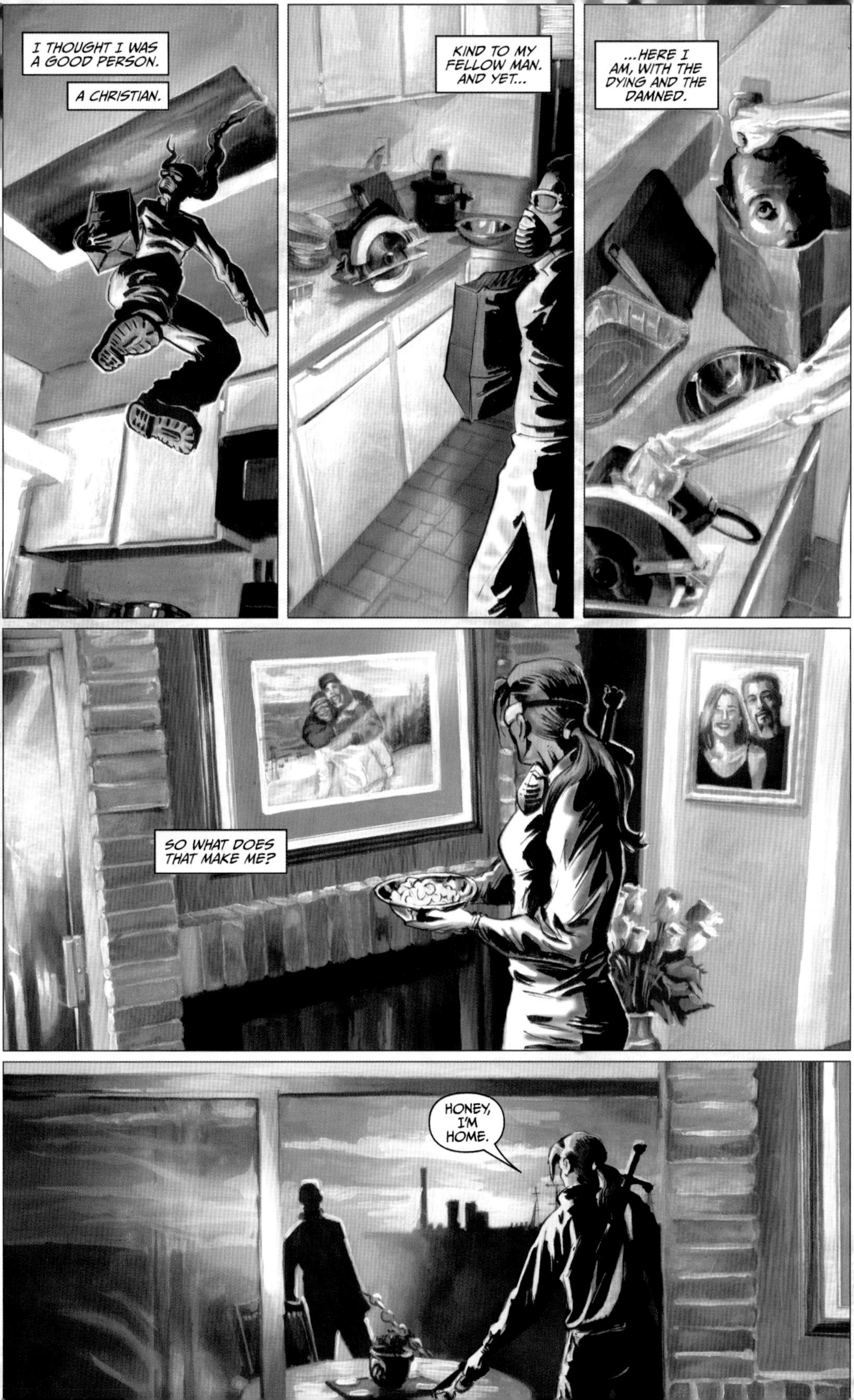
I THOUGHT I WAS A GOOD PERSON.
A CHRISTIAN.
KIND TO MY FELLOW MAN. AND YET...
...HERE I AM, WITH THE DYING AND THE DAMNED.
SO WHAT DOES THAT MAKE ME?
HONEY, I'M HOME.

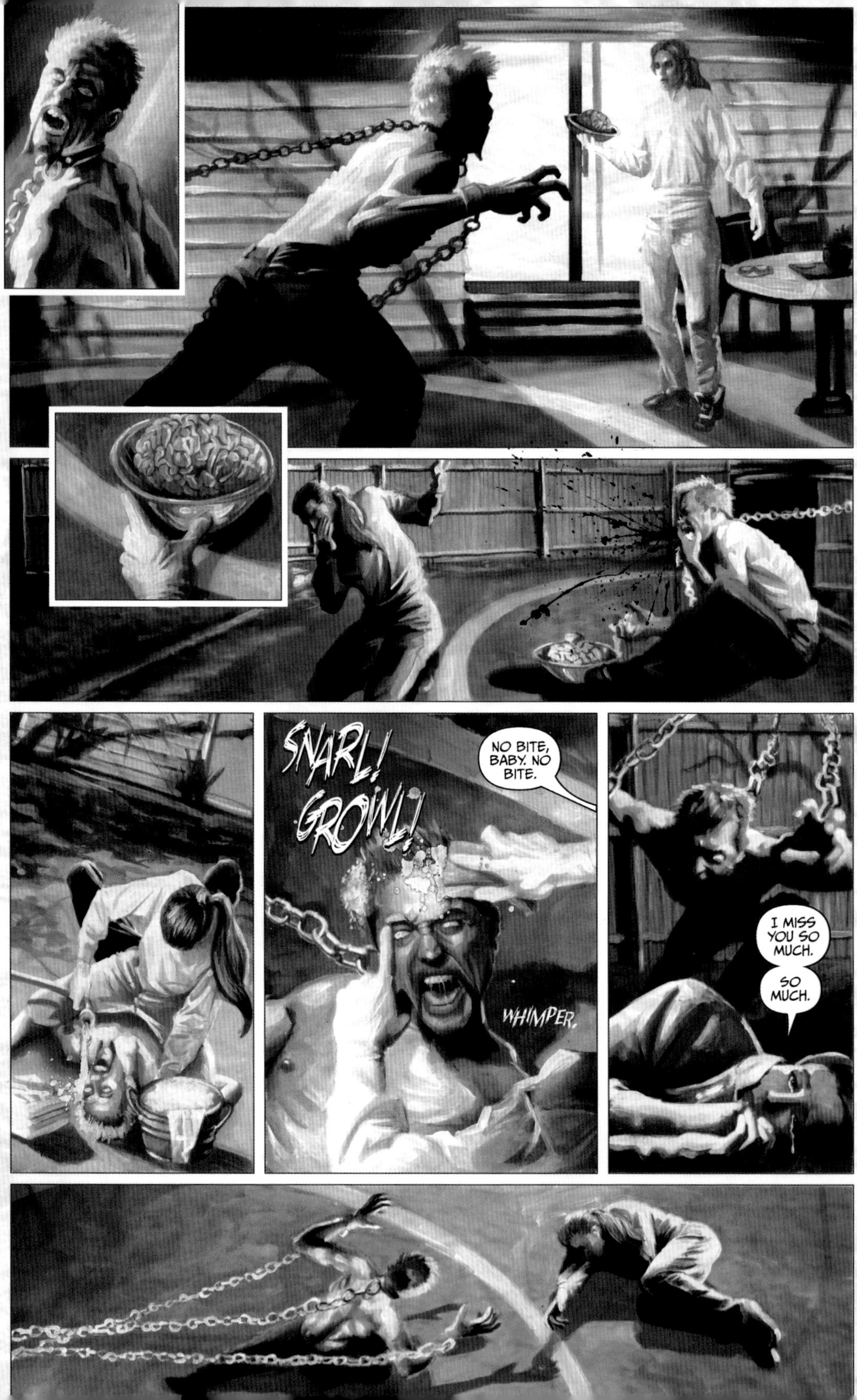
SNARL! GROWL!
NO BITE, BABY. NO BITE.
WHIMPER.
I MISS YOU SO MUCH.
SO MUCH.

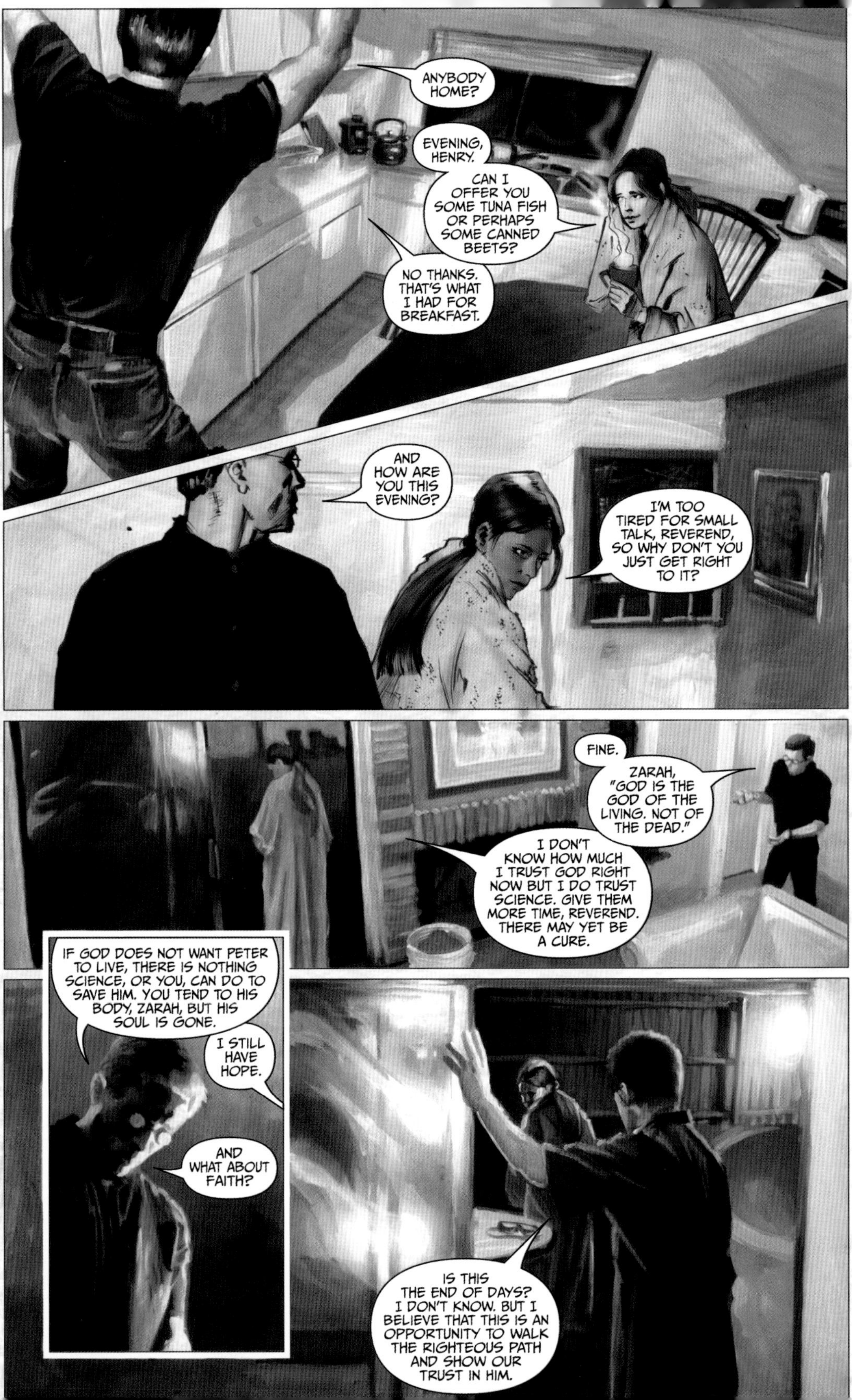
ANYBODY HOME?
EVENING, HENRY.
CAN I OFFER YOU SOME TUNA FISH OR PERHAPS SOME CANNED BEETS?
NO THANKS. THAT'S WHAT I HAD FOR BREAKFAST.
AND HOW ARE YOU THIS EVENING?
I'M TOO TIRED FOR SMALL TALK, REVEREND, SO WHY DON'T YOU JUST GET RIGHT TO IT?
FINE.
ZARAH, "GOD IS THE GOD OF THE LIVING. NOT OF THE DEAD."
I DON'T KNOW HOW MUCH I TRUST GOD RIGHT NOW BUT I DO TRUST SCIENCE. GIVE THEM MORE TIME, REVEREND. THERE MAY YET BE A CURE.
IF GOD DOES NOT WANT PETER TO LIVE, THERE IS NOTHING SCIENCE, OR YOU, CAN DO TO SAVE HIM. YOU TEND TO HIS BODY, ZARAH, BUT HIS SOUL IS GONE.
I STILL HAVE HOPE.
AND WHAT ABOUT FAITH?
IS THIS THE END OF DAYS? I DON'T KNOW. BUT I BELIEVE THAT THIS IS AN OPPORTUNITY TO WALK THE RIGHTEOUS PATH AND SHOW OUR TRUST IN HIM.

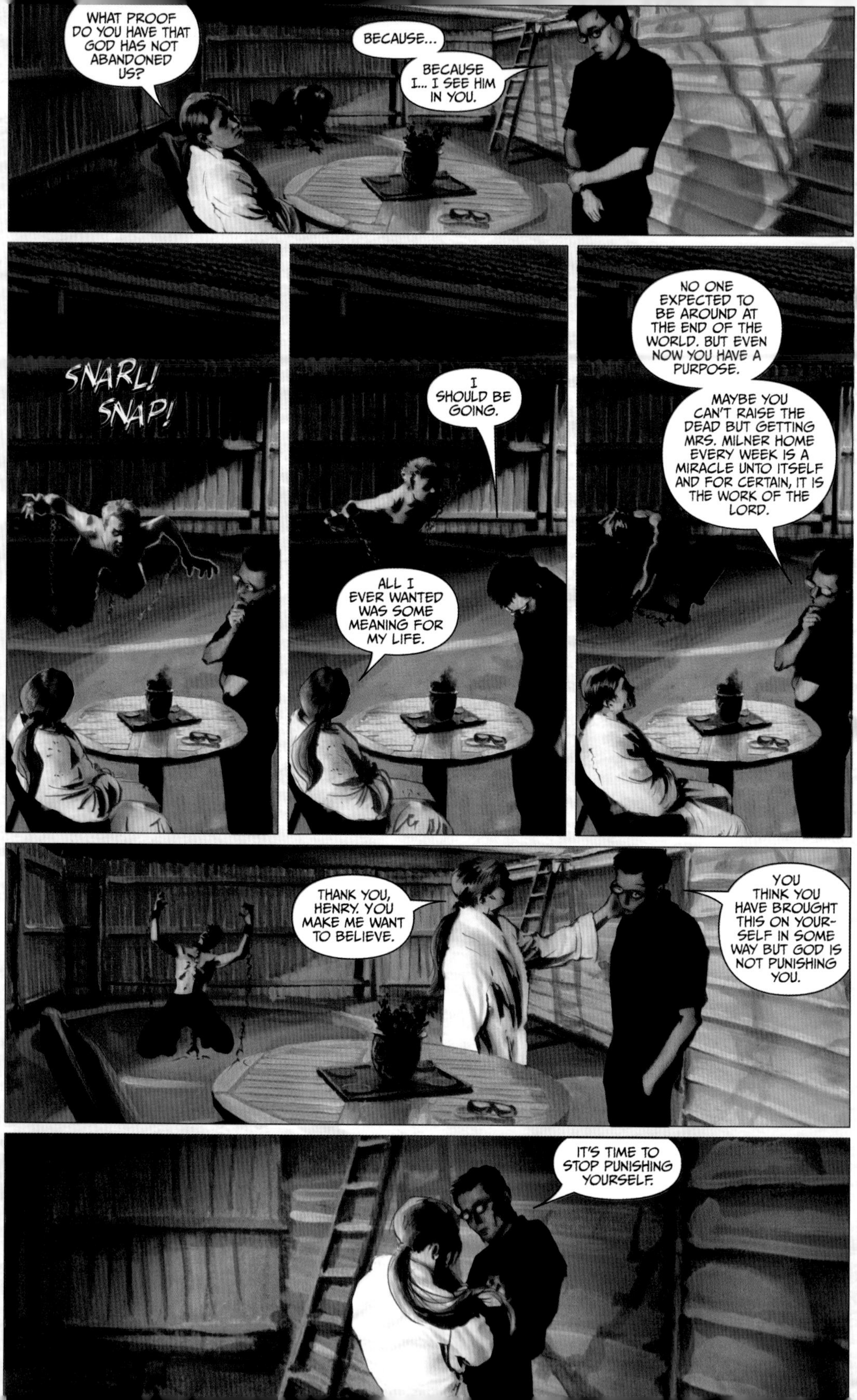
WHAT PROOF DO YOU HAVE THAT GOD HAS NOT ABANDONED US?
BECAUSE...
BECAUSE I... I SEE HIM IN YOU.
SNARL! SNAP!
I SHOULD BE GOING.
ALL I EVER WANTED WAS SOME MEANING FOR MY LIFE.
NO ONE EXPECTED TO BE AROUND AT THE END OF THE WORLD. BUT EVEN NOW YOU HAVE A PURPOSE.
MAYBE YOU CAN'T RAISE THE DEAD BUT GETTING MRS. MILNER HOME EVERY WEEK IS A MIRACLE UNTO ITSELF AND FOR CERTAIN, IT IS THE WORK OF THE LORD.
THANK YOU, HENRY. YOU MAKE ME WANT TO BELIEVE.
YOU THINK YOU HAVE BROUGHT THIS ON YOUR-SELF IN SOME WAY BUT GOD IS NOT PUNISHING YOU.
IT'S TIME TO STOP PUNISHING YOURSELF.

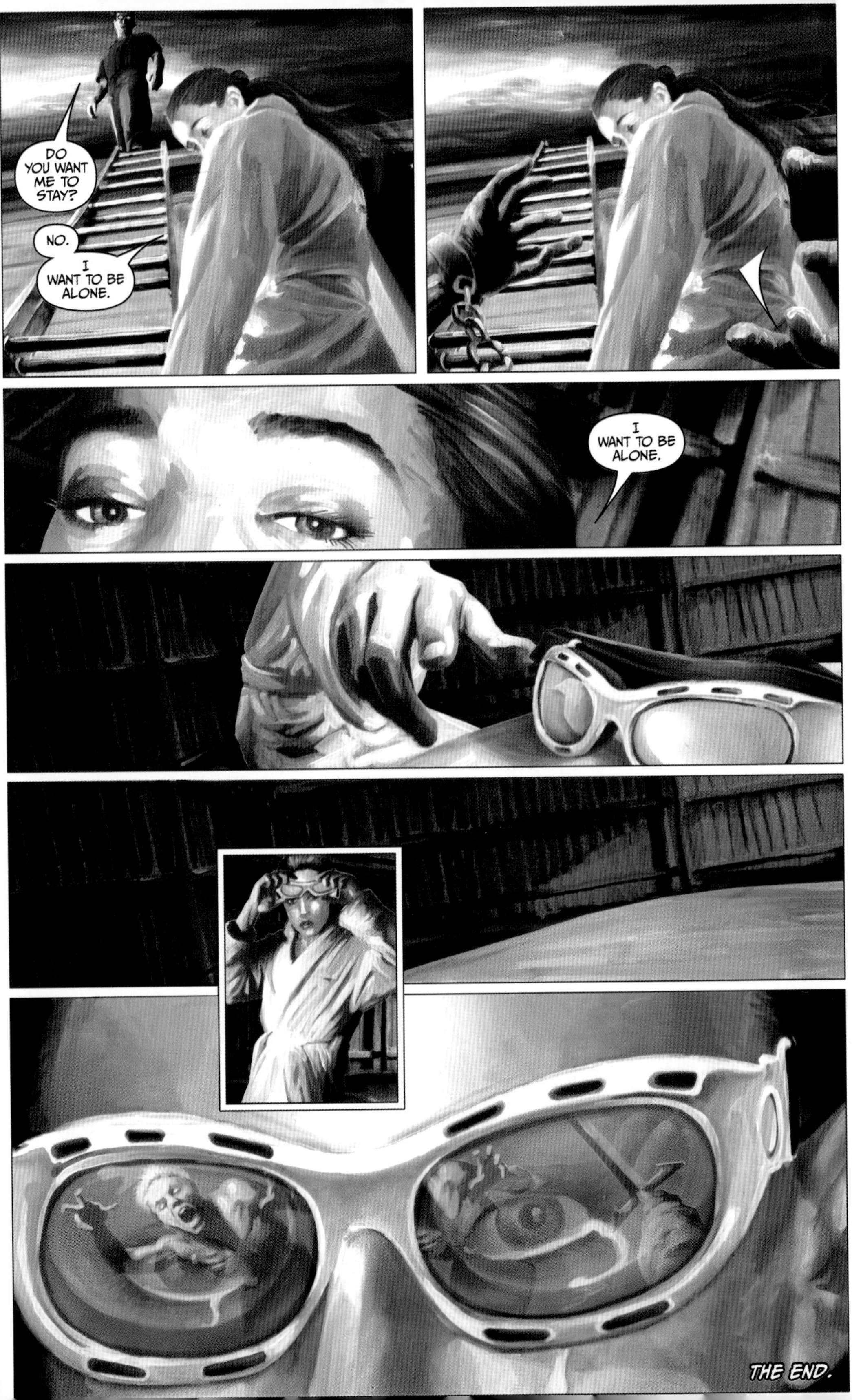
DO YOU WANT ME TO STAY?
NO.
I WANT TO BE ALONE.
I WANT TO BE ALONE.
THE END.

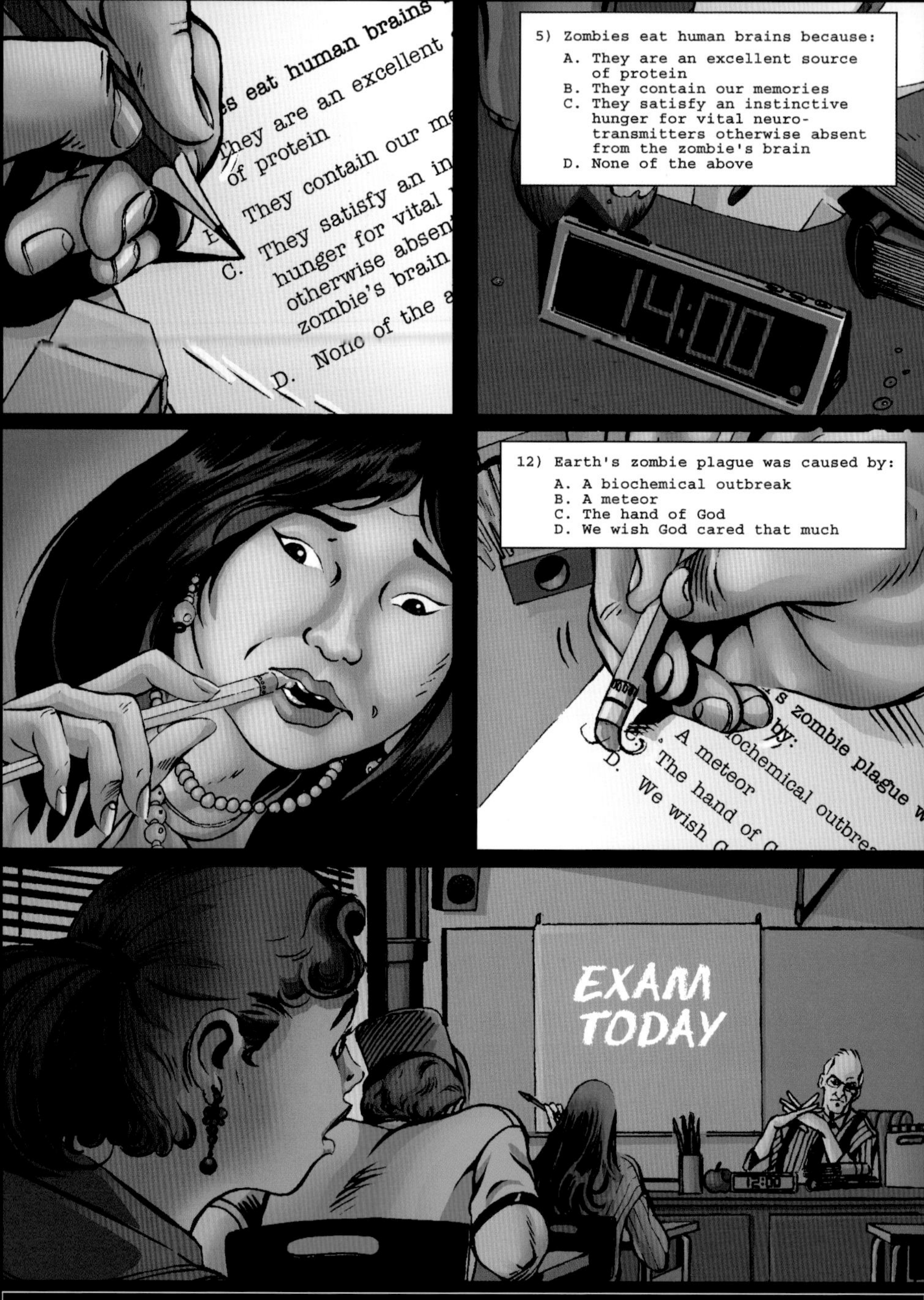
5) Zombies eat human brains because:
A. They are an excellent source of protein
B. They contain our memories
C. They satisfy an instinctive hunger for vital neuro-transmitters otherwise absent from the zombie's brain
D. None of the above
12) Earth's zombie plague was caused by:
A. A biochemical outbreak
B. A meteor
C. The hand of God
D. We wish God cared that much
EXAM TODAY

If You're So Smart...

Mark Waid
writer

Carlos Magno
artist

Matt Webb
colorist

Ed Dukeshire
letterer

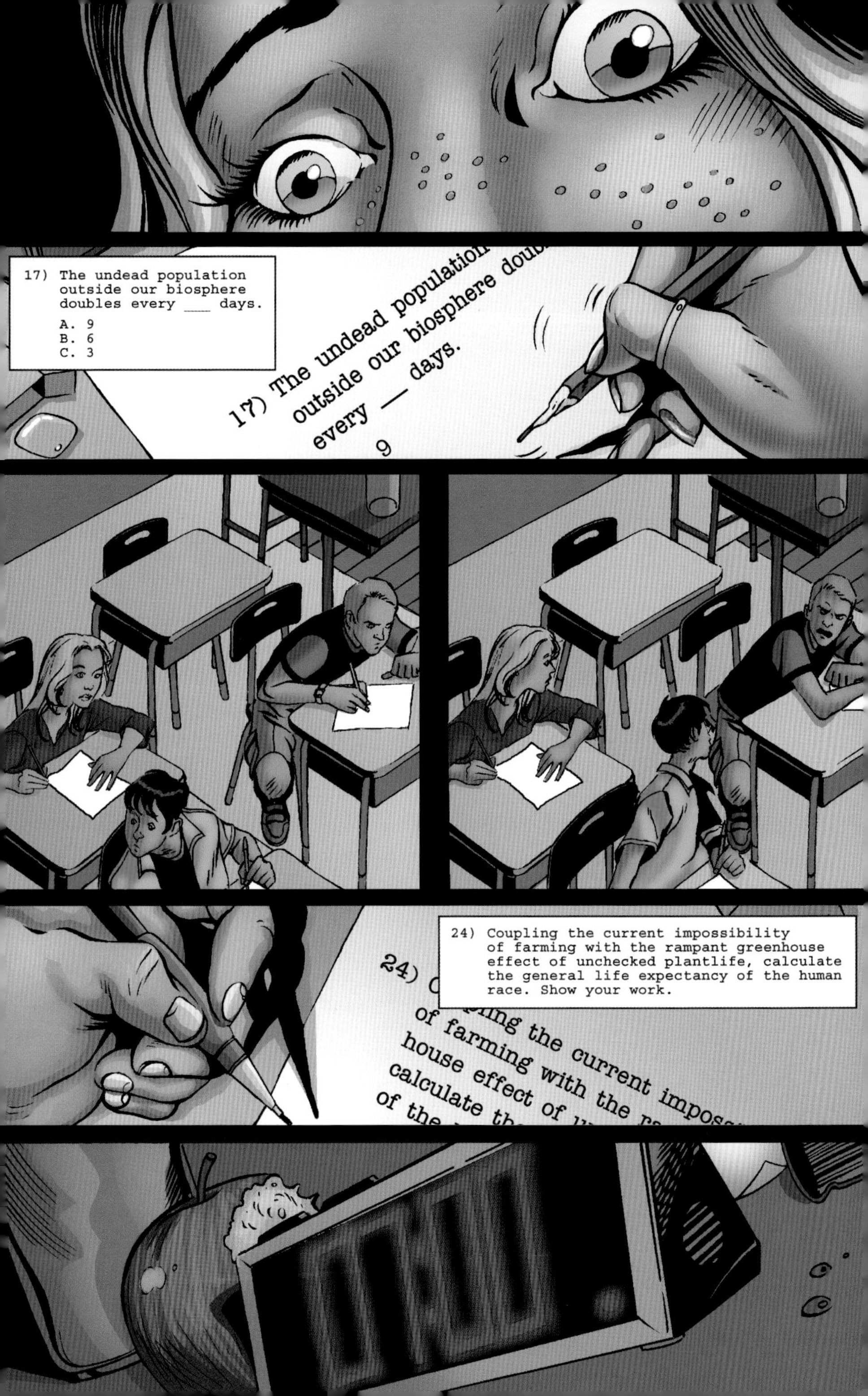

17) The undead population outside our biosphere doubles every ___ days.
A. 9
B. 6
C. 3
24) Coupling the current impossibility of farming with the rampant greenhouse effect of unchecked plantlife, calculate the general life expectancy of the human race. Show your work.

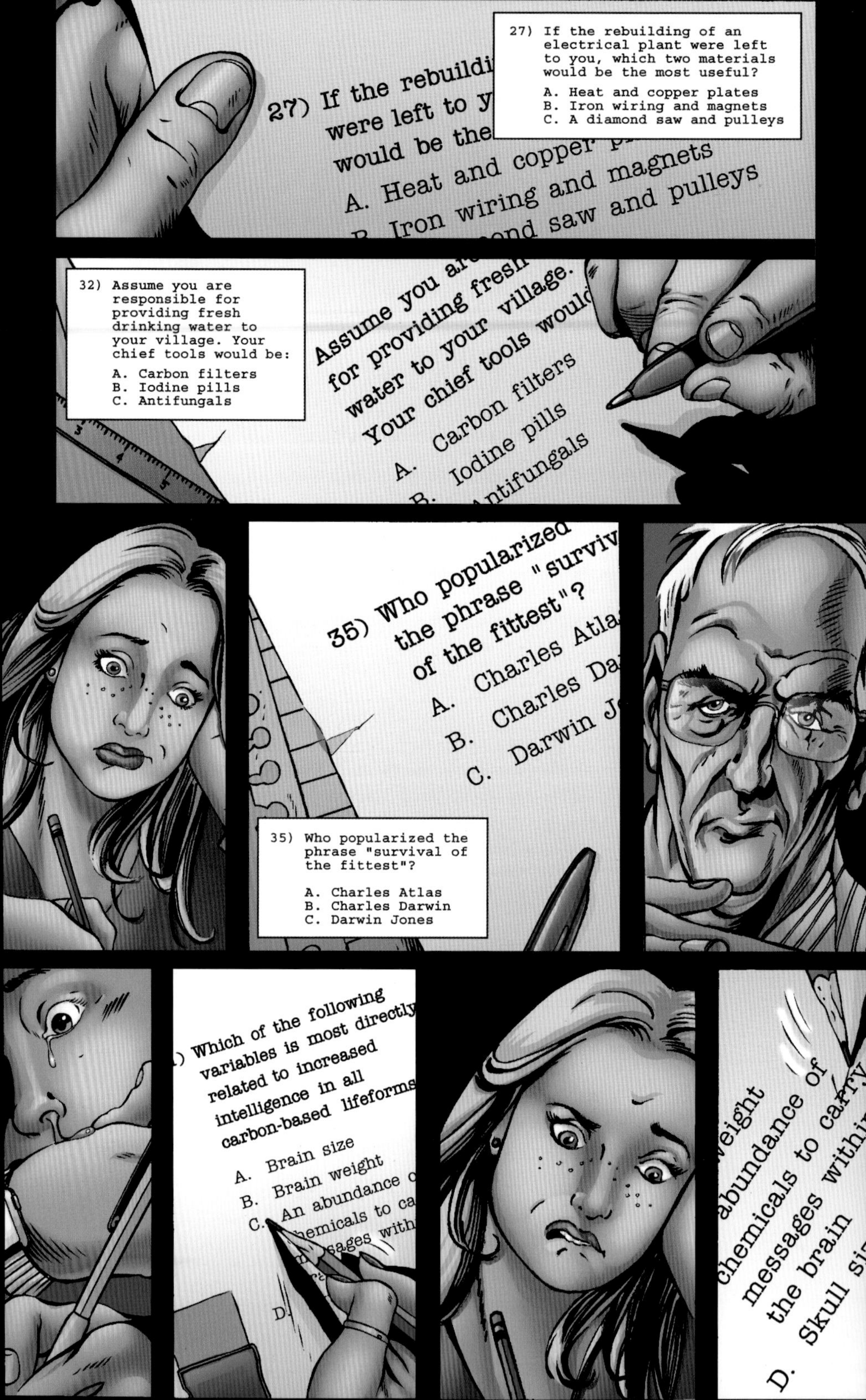

27) If the rebuilding of an electrical plant were left to you, which two materials would be the most useful?
A. Heat and copper plates
B. Iron wiring and magnets
C. A diamond saw and pulleys
32) Assume you are responsible for providing fresh drinking water to your village. Your chief tools would be:
A. Carbon filters
B. Iodine pills
C. Antifungals
35) Who popularized the phrase "survival of the fittest"?
A. Charles Atlas
B. Charles Darwin
C. Darwin Jones
Which of the following variables is most directly related to increased intelligence in all carbon-based lifeforms
A. Brain size
B. Brain weight
chemicals to carry
messages within
the brain
D. Skull

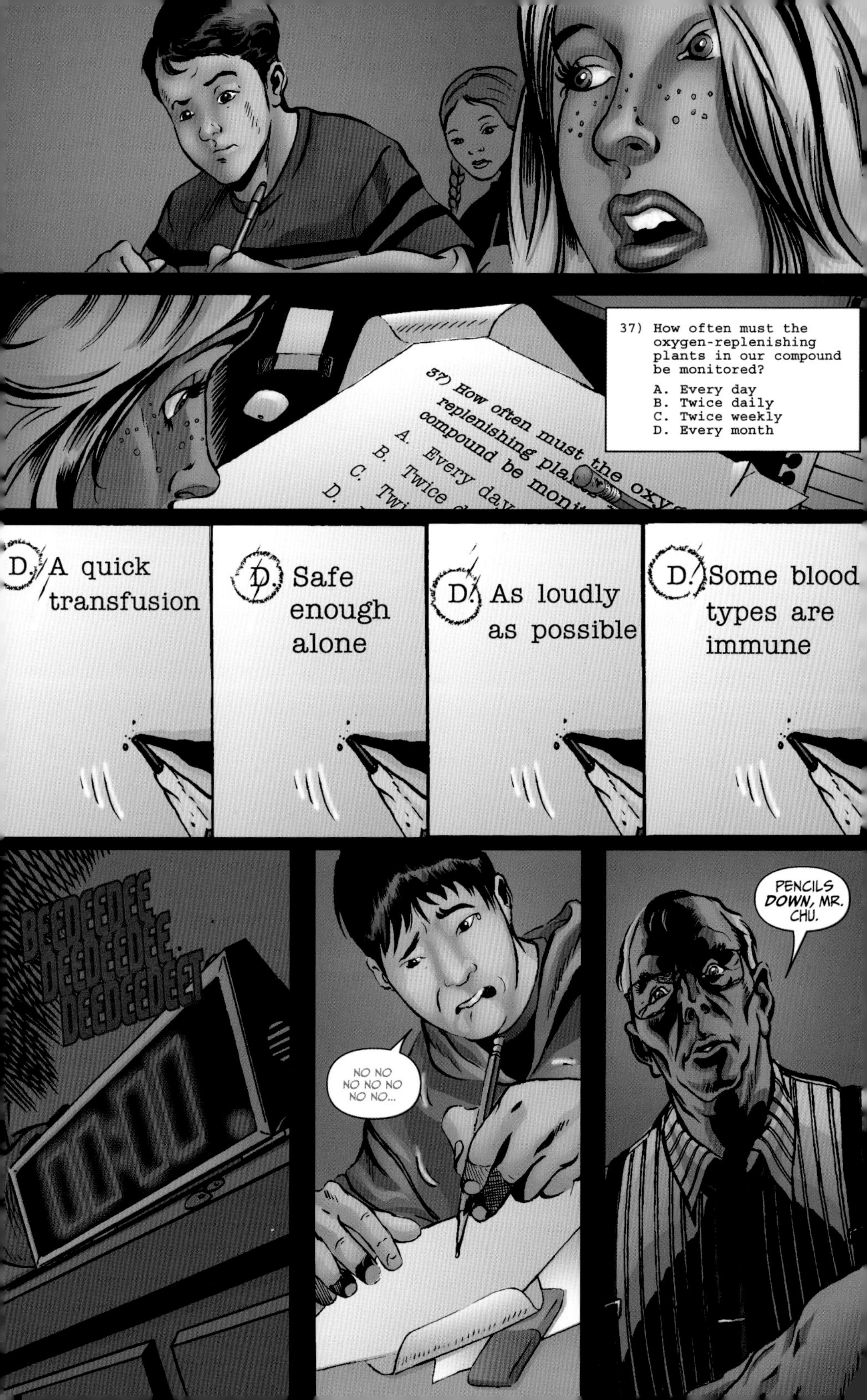

37) How often must the oxygen-replenishing plants in our compound be monitored?
A. Every day
B. Twice daily
C. Twice weekly
D. Every month
D. A quick transfusion
D. Safe enough alone
D. As loudly as possible
D. Some blood types are immune
DEEDEEDEE DEEDEEDEE DEEDEEDEET
NO NO NO NO NO NO NO...
PENCILS DOWN, MR. CHU.

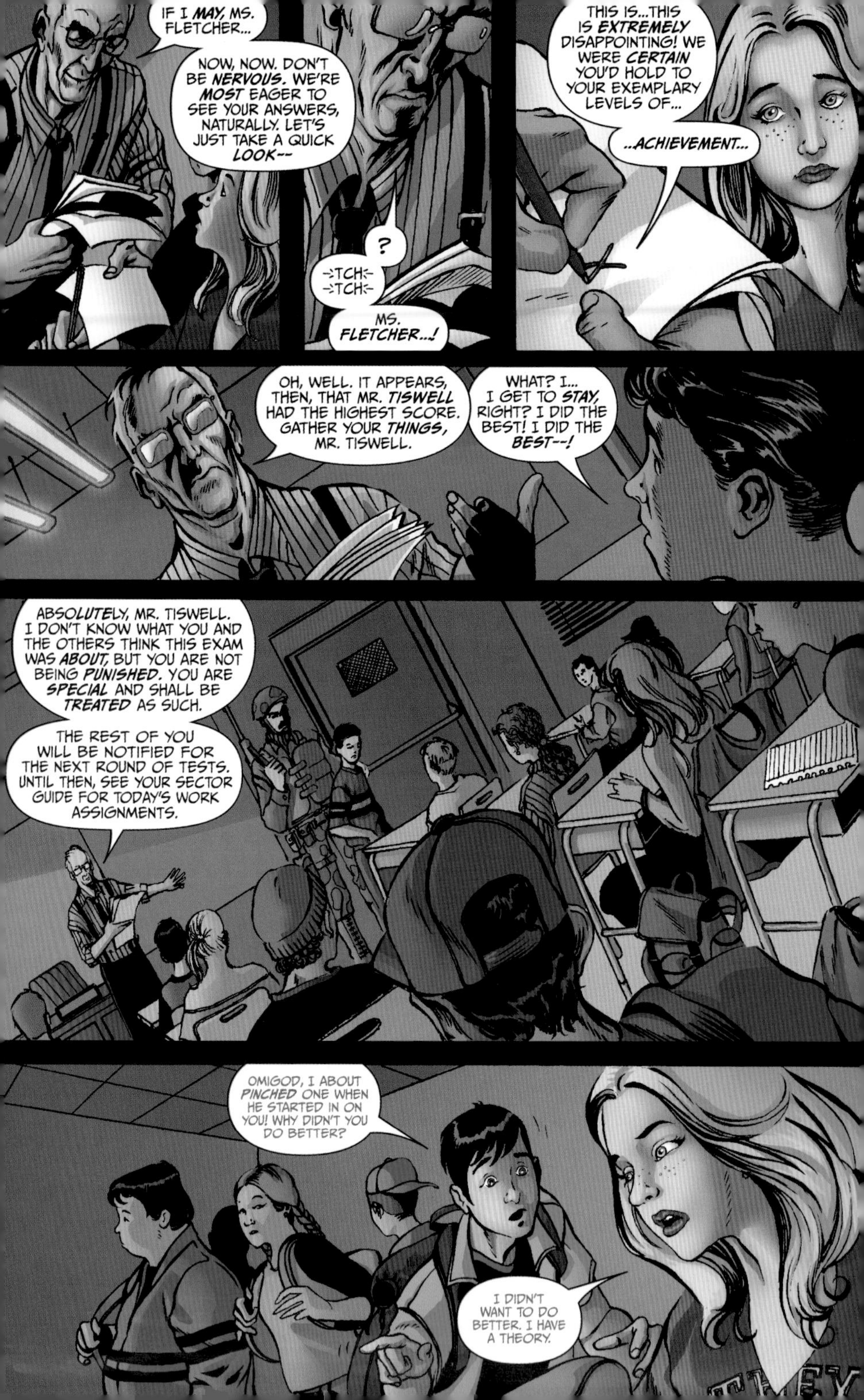
IF I MAY, MS. FLETCHER...
NOW, NOW. DON'T BE NERVOUS. WE'RE MOST EAGER TO SEE YOUR ANSWERS, NATURALLY. LET'S JUST TAKE A QUICK LOOK--
?
-TCH-
-TCH-
MS. FLETCHER...!
THIS IS...THIS IS EXTREMELY DISAPPOINTING! WE WERE CERTAIN YOU'D HOLD TO YOUR EXEMPLARY LEVELS OF...
...ACHIEVEMENT...
OH, WELL. IT APPEARS, THEN, THAT MR. TISWELL HAD THE HIGHEST SCORE. GATHER YOUR THINGS, MR. TISWELL.
WHAT? I... I GET TO STAY, RIGHT? I DID THE BEST! I DID THE BEST--!
ABSOLUTELY, MR. TISWELL. I DON'T KNOW WHAT YOU AND THE OTHERS THINK THIS EXAM WAS ABOUT, BUT YOU ARE NOT BEING PUNISHED. YOU ARE SPECIAL AND SHALL BE TREATED AS SUCH.
THE REST OF YOU WILL BE NOTIFIED FOR THE NEXT ROUND OF TESTS. UNTIL THEN, SEE YOUR SECTOR GUIDE FOR TODAY'S WORK ASSIGNMENTS.
OMIGOD, I ABOUT PINCHED ONE WHEN HE STARTED IN ON YOU! WHY DIDN'T YOU DO BETTER?
I DIDN'T WANT TO DO BETTER. I HAVE A THEORY.

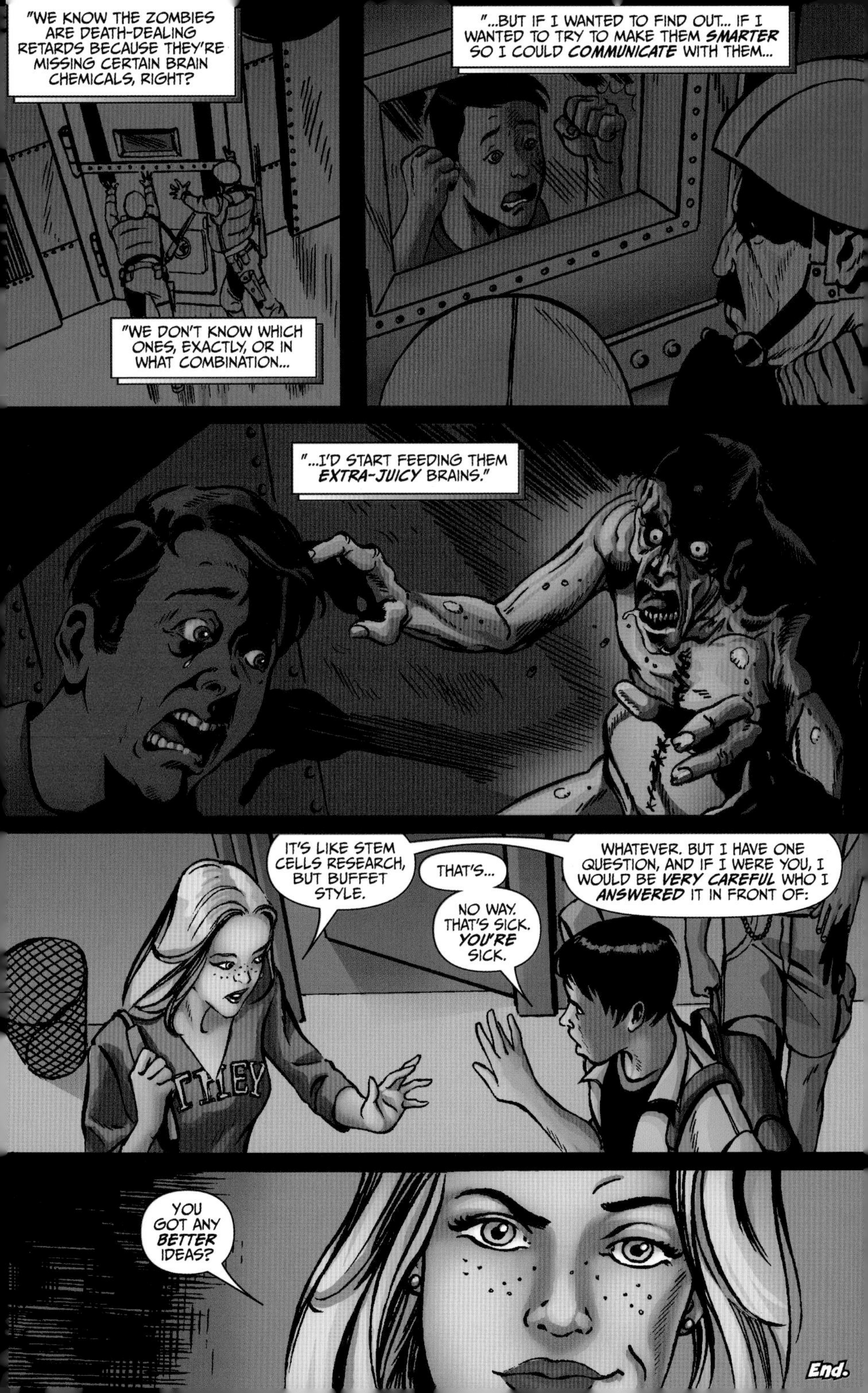
"WE KNOW THE ZOMBIES ARE DEATH-DEALING RETARDS BECAUSE THEY'RE MISSING CERTAIN BRAIN CHEMICALS, RIGHT?
"WE DON'T KNOW WHICH ONES, EXACTLY, OR IN WHAT COMBINATION...
"...BUT IF I WANTED TO FIND OUT... IF I WANTED TO TRY TO MAKE THEM SMARTER SO I COULD COMMUNICATE WITH THEM...
"...I'D START FEEDING THEM EXTRA-JUICY BRAINS."
IT'S LIKE STEM CELLS RESEARCH, BUT BUFFET STYLE.
THAT'S...
NO WAY. THAT'S SICK. YOU'RE SICK.
WHATEVER. BUT I HAVE ONE QUESTION, AND IF I WERE YOU, I WOULD BE VERY CAREFUL WHO I ANSWERED IT IN FRONT OF:
YOU GOT ANY BETTER IDEAS?
End.

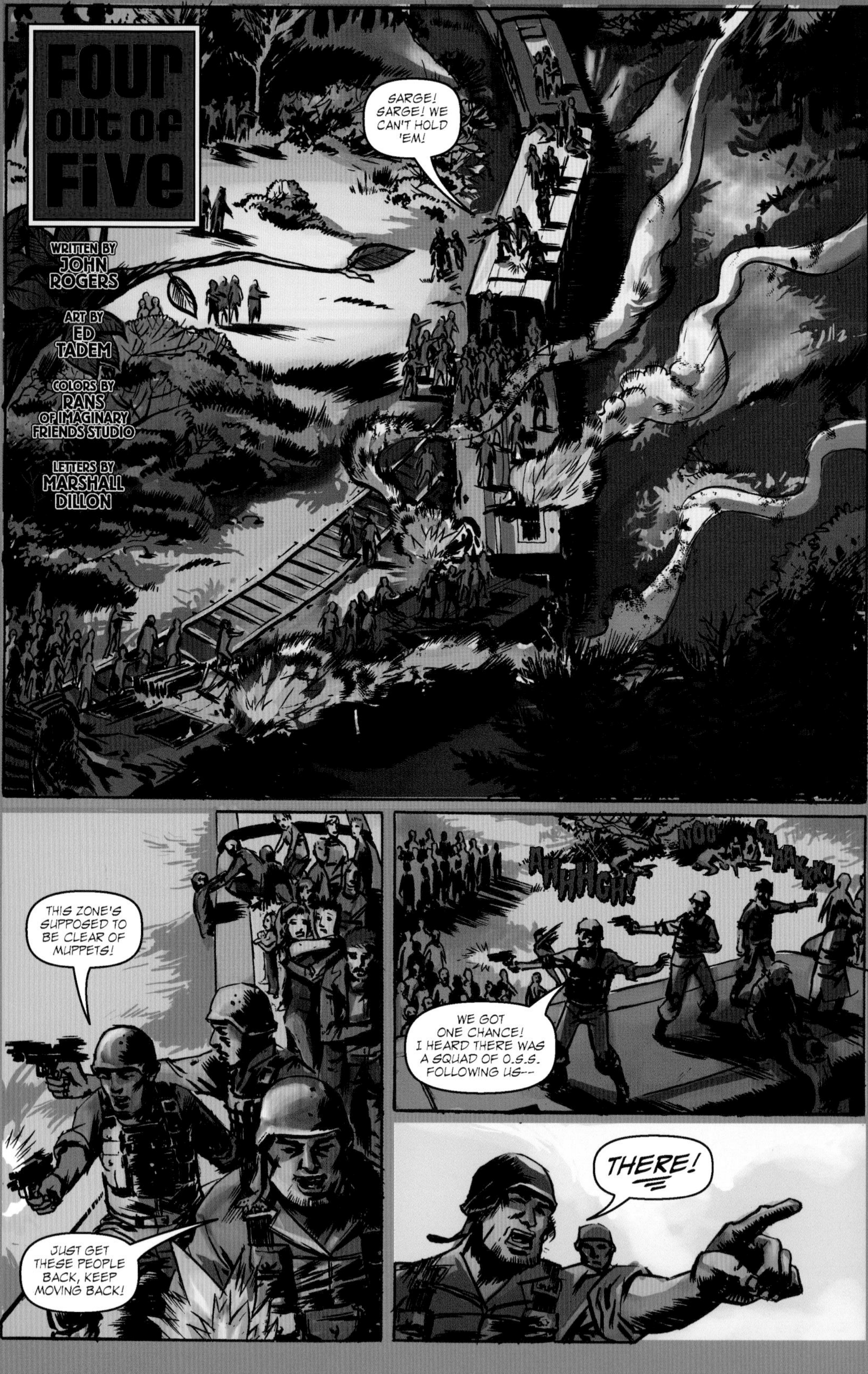
FOUR OUT OF FIVE
WRITTEN BY JOHN ROGERS
ART BY ED TADEM
COLORS BY RANS OF IMAGINARY FRIENDS STUDIO
LETTERS BY MARSHALL DILLON
SARGE! SARGE! WE CAN'T HOLD 'EM!
THIS ZONE'S SUPPOSED TO BE CLEAR OF MUPPETS!
JUST GET THESE PEOPLE BACK, KEEP MOVING BACK!
AHHHGH!
NOO
WE GOT ONE CHANCE! I HEARD THERE WAS A SQUAD OF O.S.S. FOLLOWING US--
THERE!

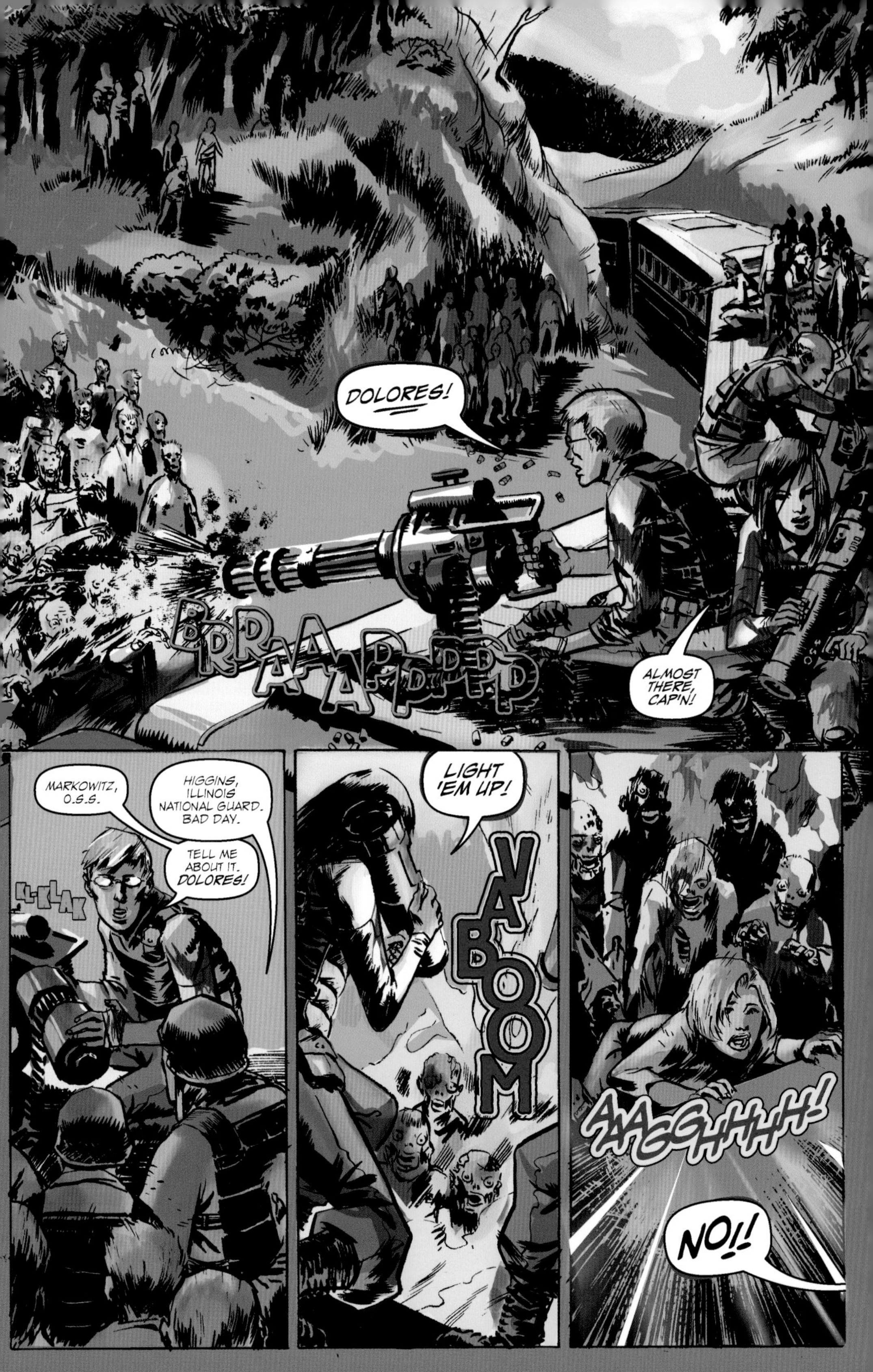

DOLORES!
BRRAAAPPPPPP
ALMOST THERE, CAP'N!
MARKOWITZ, O.S.S.
HIGGINS, ILLINOIS NATIONAL GUARD. BAD DAY.
TELL ME ABOUT IT. DOLORES!
KL-KLAK
LIGHT 'EM UP!
VABOOM
AAAGHHHH!
NO!!

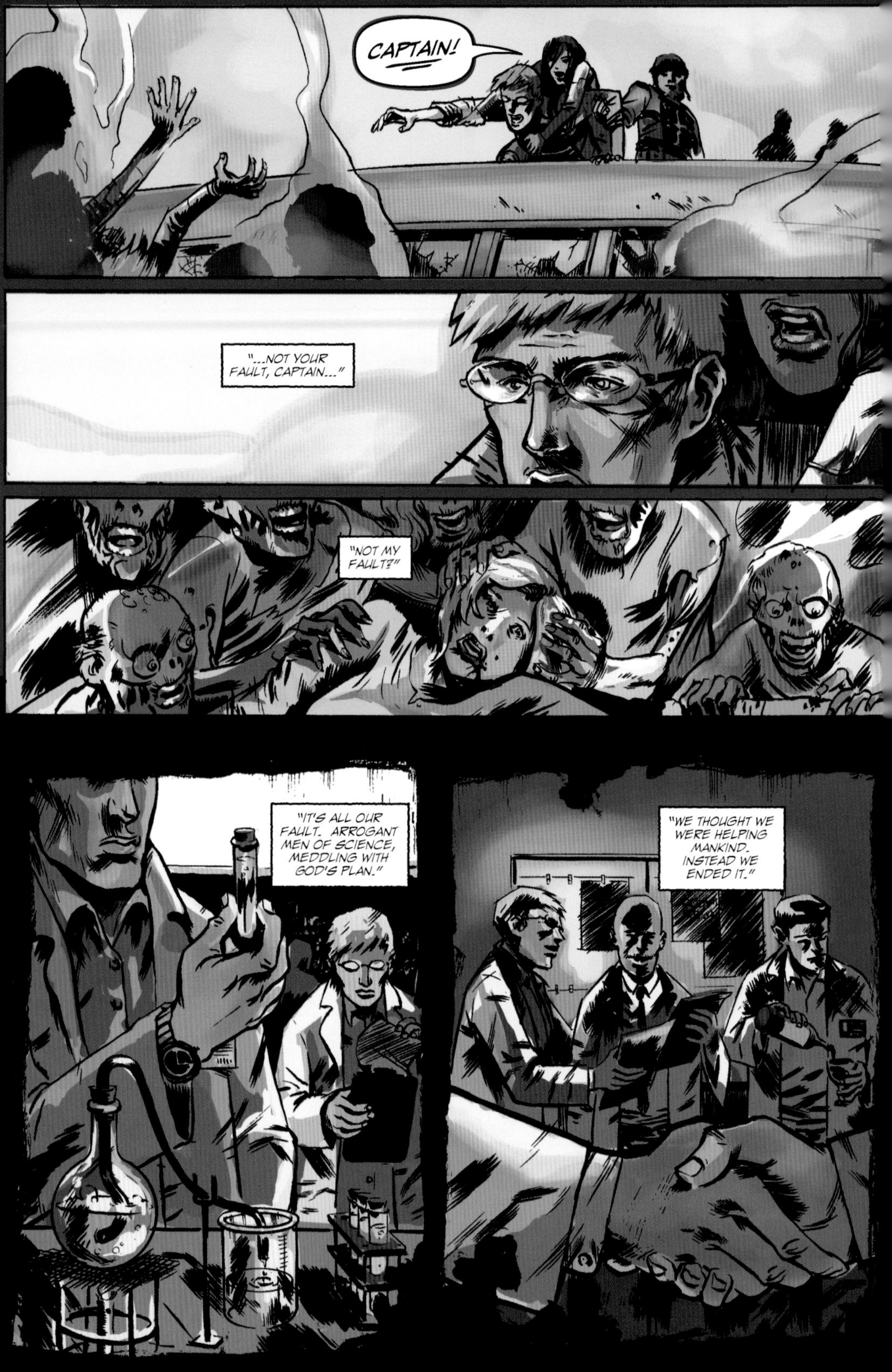
CAPTAIN!
"...NOT YOUR FAULT, CAPTAIN..."
"NOT MY FAULT?"
"IT'S ALL OUR FAULT. ARROGANT MEN OF SCIENCE, MEDDLING WITH GOD'S PLAN."
"WE THOUGHT WE WERE HELPING MANKIND. INSTEAD WE ENDED IT."

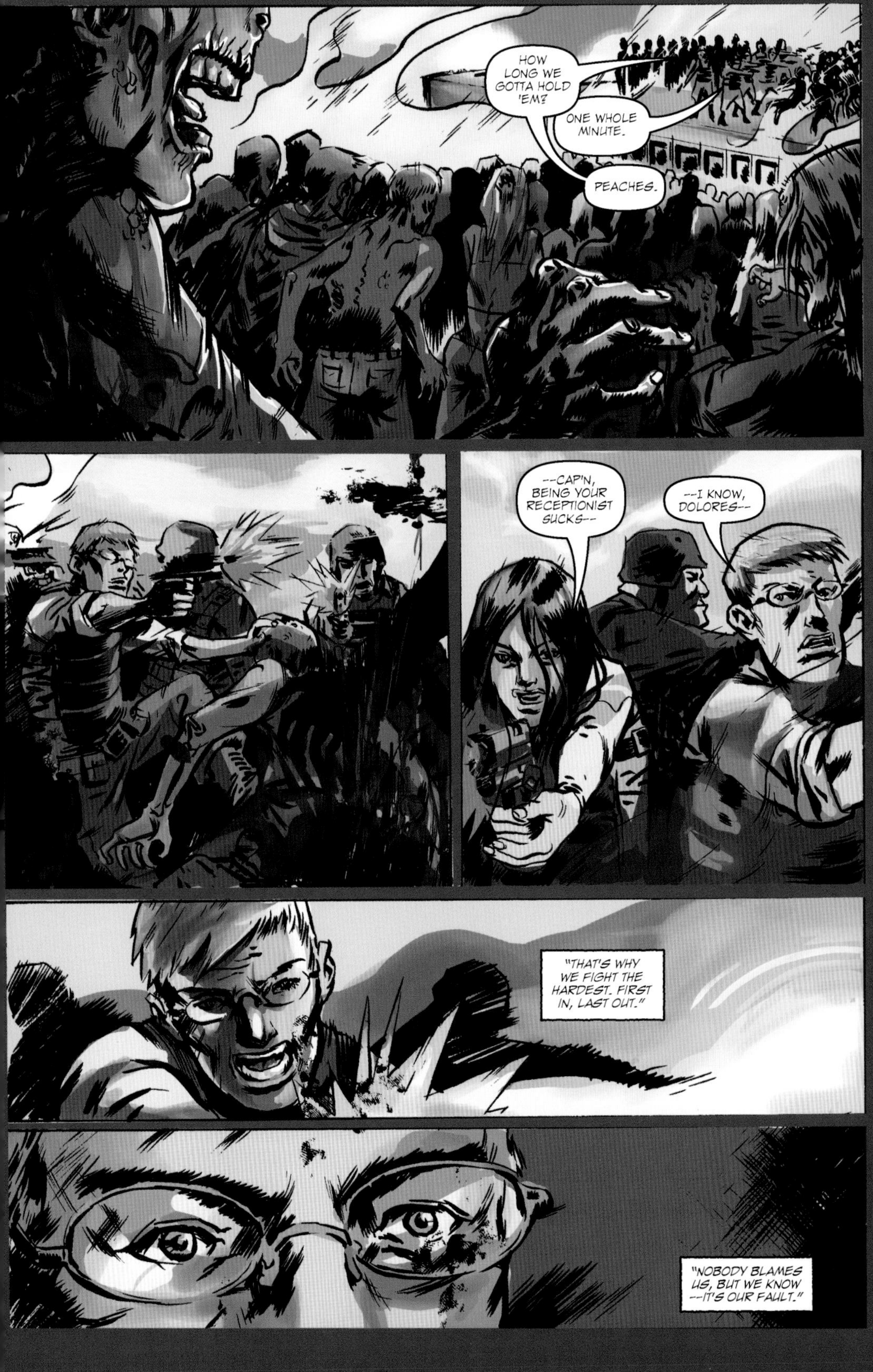
HOW LONG WE GOTTA HOLD 'EM?
ONE WHOLE MINUTE.
PEACHES.
--CAP'N, BEING YOUR RECEPTIONIST SUCKS--
--I KNOW, DOLORES--
"THAT'S WHY WE FIGHT THE HARDEST. FIRST IN, LAST OUT."
"NOBODY BLAMES US, BUT WE KNOW --IT'S OUR FAULT."

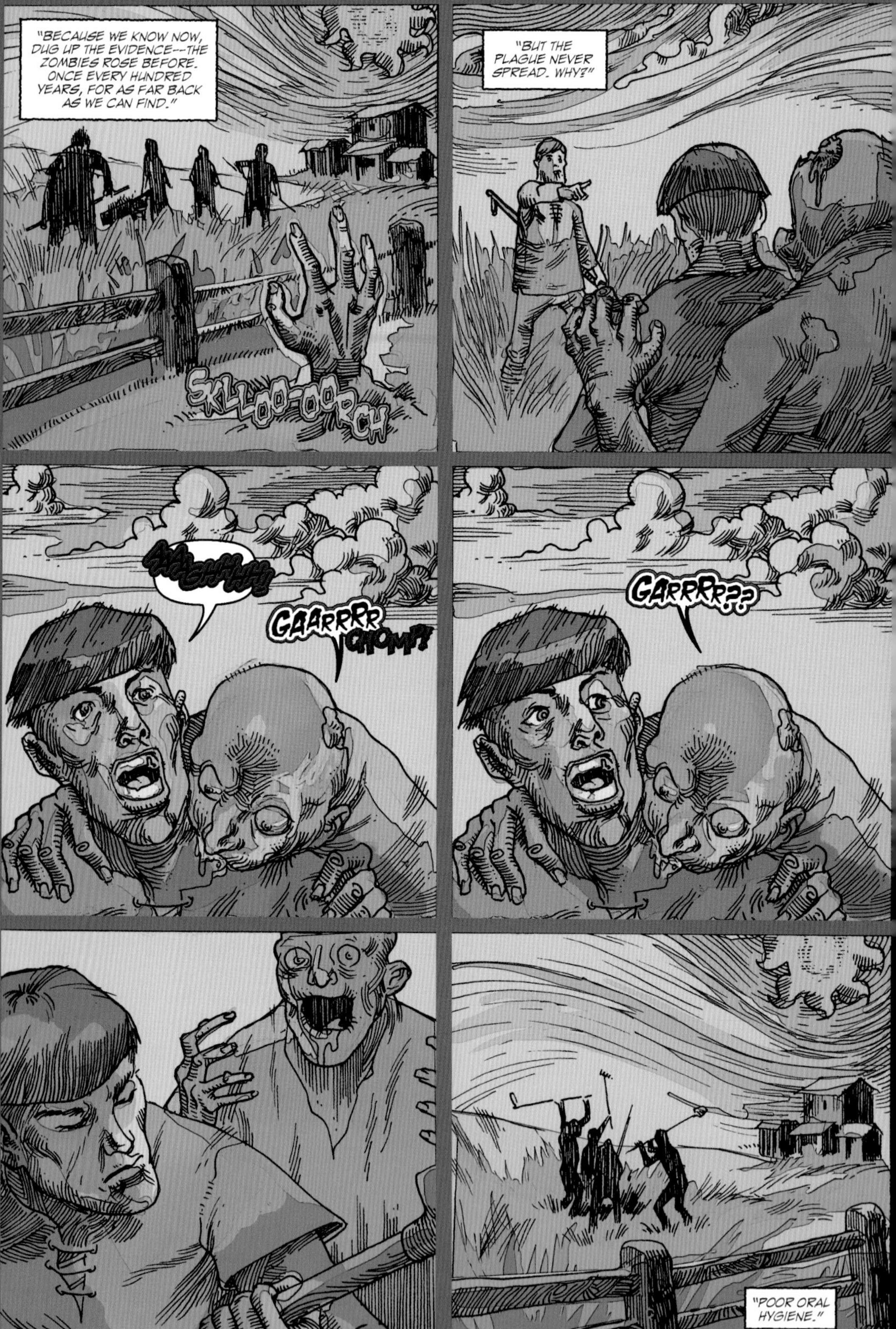
"BECAUSE WE KNOW NOW, DUG UP THE EVIDENCE--THE ZOMBIES ROSE BEFORE. ONCE EVERY HUNDRED YEARS, FOR AS FAR BACK AS WE CAN FIND."
SKLLOO-OORCH
"BUT THE PLAGUE NEVER SPREAD. WHY?"
AAAGHHHH!
GAARRRR CHOMP!
GARRRR??
"POOR ORAL HYGIENE."

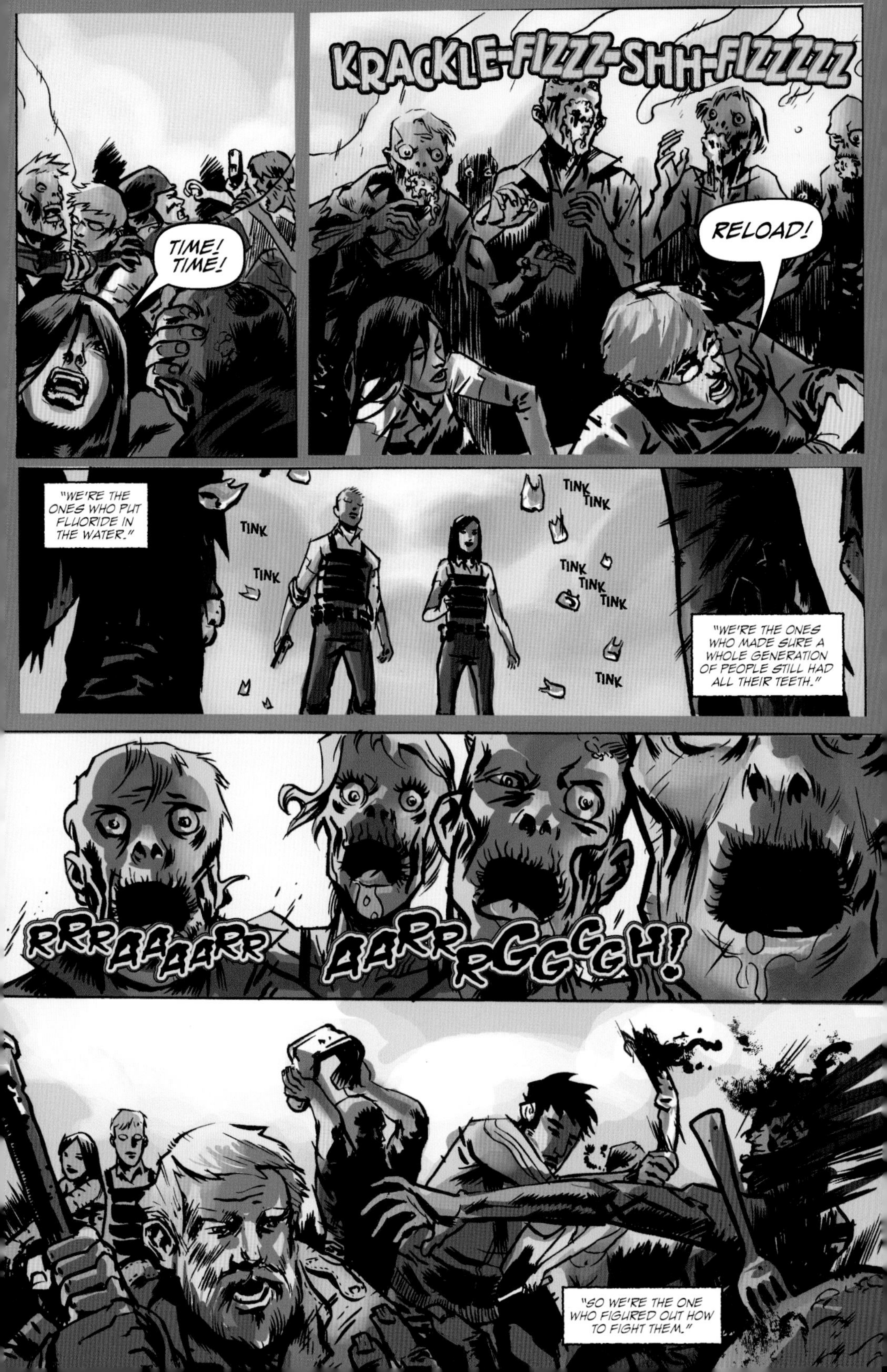
TIME! TIME!
KRACKLE-FIZZZ-SHH-FIZZZZZ
RELOAD!
"WE'RE THE ONES WHO PUT FLUORIDE IN THE WATER."
TINK
TINK
TINK TINK
TINK TINK TINK
TINK
"WE'RE THE ONES WHO MADE SURE A WHOLE GENERATION OF PEOPLE STILL HAD ALL THEIR TEETH."
RRRAAAAARR
AARRRGGGGH!
"SO WE'RE THE ONE WHO FIGURED OUT HOW TO FIGHT THEM."

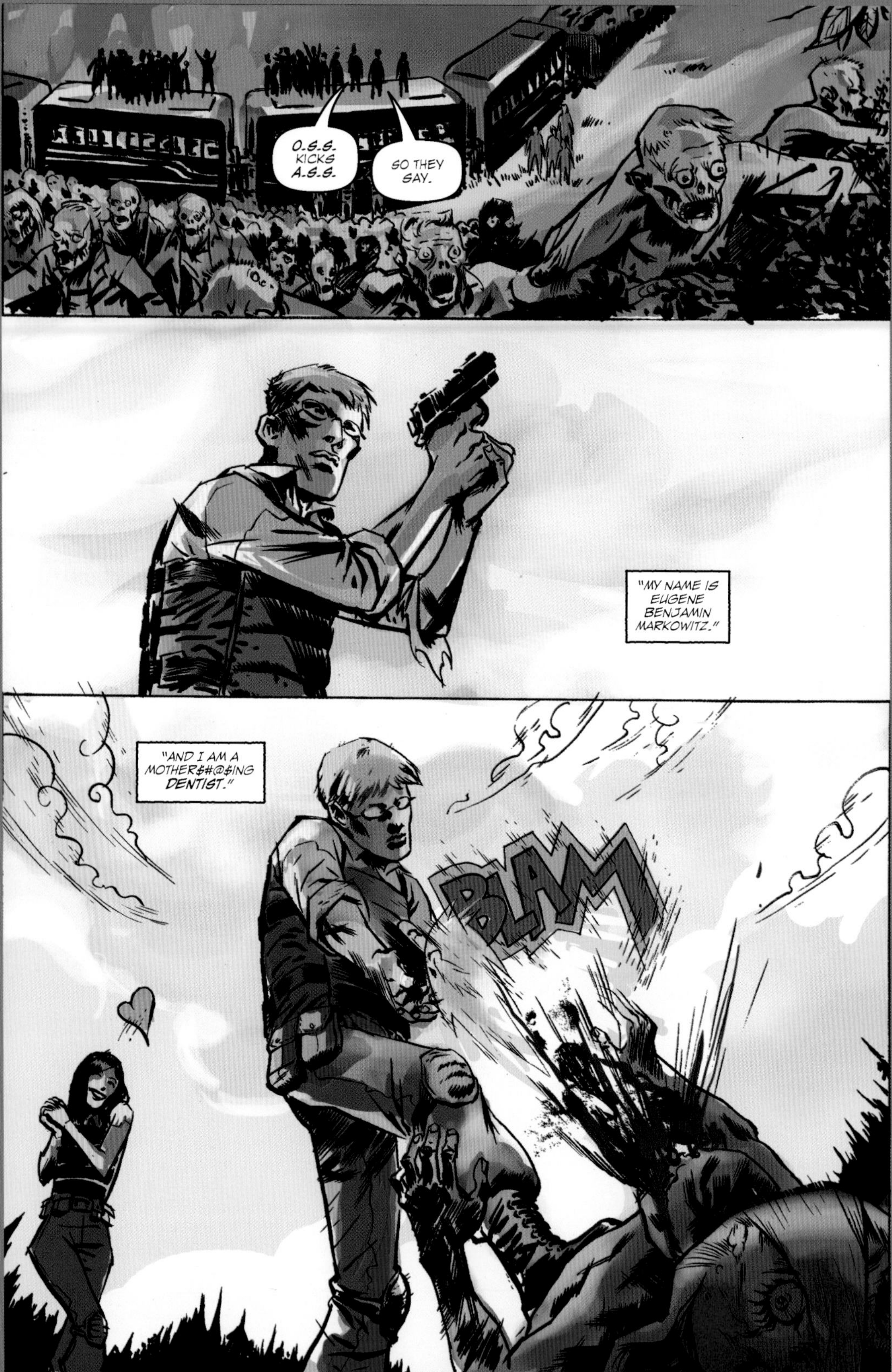
O.S.S. KICKS A.S.S.
SO THEY SAY.
"MY NAME IS EUGENE BENJAMIN MARKOWITZ."
"AND I AM A MOTHER$#@$ING DENTIST."
BLAM

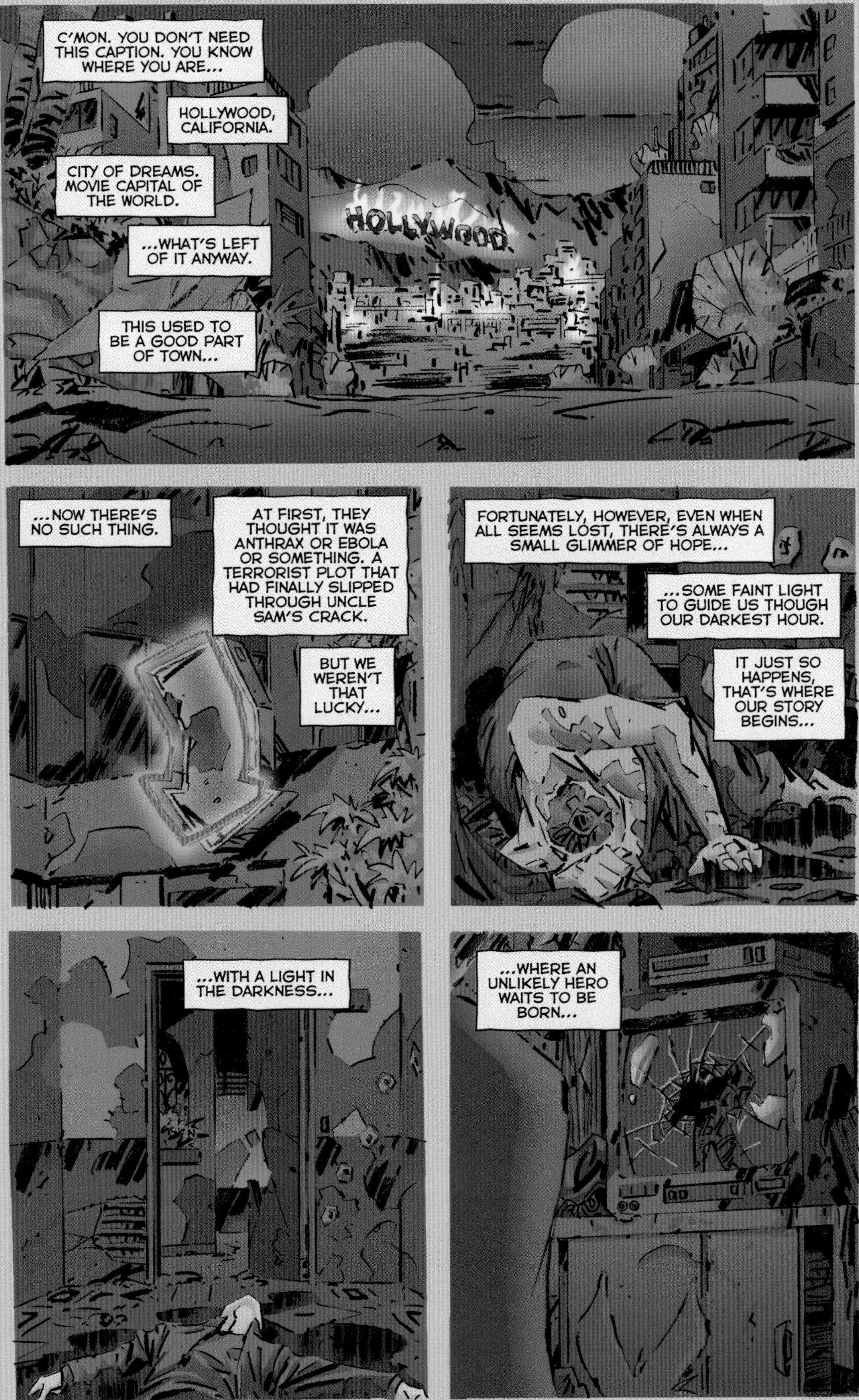
C'MON. YOU DON'T NEED THIS CAPTION. YOU KNOW WHERE YOU ARE...
HOLLYWOOD, CALIFORNIA.
CITY OF DREAMS. MOVIE CAPITAL OF THE WORLD.
...WHAT'S LEFT OF IT ANYWAY.
HOLLYWOOD
THIS USED TO BE A GOOD PART OF TOWN...
...NOW THERE'S NO SUCH THING.
AT FIRST, THEY THOUGHT IT WAS ANTHRAX OR EBOLA OR SOMETHING. A TERRORIST PLOT THAT HAD FINALLY SLIPPED THROUGH UNCLE SAM'S CRACK.
BUT WE WEREN'T THAT LUCKY...
FORTUNATELY, HOWEVER, EVEN WHEN ALL SEEMS LOST, THERE'S ALWAYS A SMALL GLIMMER OF HOPE...
...SOME FAINT LIGHT TO GUIDE US THOUGH OUR DARKEST HOUR.
IT JUST SO HAPPENS, THAT'S WHERE OUR STORY BEGINS...
...WITH A LIGHT IN THE DARKNESS...
...WHERE AN UNLIKELY HERO WAITS TO BE BORN...

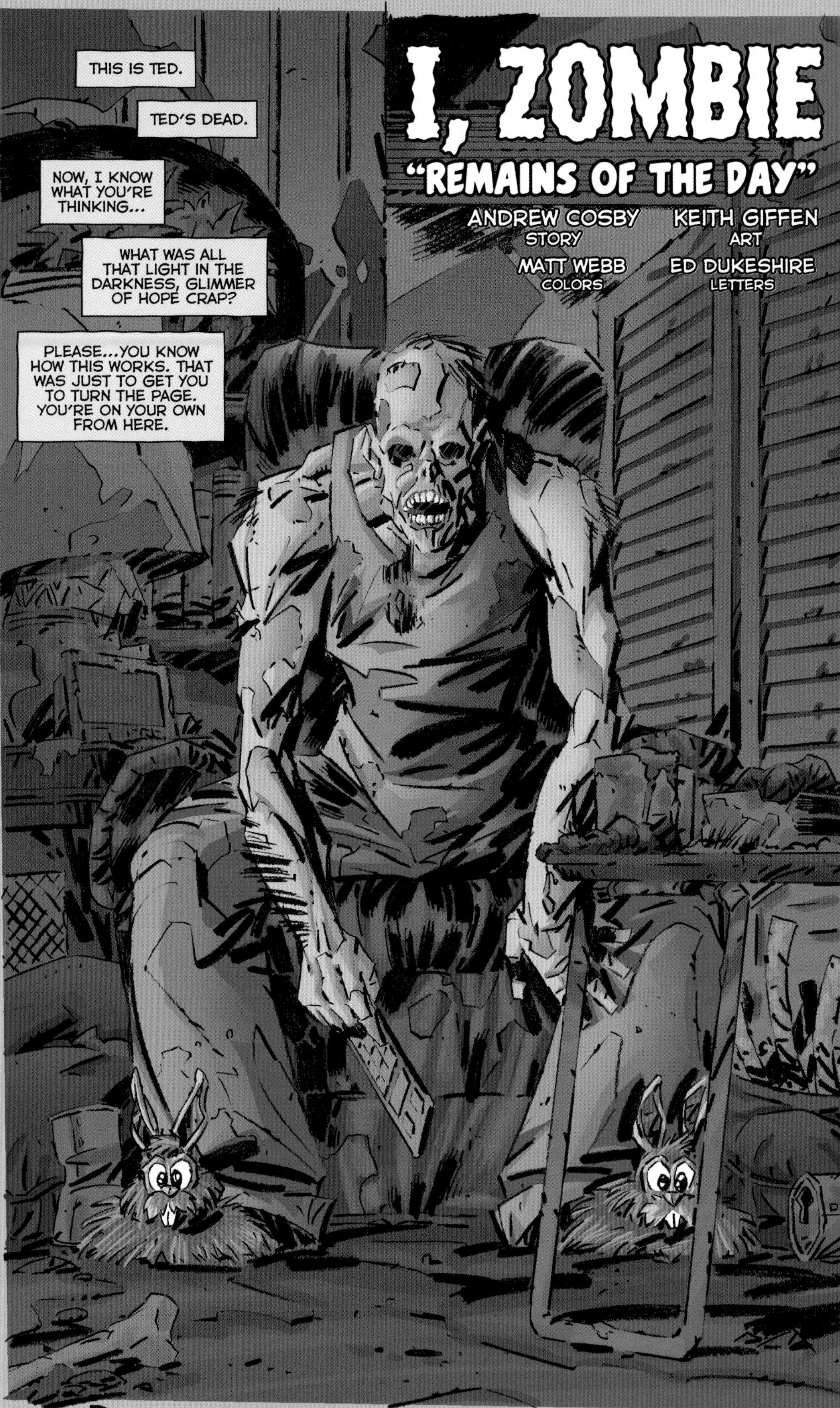
THIS IS TED.
TED'S DEAD.
NOW, I KNOW WHAT YOU'RE THINKING...
WHAT WAS ALL THAT LIGHT IN THE DARKNESS, GLIMMER OF HOPE CRAP?
PLEASE...YOU KNOW HOW THIS WORKS. THAT WAS JUST TO GET YOU TO TURN THE PAGE. YOU'RE ON YOUR OWN FROM HERE.
I, ZOMBIE
"REMAINS OF THE DAY"
ANDREW COSBY STORY
KEITH GIFFEN ART
MATT WEBB COLORS
ED DUKESHIRE LETTERS

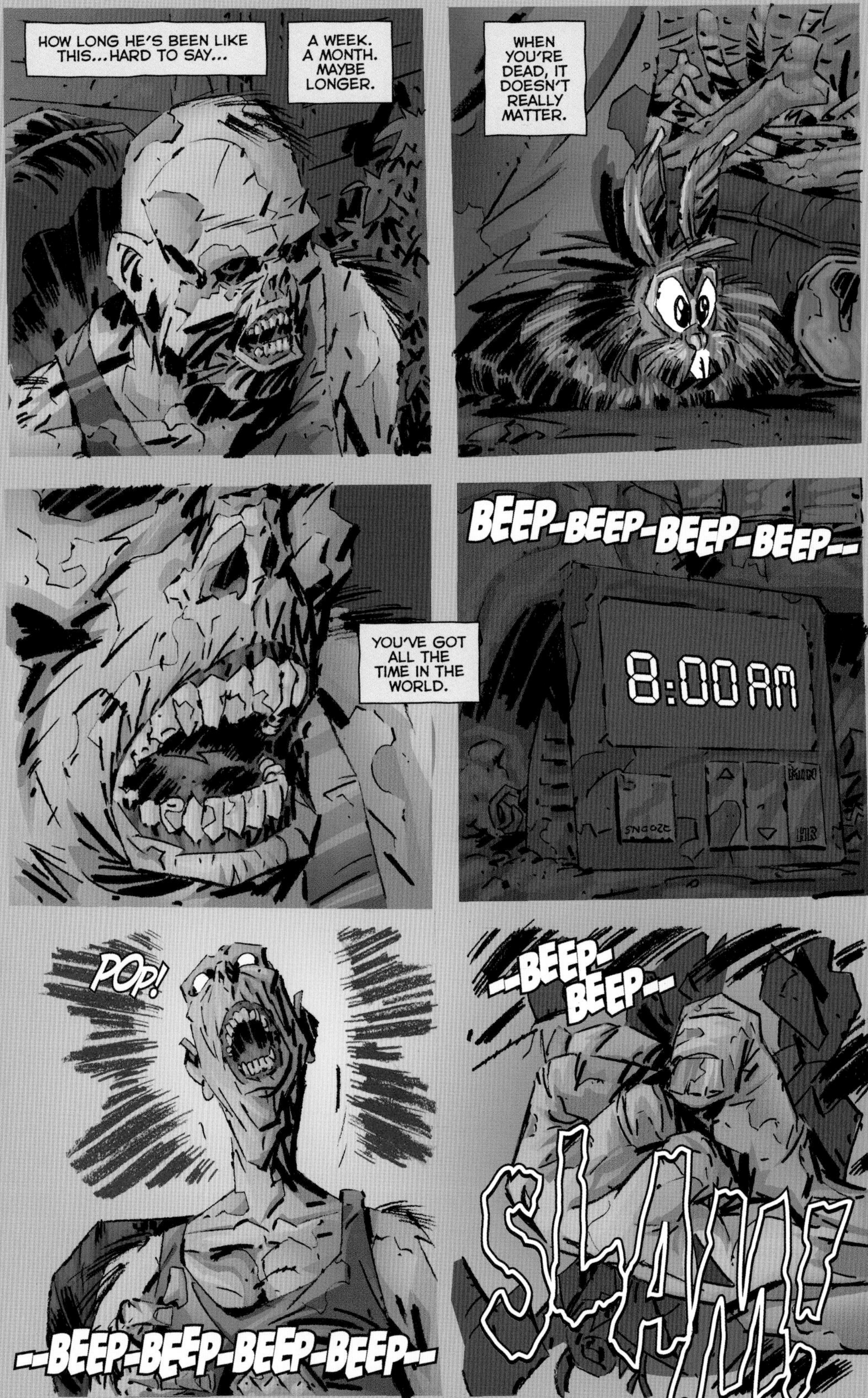

HOW LONG HE'S BEEN LIKE THIS...HARD TO SAY...
A WEEK. A MONTH. MAYBE LONGER.
WHEN YOU'RE DEAD, IT DOESN'T REALLY MATTER.
YOU'VE GOT ALL THE TIME IN THE WORLD.
BEEP-BEEP-BEEP-BEEP--
8:00AM
SNOOZE
MIN
HR
POP!
--BEEP-BEEP-BEEP-BEEP--
--BEEP-BEEP--
SLAM!

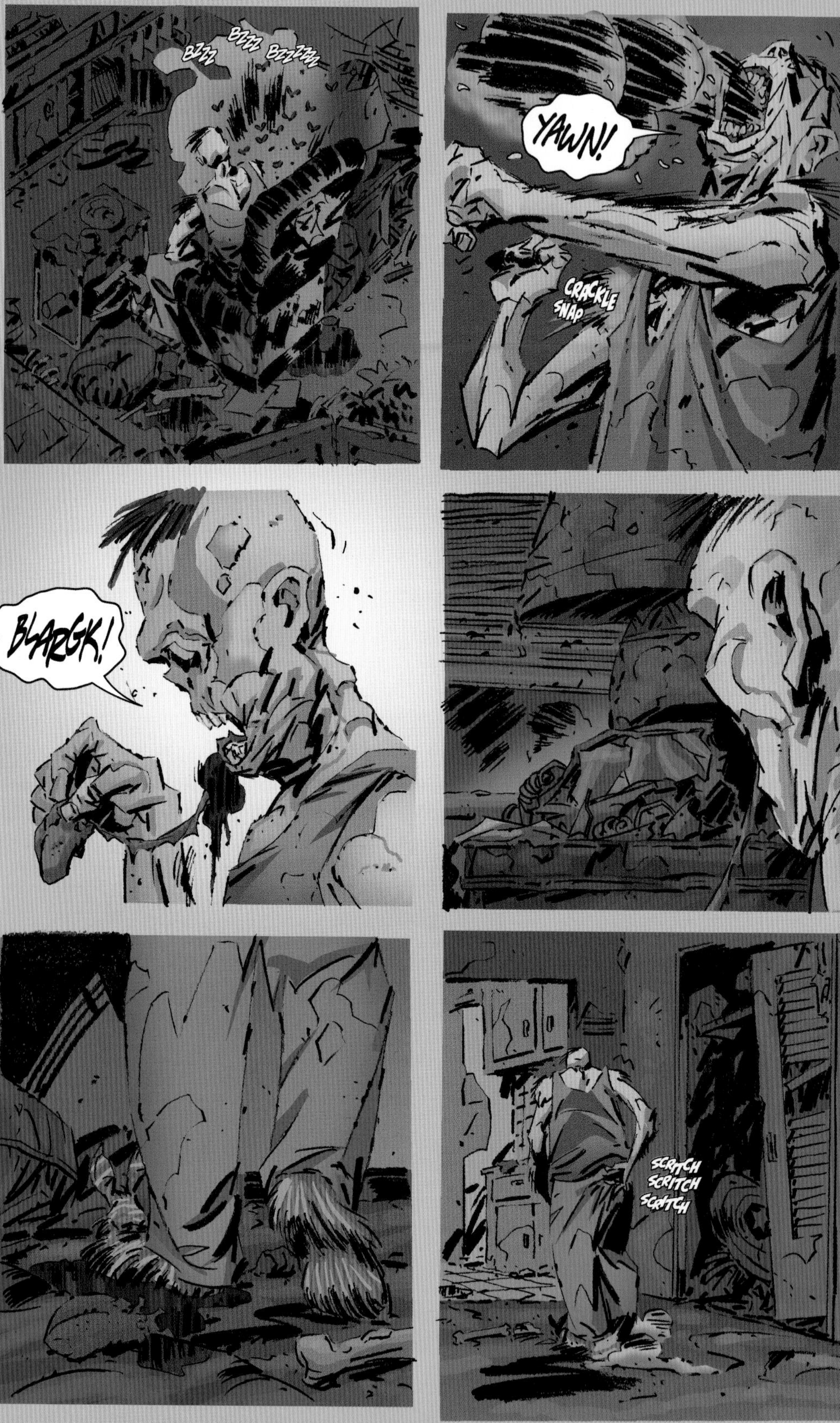
BZZZ
BZZZ
BZZZZZZ
YAWN!
CRACKLE
SNAP
BLARGK!
SCRITCH
SCRITCH
SCRITCH

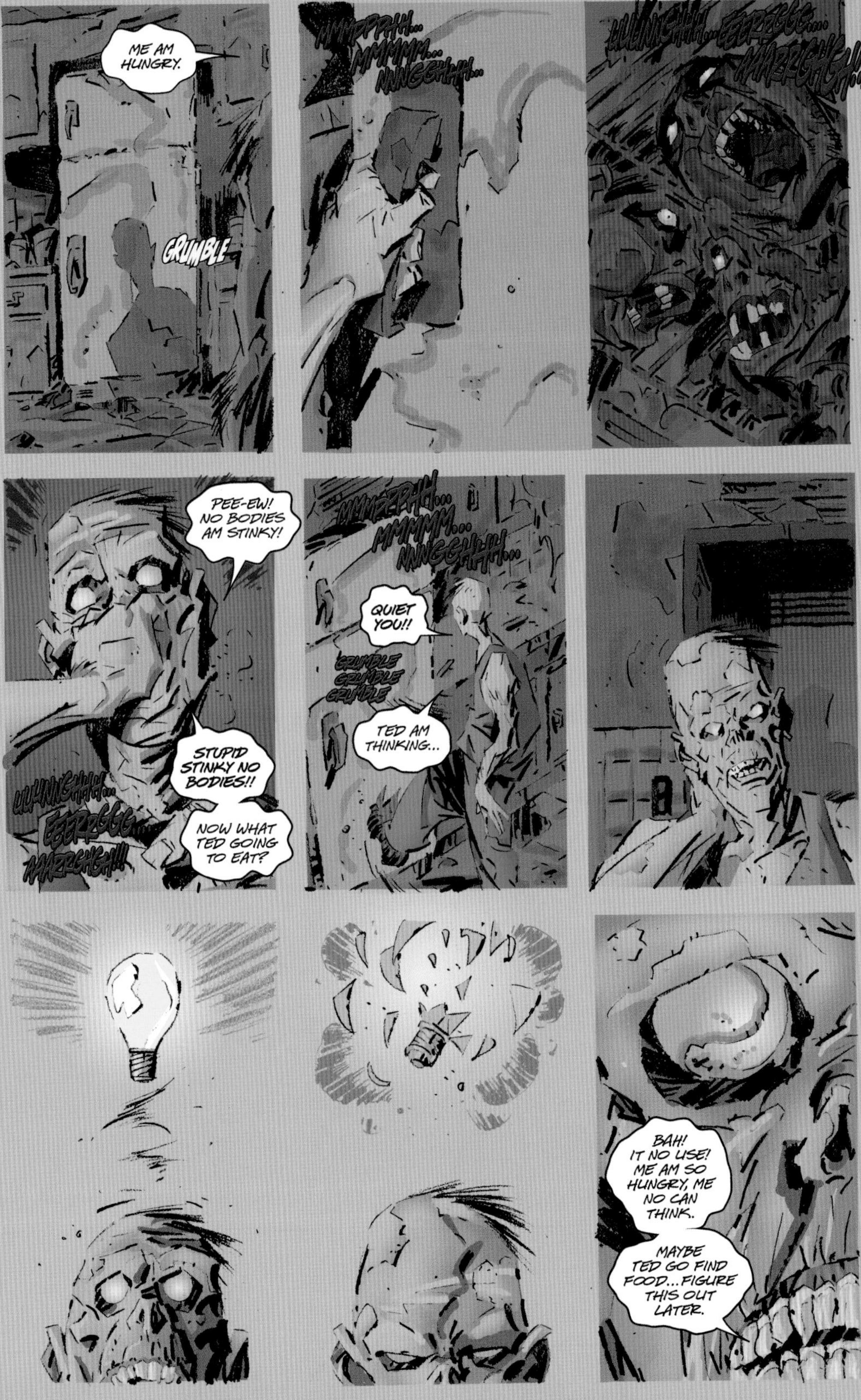
ME AM HUNGRY.
GRUMBLE
MMMPPPHH... MMMMM... NNNGGHHH...
LLLUNNGHHH... EEERRGGG... AAARRGHGH!!!
PEE-EW! NO BODIES AM STINKY!
STUPID STINKY NO BODIES!!
LLLUNNGHHH... EEERRGGG... AAARRGHGH!!!
NOW WHAT TED GOING TO EAT?
MMMPPPHH... MMMMM... NNNGGHHH...
QUIET YOU!!
GRUMBLE GRUMBLE GRUMBLE
TED AM THINKING...
BAH! IT NO USE! ME AM SO HUNGRY, ME NO CAN THINK.
MAYBE TED GO FIND FOOD... FIGURE THIS OUT LATER.

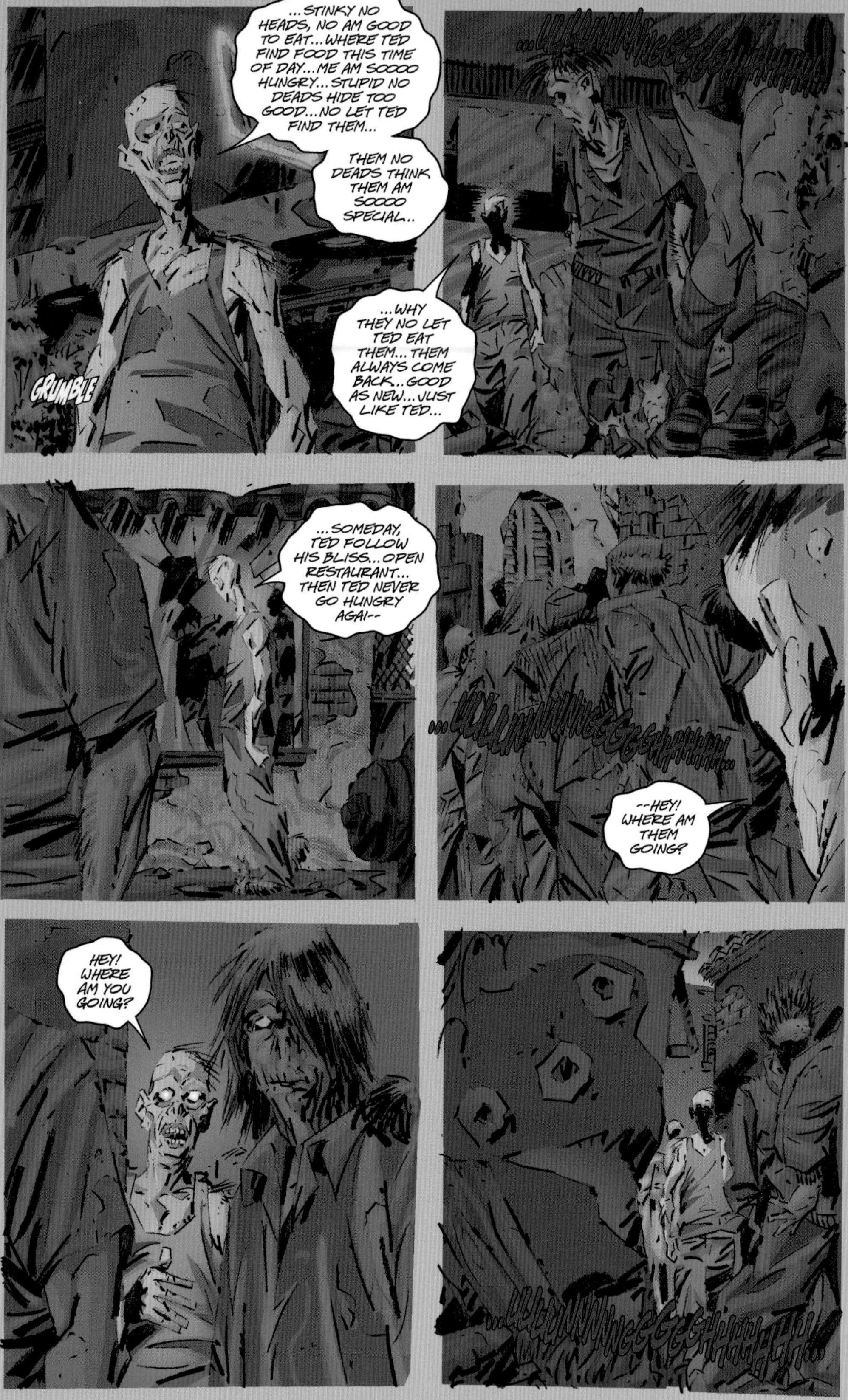
...STINKY NO HEADS, NO AM GOOD TO EAT...WHERE TED FIND FOOD THIS TIME OF DAY...ME AM SOOOO HUNGRY...STUPID NO DEADS HIDE TOO GOOD...NO LET TED FIND THEM...
THEM NO DEADS THINK THEM AM SOOOO SPECIAL...
GRUMBLE
...WHY THEY NO LET TED EAT THEM...THEM ALWAYS COME BACK...GOOD AS NEW...JUST LIKE TED...
...SOMEDAY, TED FOLLOW HIS BLISS...OPEN RESTAURANT...THEN TED NEVER GO HUNGRY AGAI--
--HEY! WHERE AM THEM GOING?
HEY! WHERE AM YOU GOING?

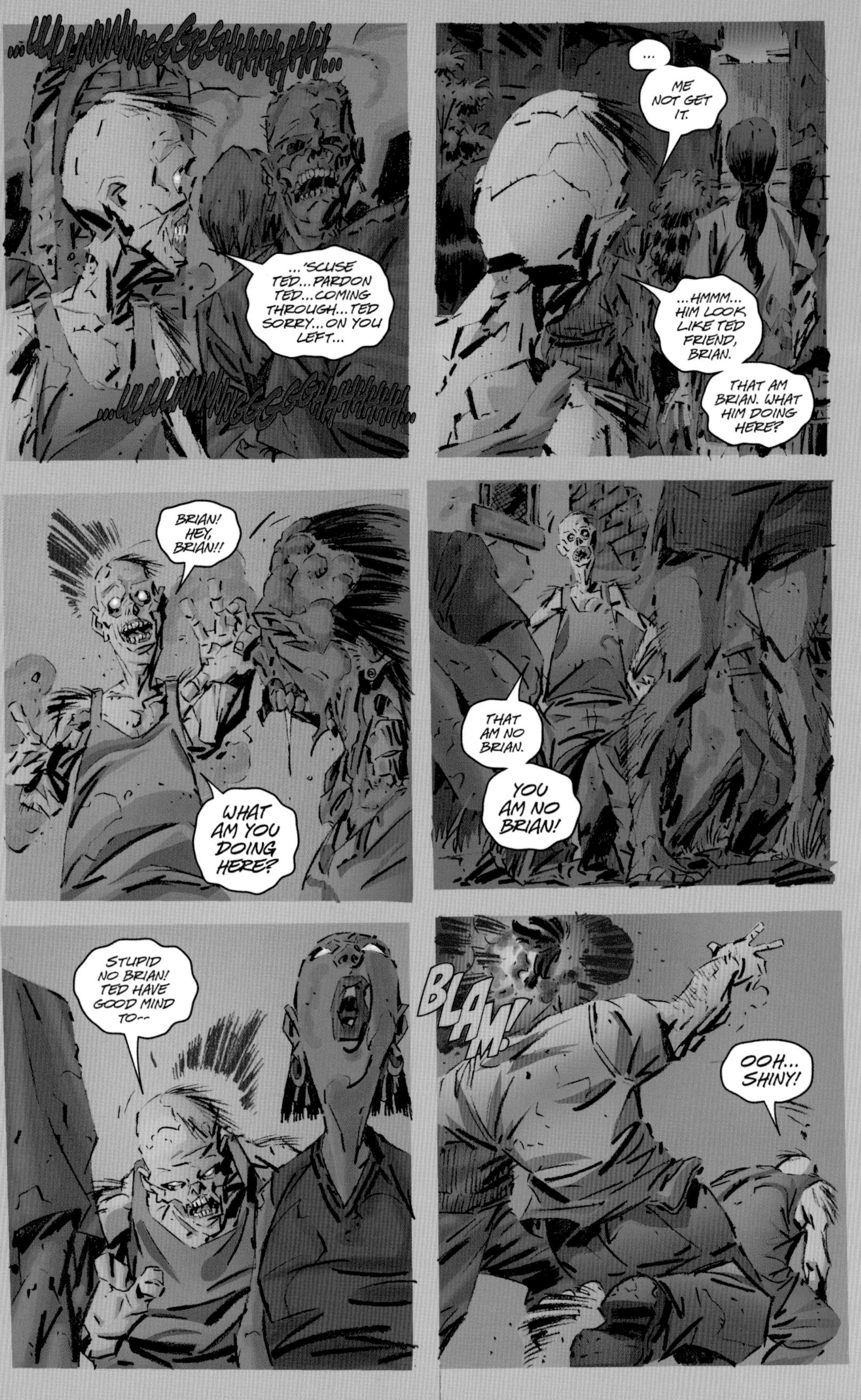
...UUUUUNNNNNGGGGGHHHHHHHH...
...'SCUSE TED...PARDON TED...COMING THROUGH...TED SORRY...ON YOU LEFT...
...UUUUUNNNNNGGGGGHHHHHH...
...
ME NOT GET IT.
...HMMM... HIM LOOK LIKE TED FRIEND, BRIAN.
THAT AM BRIAN. WHAT HIM DOING HERE?
BRIAN! HEY, BRIAN!!
WHAT AM YOU DOING HERE?
THAT AM NO BRIAN.
YOU AM NO BRIAN!
STUPID NO BRIAN! TED HAVE GOOD MIND TO--
BLAM!
OOH... SHINY!

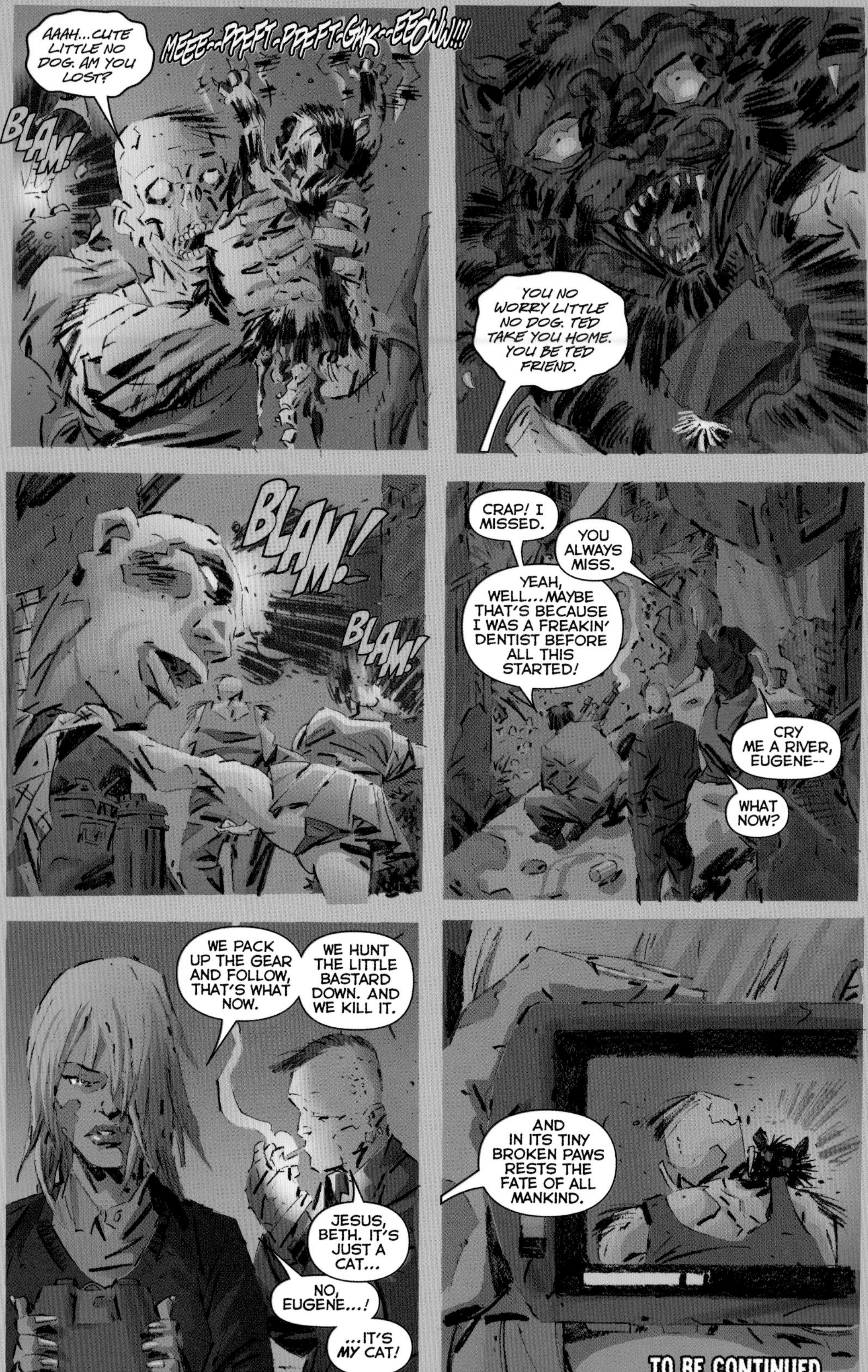
AAAH...CUTE LITTLE NO DOG. AM YOU LOST?
MEEE--PPFFT-PPFFT-GAK--EEOWW!!!
BLAM!
YOU NO WORRY LITTLE NO DOG. TED TAKE YOU HOME. YOU BE TED FRIEND.
BLAM!
BLAM!
CRAP! I MISSED.
YOU ALWAYS MISS.
YEAH, WELL... MAYBE THAT'S BECAUSE I WAS A FREAKIN' DENTIST BEFORE ALL THIS STARTED!
CRY ME A RIVER, EUGENE--
WHAT NOW?
WE PACK UP THE GEAR AND FOLLOW, THAT'S WHAT NOW.
WE HUNT THE LITTLE BASTARD DOWN. AND WE KILL IT.
JESUS, BETH. IT'S JUST A CAT...
NO, EUGENE...!
...IT'S MY CAT!
AND IN ITS TINY BROKEN PAWS RESTS THE FATE OF ALL MANKIND.
TO BE CONTINUED...

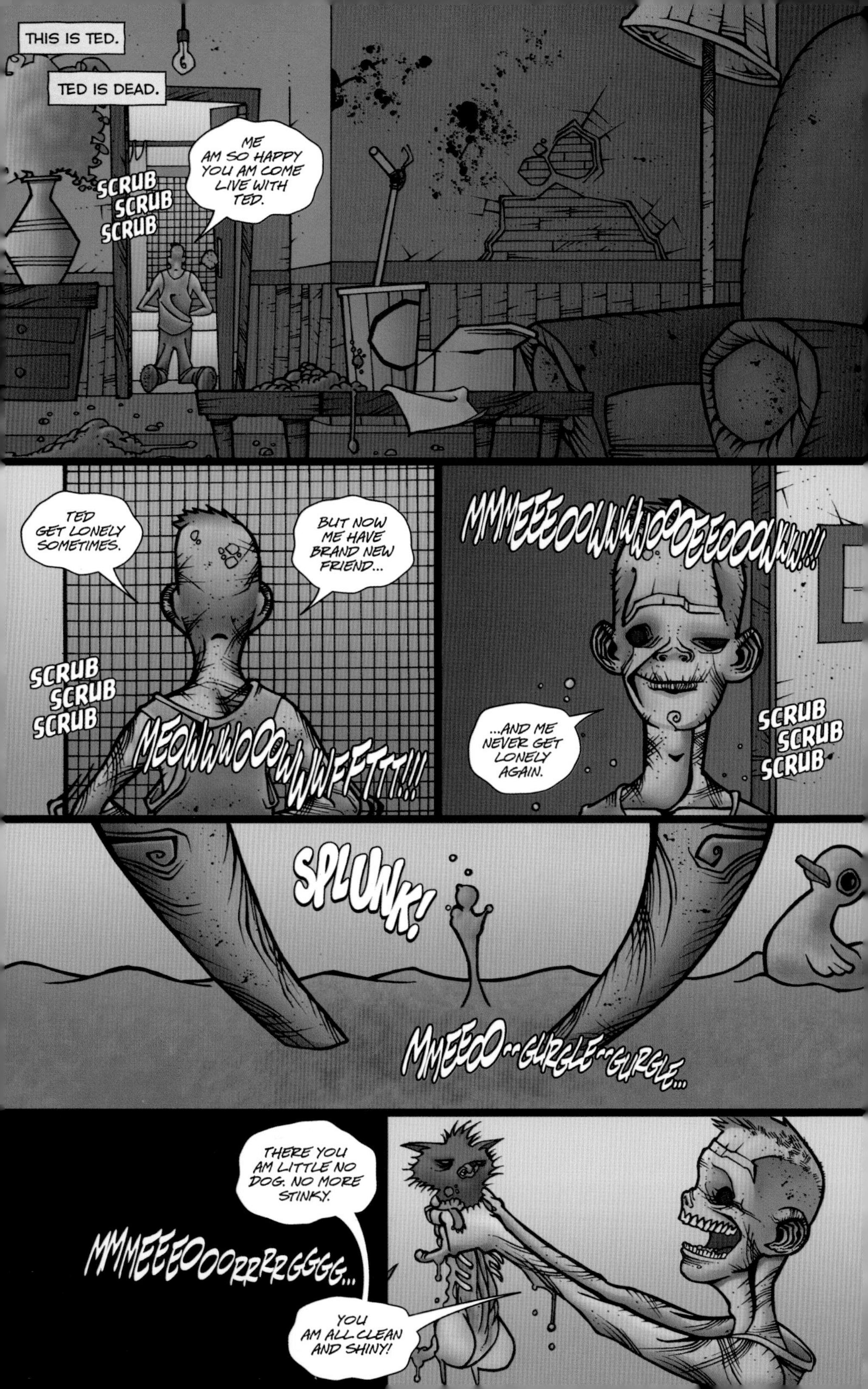
THIS IS TED.
TED IS DEAD.
SCRUB SCRUB SCRUB
ME AM SO HAPPY YOU AM COME LIVE WITH TED.
TED GET LONELY SOMETIMES.
BUT NOW ME HAVE BRAND NEW FRIEND...
SCRUB SCRUB SCRUB
MEOWWWOOOOWWWFFTTT!!!
MMMEEEEOOWWWWOOOEEOOOWWW!!!
...AND ME NEVER GET LONELY AGAIN.
SCRUB SCRUB SCRUB
SPLUNK!
MMEEOO--GURGLE--GURGLE...
THERE YOU AM LITTLE NO DOG. NO MORE STINKY.
MMMEEEEOOORRRRGGGG...
YOU AM ALL CLEAN AND SHINY!

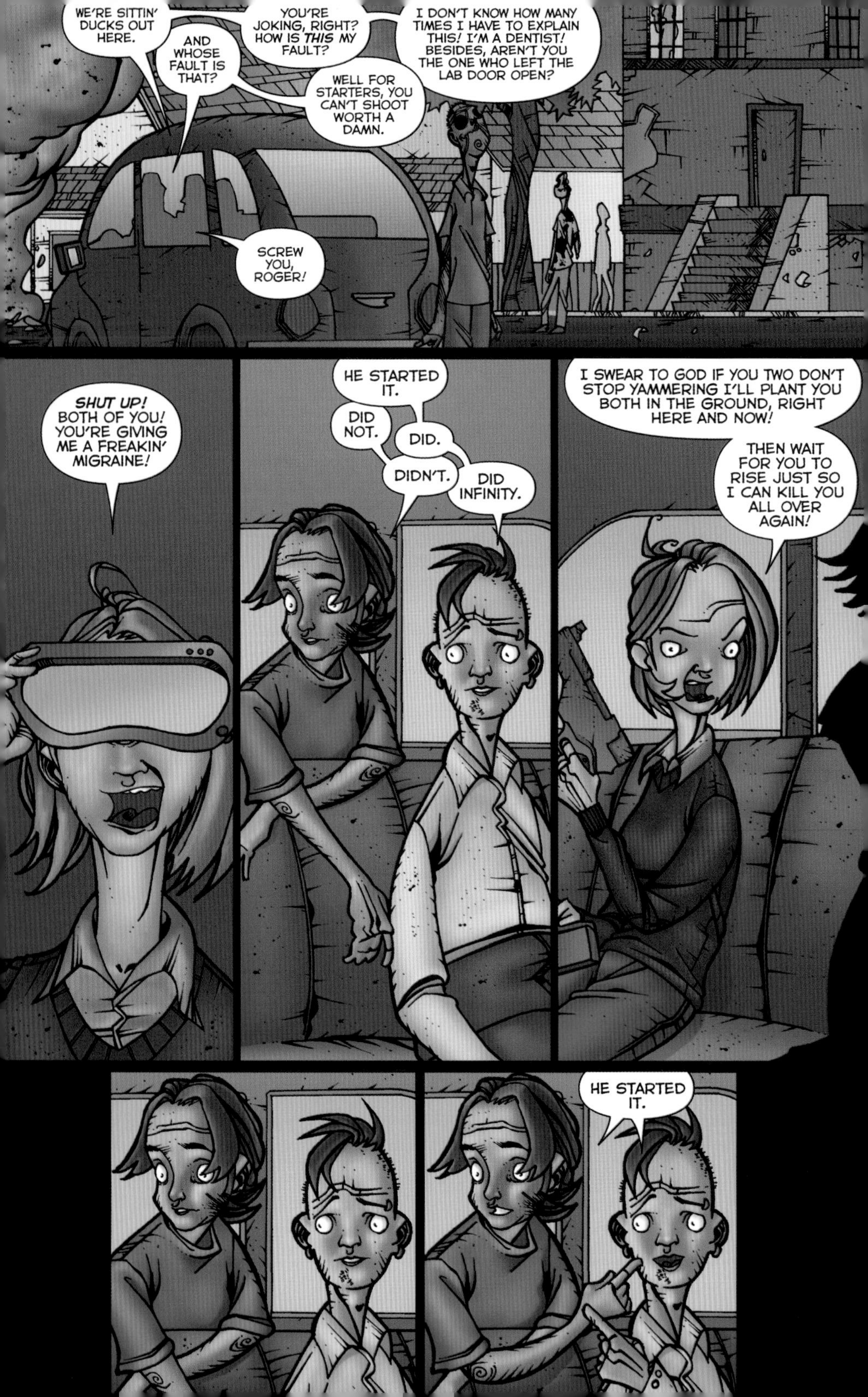
WE'RE SITTIN' DUCKS OUT HERE.
AND WHOSE FAULT IS THAT?
YOU'RE JOKING, RIGHT? HOW IS *THIS* MY FAULT?
WELL FOR STARTERS, YOU CAN'T SHOOT WORTH A DAMN.
I DON'T KNOW HOW MANY TIMES I HAVE TO EXPLAIN THIS! I'M A DENTIST! BESIDES, AREN'T YOU THE ONE WHO LEFT THE LAB DOOR OPEN?
SCREW YOU, ROGER!
SHUT UP! BOTH OF YOU! YOU'RE GIVING ME A FREAKIN' MIGRAINE!
HE STARTED IT.
DID NOT.
DID.
DIDN'T.
DID INFINITY.
I SWEAR TO GOD IF YOU TWO DON'T STOP YAMMERING I'LL PLANT YOU BOTH IN THE GROUND, RIGHT HERE AND NOW!
THEN WAIT FOR YOU TO RISE JUST SO I CAN KILL YOU ALL OVER AGAIN!
HE STARTED IT.

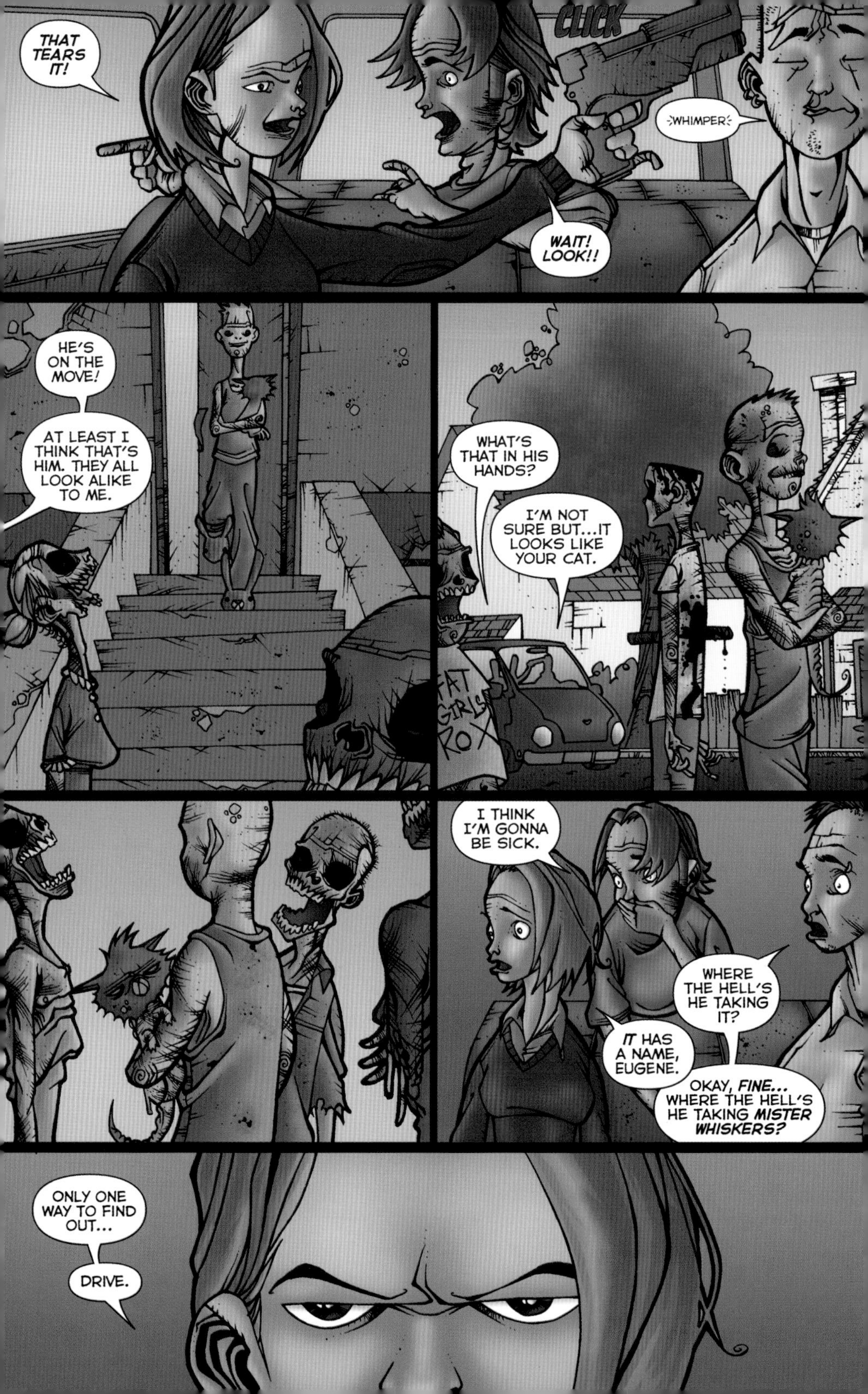
CLICK
THAT TEARS IT!
WHIMPER
WAIT! LOOK!!
HE'S ON THE MOVE!
AT LEAST I THINK THAT'S HIM. THEY ALL LOOK ALIKE TO ME.
WHAT'S THAT IN HIS HANDS?
I'M NOT SURE BUT...IT LOOKS LIKE YOUR CAT.
FAT GIRLS ROX
I THINK I'M GONNA BE SICK.
WHERE THE HELL'S HE TAKING IT?
IT HAS A NAME, EUGENE.
OKAY, FINE... WHERE THE HELL'S HE TAKING MISTER WHISKERS?
ONLY ONE WAY TO FIND OUT...
DRIVE.

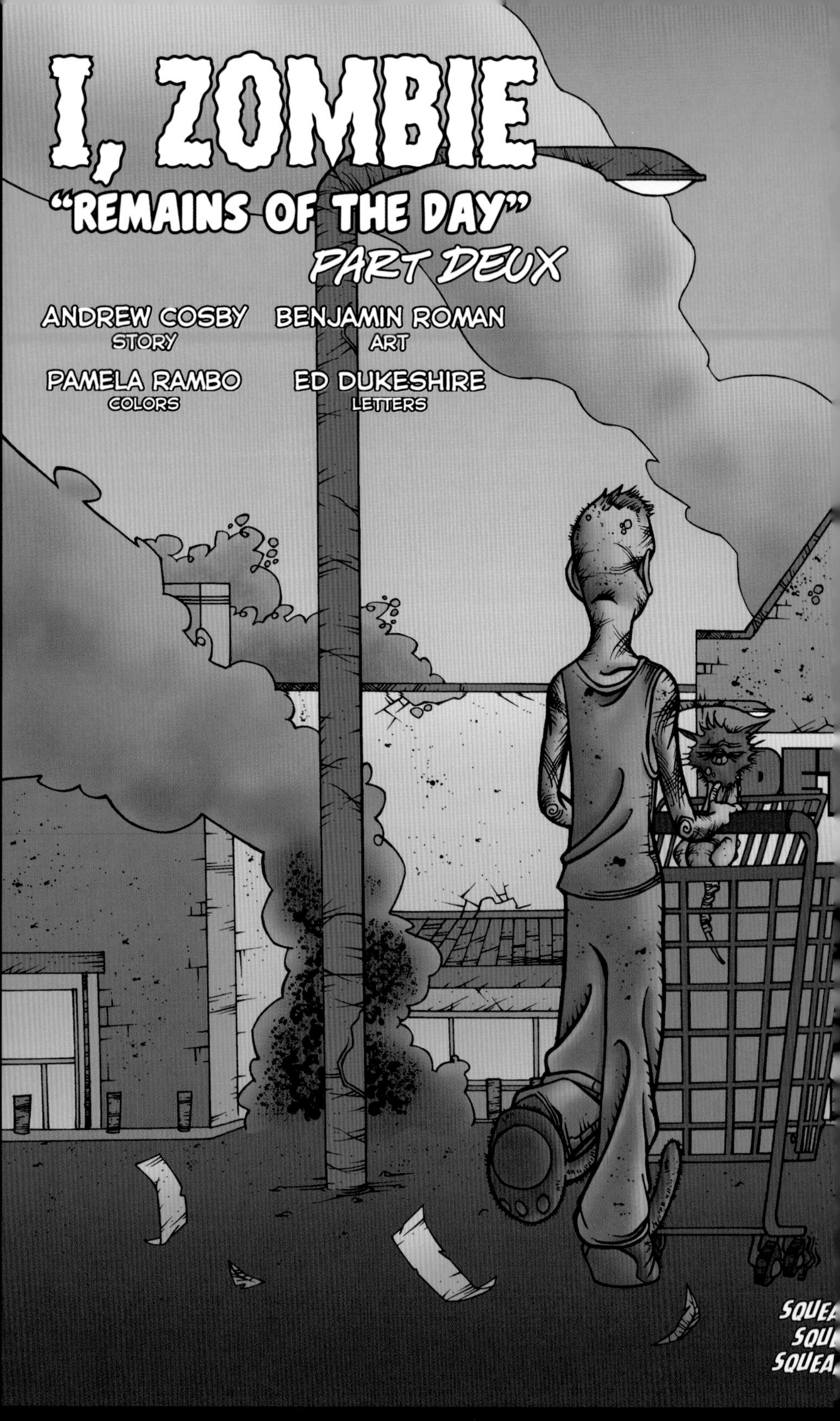
I, ZOMBIE
"REMAINS OF THE DAY"
PART DEUX
ANDREW COSBY
STORY
BENJAMIN ROMAN
ART
PAMELA RAMBO
COLORS
ED DUKESHIRE
LETTERS

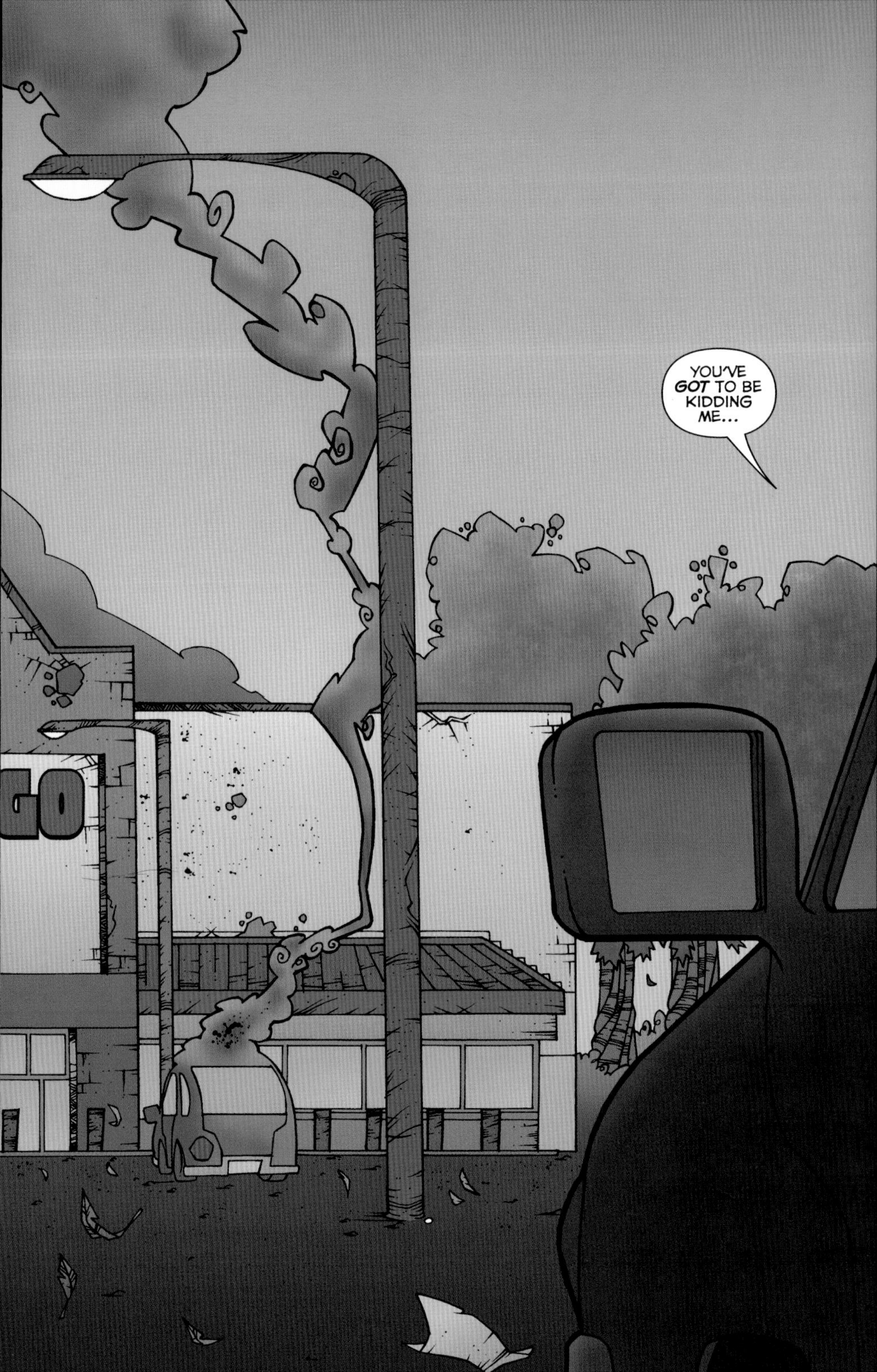
YOU'VE GOT TO BE KIDDING ME...
GO

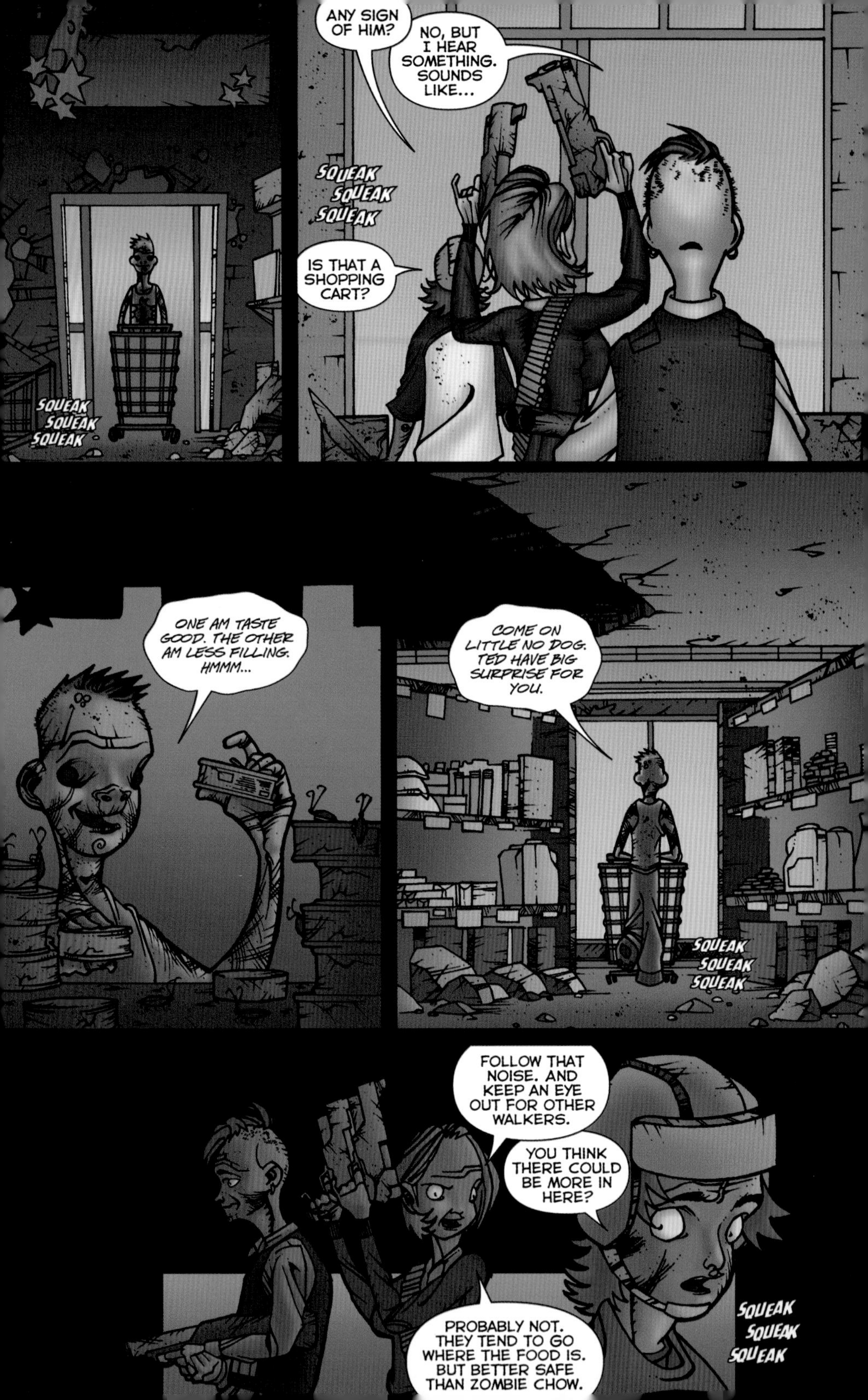
SQUEAK
SQUEAK
SQUEAK
ANY SIGN OF HIM?
NO, BUT I HEAR SOMETHING. SOUNDS LIKE...
SQUEAK
SQUEAK
SQUEAK
IS THAT A SHOPPING CART?
ONE AM TASTE GOOD. THE OTHER AM LESS FILLING. HMMM...
COME ON LITTLE NO DOG. TED HAVE BIG SURPRISE FOR YOU.
SQUEAK
SQUEAK
SQUEAK
FOLLOW THAT NOISE. AND KEEP AN EYE OUT FOR OTHER WALKERS.
YOU THINK THERE COULD BE MORE IN HERE?
PROBABLY NOT. THEY TEND TO GO WHERE THE FOOD IS. BUT BETTER SAFE THAN ZOMBIE CHOW.
SQUEAK
SQUEAK
SQUEAK

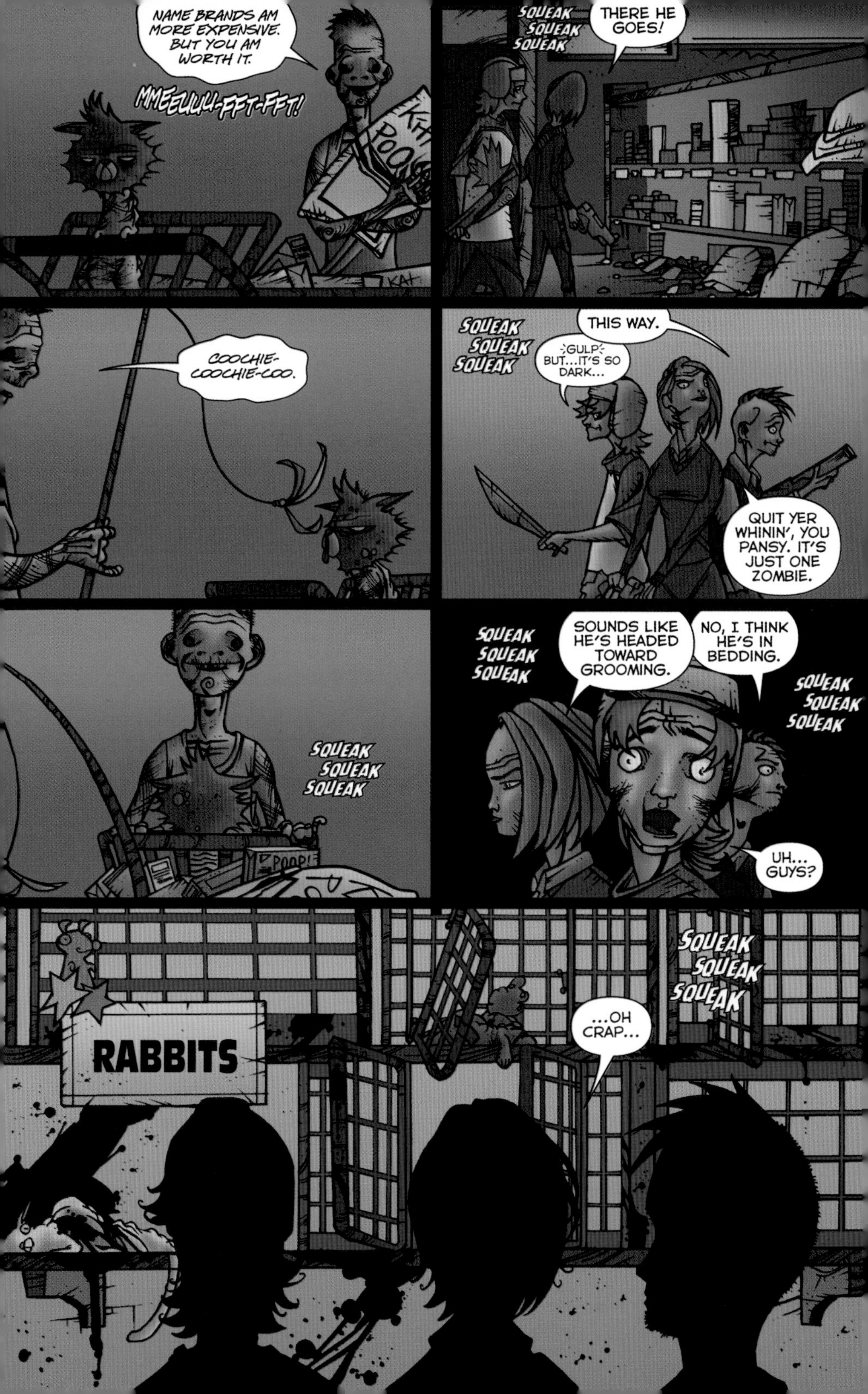
NAME BRANDS AM MORE EXPENSIVE. BUT YOU AM WORTH IT.
MMEEUUU-FFT-FFT!
SQUEAK SQUEAK SQUEAK
THERE HE GOES!
COOCHIE-COOCHIE-COO.
SQUEAK SQUEAK SQUEAK
THIS WAY.
GULP BUT...IT'S SO DARK...
QUIT YER WHININ', YOU PANSY. IT'S JUST ONE ZOMBIE.
SQUEAK SQUEAK SQUEAK
SQUEAK SQUEAK SQUEAK
SOUNDS LIKE HE'S HEADED TOWARD GROOMING.
NO, I THINK HE'S IN BEDDING.
SQUEAK SQUEAK SQUEAK
UH... GUYS?
RABBITS
SQUEAK SQUEAK SQUEAK
...OH CRAP...

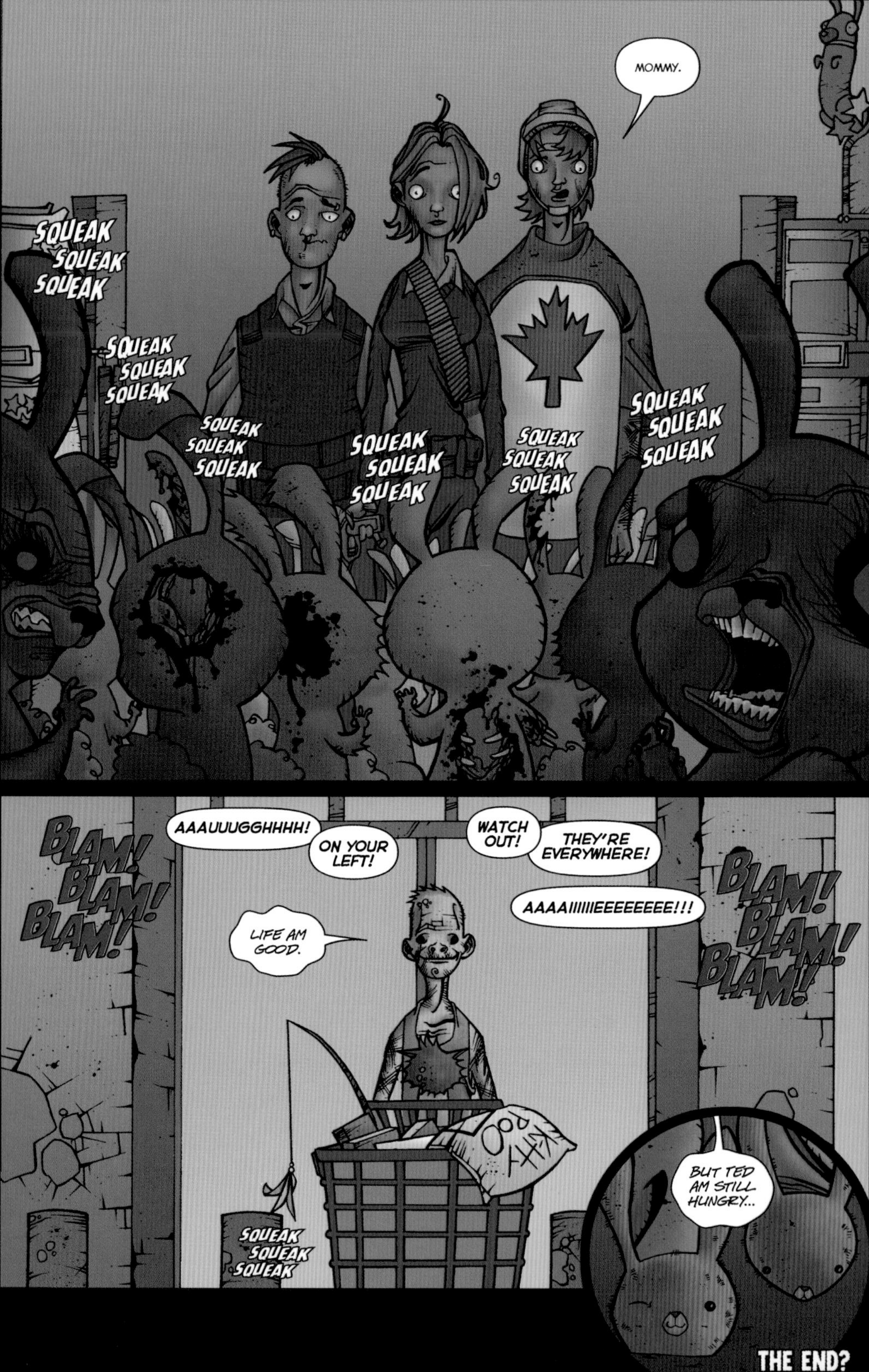
MOMMY.
SQUEAK SQUEAK SQUEAK
SQUEAK SQUEAK SQUEAK
SQUEAK SQUEAK SQUEAK
SQUEAK SQUEAK SQUEAK
SQUEAK SQUEAK SQUEAK
SQUEAK SQUEAK SQUEAK
BLAM! BLAM! BLAM!
AAAUUUGGHHHH!
ON YOUR LEFT!
WATCH OUT!
THEY'RE EVERYWHERE!
BLAM! BLAM! BLAM!
AAAAIIIIIIEEEEEEEE!!!
LIFE AM GOOD.
SQUEAK SQUEAK SQUEAK
BUT TED AM STILL HUNGRY...
THE END?

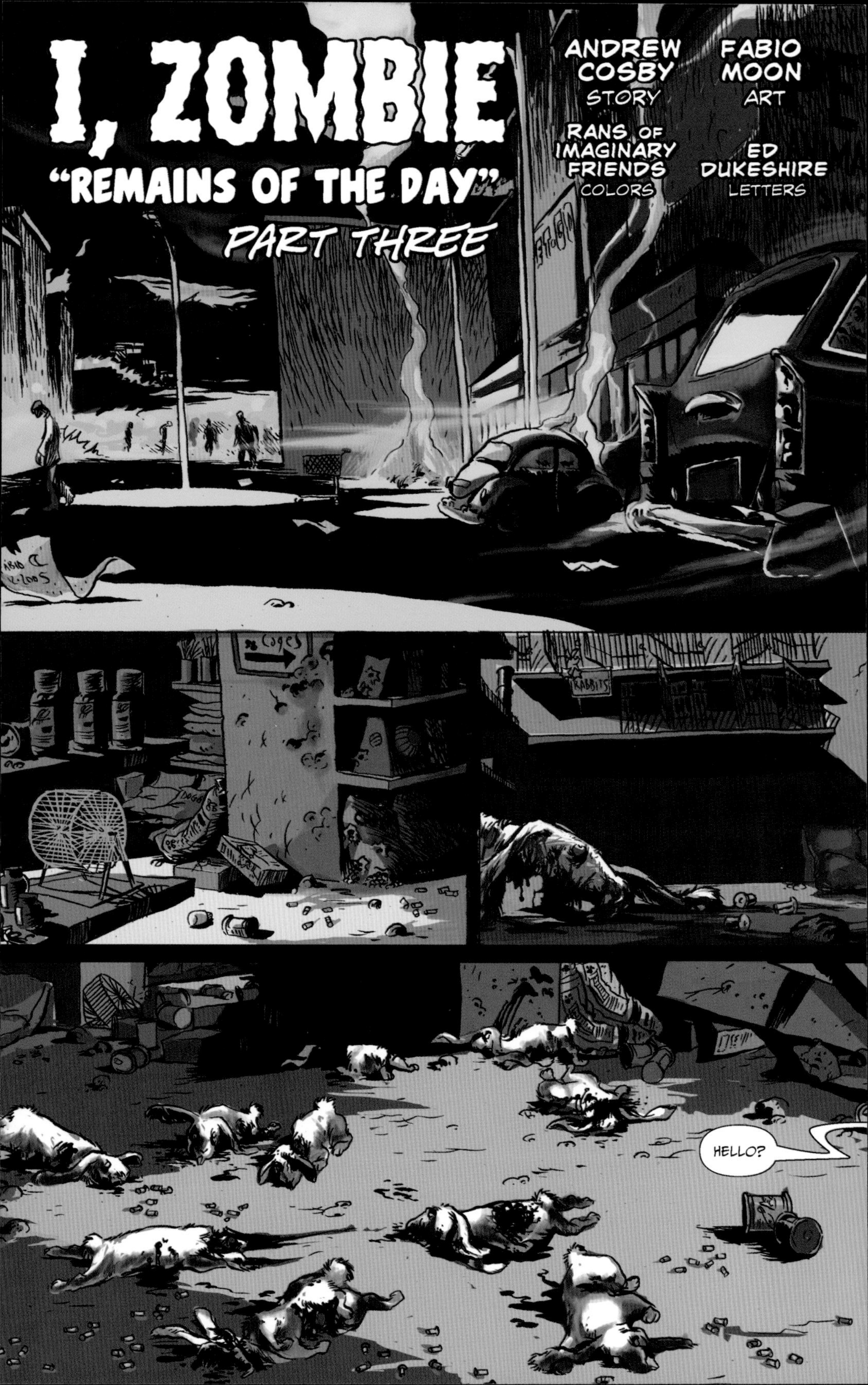
I, ZOMBIE
"REMAINS OF THE DAY"
PART THREE
ANDREW COSBY
STORY
FABIO MOON
ART
RANS OF IMAGINARY FRIENDS
COLORS
ED DUKESHIRE
LETTERS
CAGES
RABBITS
HELLO?

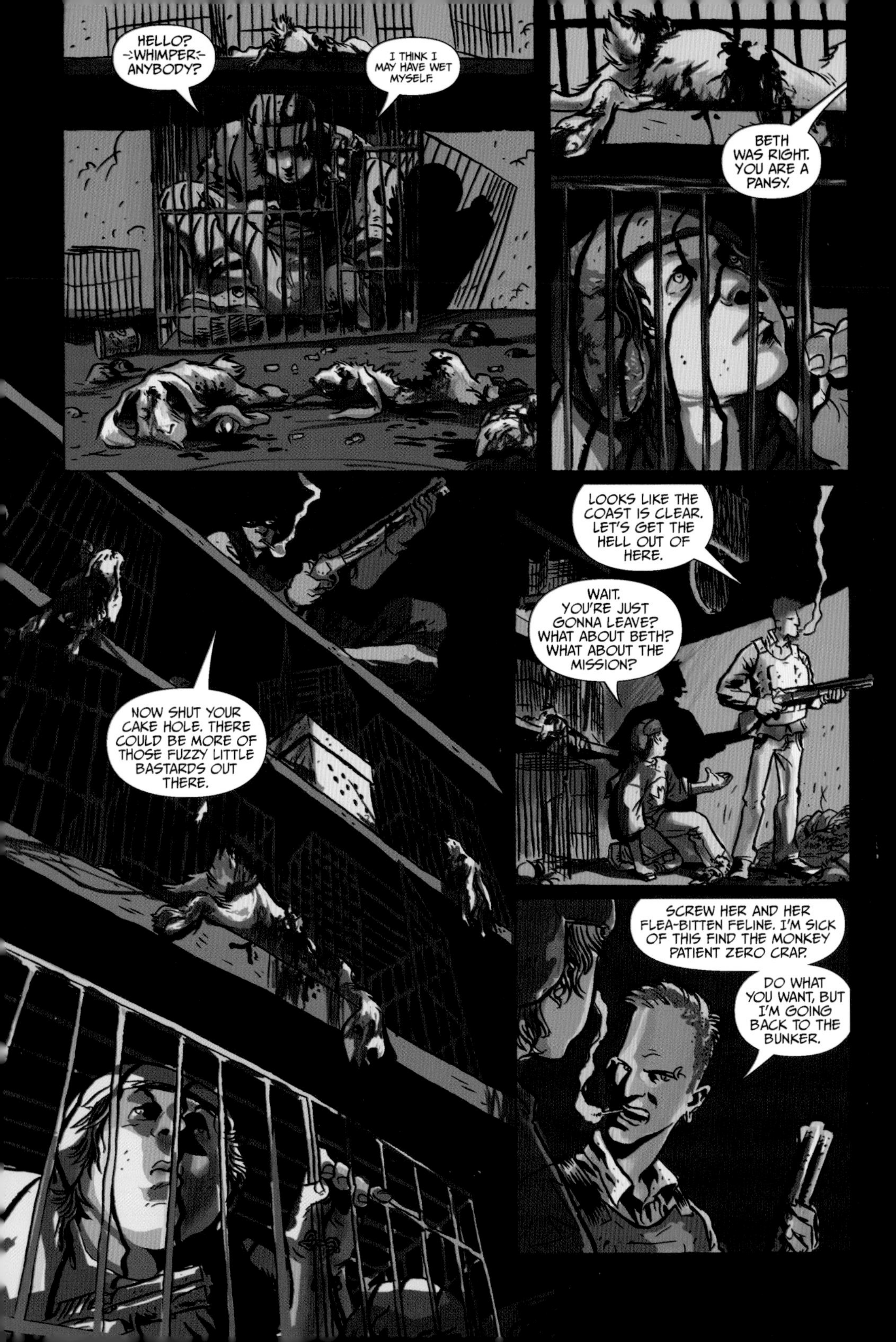
HELLO? -WHIMPER- ANYBODY?
I THINK I MAY HAVE WET MYSELF.
BETH WAS RIGHT. YOU ARE A PANSY.
NOW SHUT YOUR CAKE HOLE. THERE COULD BE MORE OF THOSE FUZZY LITTLE BASTARDS OUT THERE.
LOOKS LIKE THE COAST IS CLEAR. LET'S GET THE HELL OUT OF HERE.
WAIT. YOU'RE JUST GONNA LEAVE? WHAT ABOUT BETH? WHAT ABOUT THE MISSION?
SCREW HER AND HER FLEA-BITTEN FELINE. I'M SICK OF THIS FIND THE MONKEY PATIENT ZERO CRAP.
DO WHAT YOU WANT, BUT I'M GOING BACK TO THE BUNKER.

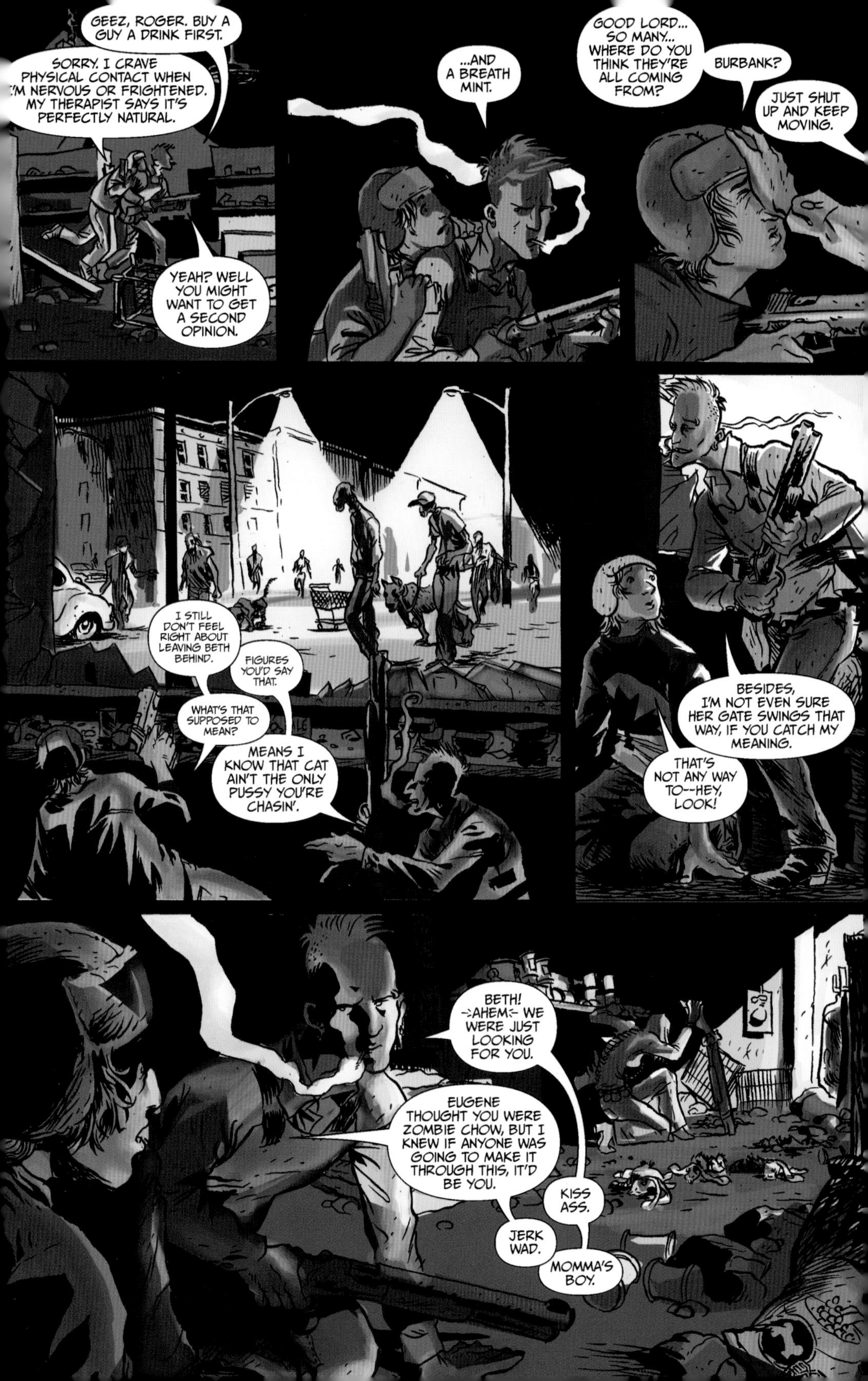

GEEZ, ROGER. BUY A GUY A DRINK FIRST.
SORRY. I CRAVE PHYSICAL CONTACT WHEN I'M NERVOUS OR FRIGHTENED. MY THERAPIST SAYS IT'S PERFECTLY NATURAL.
YEAH? WELL YOU MIGHT WANT TO GET A SECOND OPINION.
...AND A BREATH MINT.
GOOD LORD... SO MANY... WHERE DO YOU THINK THEY'RE ALL COMING FROM?
BURBANK?
JUST SHUT UP AND KEEP MOVING.
I STILL DON'T FEEL RIGHT ABOUT LEAVING BETH BEHIND.
FIGURES YOU'D SAY THAT.
WHAT'S THAT SUPPOSED TO MEAN?
MEANS I KNOW THAT CAT AIN'T THE ONLY PUSSY YOU'RE CHASIN'.
BESIDES, I'M NOT EVEN SURE HER GATE SWINGS THAT WAY, IF YOU CATCH MY MEANING.
THAT'S NOT ANY WAY TO--HEY, LOOK!
BETH! -AHEM- WE WERE JUST LOOKING FOR YOU.
EUGENE THOUGHT YOU WERE ZOMBIE CHOW, BUT I KNEW IF ANYONE WAS GOING TO MAKE IT THROUGH THIS, IT'D BE YOU.
KISS ASS.
JERK WAD.
MOMMA'S BOY.

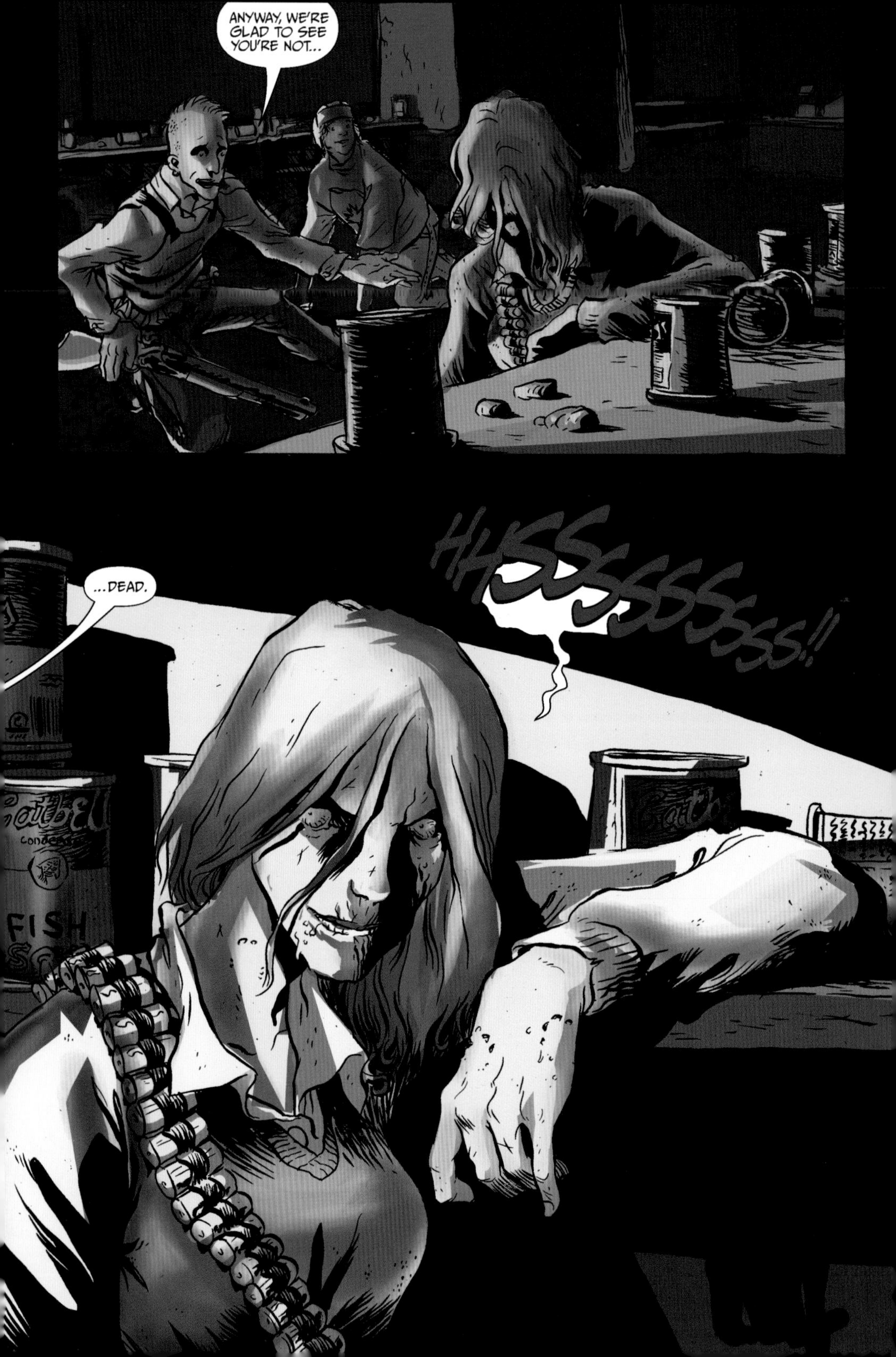
ANYWAY, WE'RE GLAD TO SEE YOU'RE NOT...
...DEAD.
HHSSSSSSSSSS!!

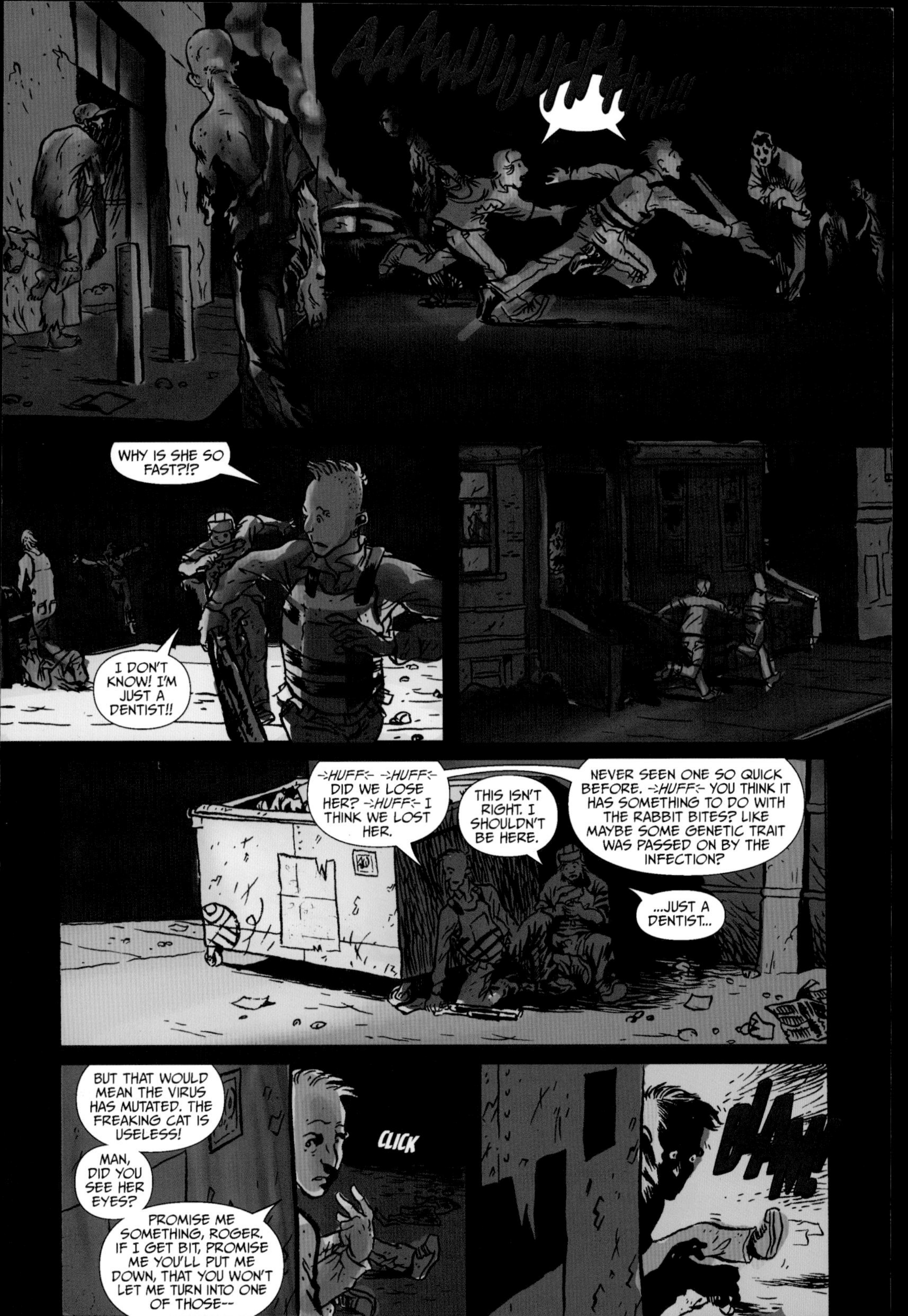

AAAAAUUUUUHHHHHHH!!!
WHY IS SHE SO FAST?!?
I DON'T KNOW! I'M JUST A DENTIST!!
-HUFF- -HUFF- DID WE LOSE HER? -HUFF- I THINK WE LOST HER.
THIS ISN'T RIGHT. I SHOULDN'T BE HERE.
NEVER SEEN ONE SO QUICK BEFORE. -HUFF- YOU THINK IT HAS SOMETHING TO DO WITH THE RABBIT BITES? LIKE MAYBE SOME GENETIC TRAIT WAS PASSED ON BY THE INFECTION?
...JUST A DENTIST...
BUT THAT WOULD MEAN THE VIRUS HAS MUTATED. THE FREAKING CAT IS USELESS!
MAN, DID YOU SEE HER EYES?
PROMISE ME SOMETHING, ROGER. IF I GET BIT, PROMISE ME YOU'LL PUT ME DOWN, THAT YOU WON'T LET ME TURN INTO ONE OF THOSE--
CLICK

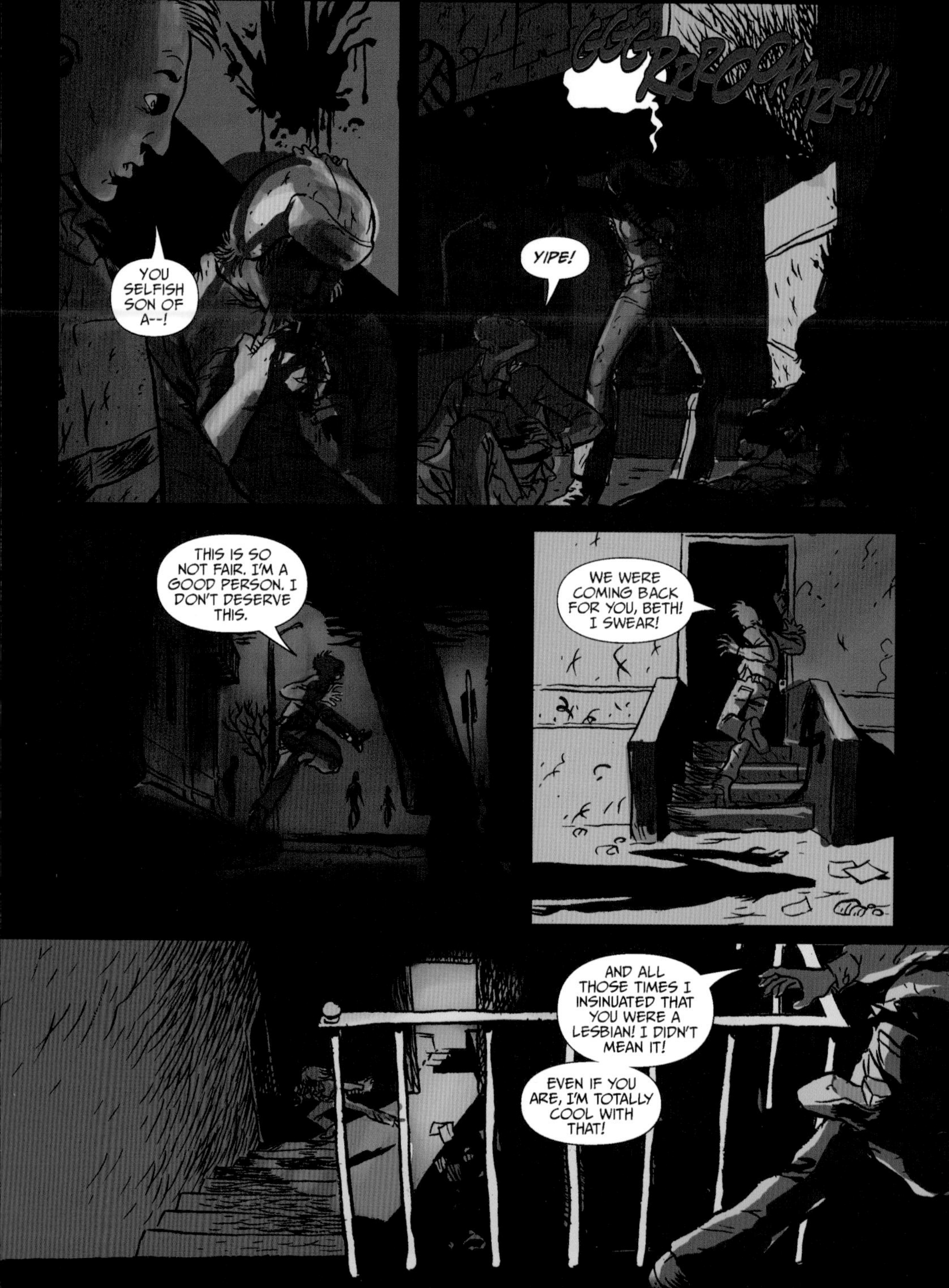
YOU SELFISH SON OF A--!
GGGRRROOAARR!!!
YIPE!
THIS IS SO NOT FAIR. I'M A GOOD PERSON. I DON'T DESERVE THIS.
WE WERE COMING BACK FOR YOU, BETH! I SWEAR!
AND ALL THOSE TIMES I INSINUATED THAT YOU WERE A LESBIAN! I DIDN'T MEAN IT!
EVEN IF YOU ARE, I'M TOTALLY COOL WITH THAT!

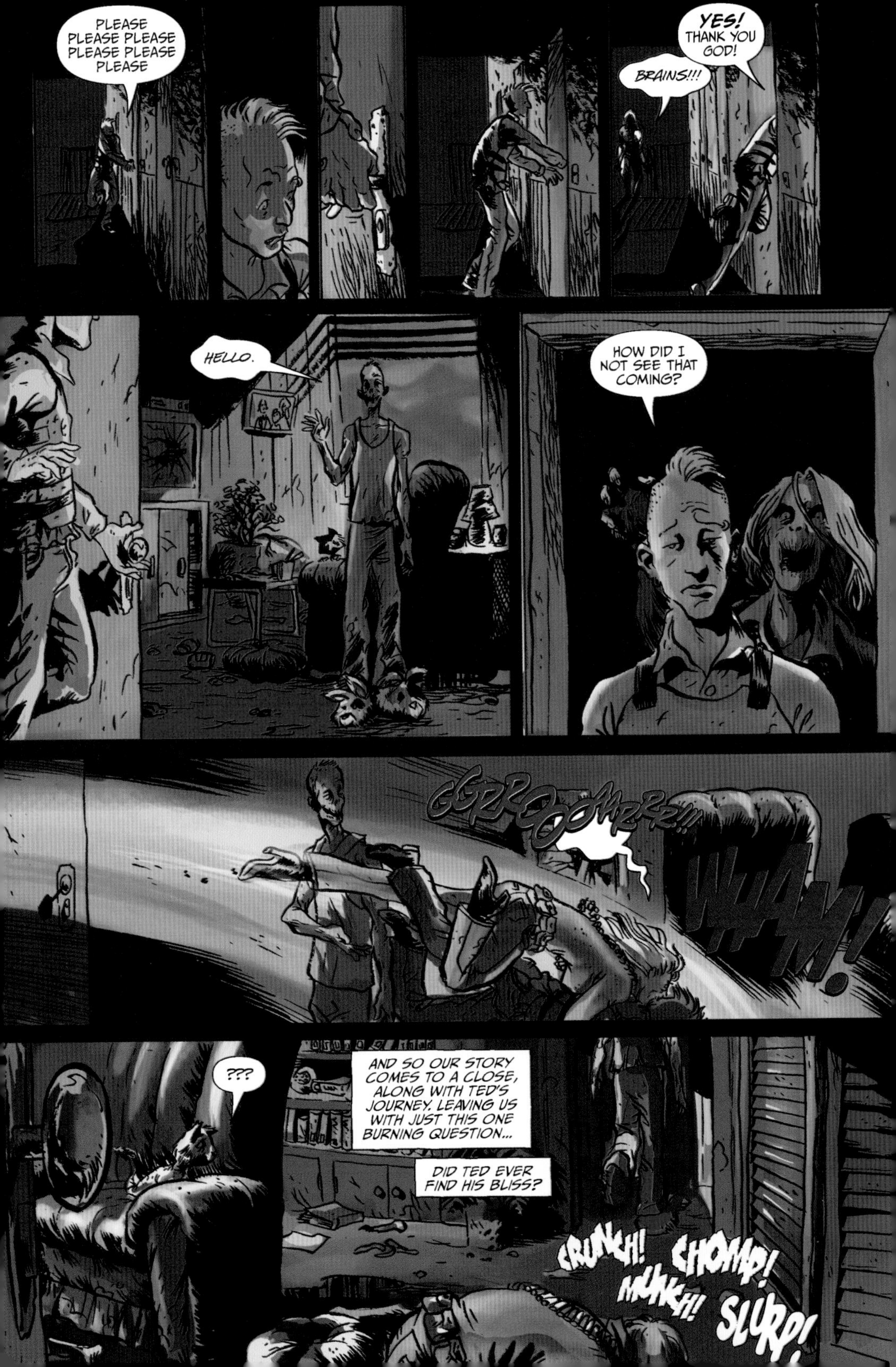
PLEASE PLEASE PLEASE PLEASE PLEASE PLEASE
YES! THANK YOU GOD!
BRAINS!!!
HELLO.
HOW DID I NOT SEE THAT COMING?
GGRROOOARRR!!!
WHAM!!
???
AND SO OUR STORY COMES TO A CLOSE, ALONG WITH TED'S JOURNEY. LEAVING US WITH JUST THIS ONE BURNING QUESTION...
DID TED EVER FIND HIS BLISS?
CRUNCH! CHOMP! MUNCH! SLURP!

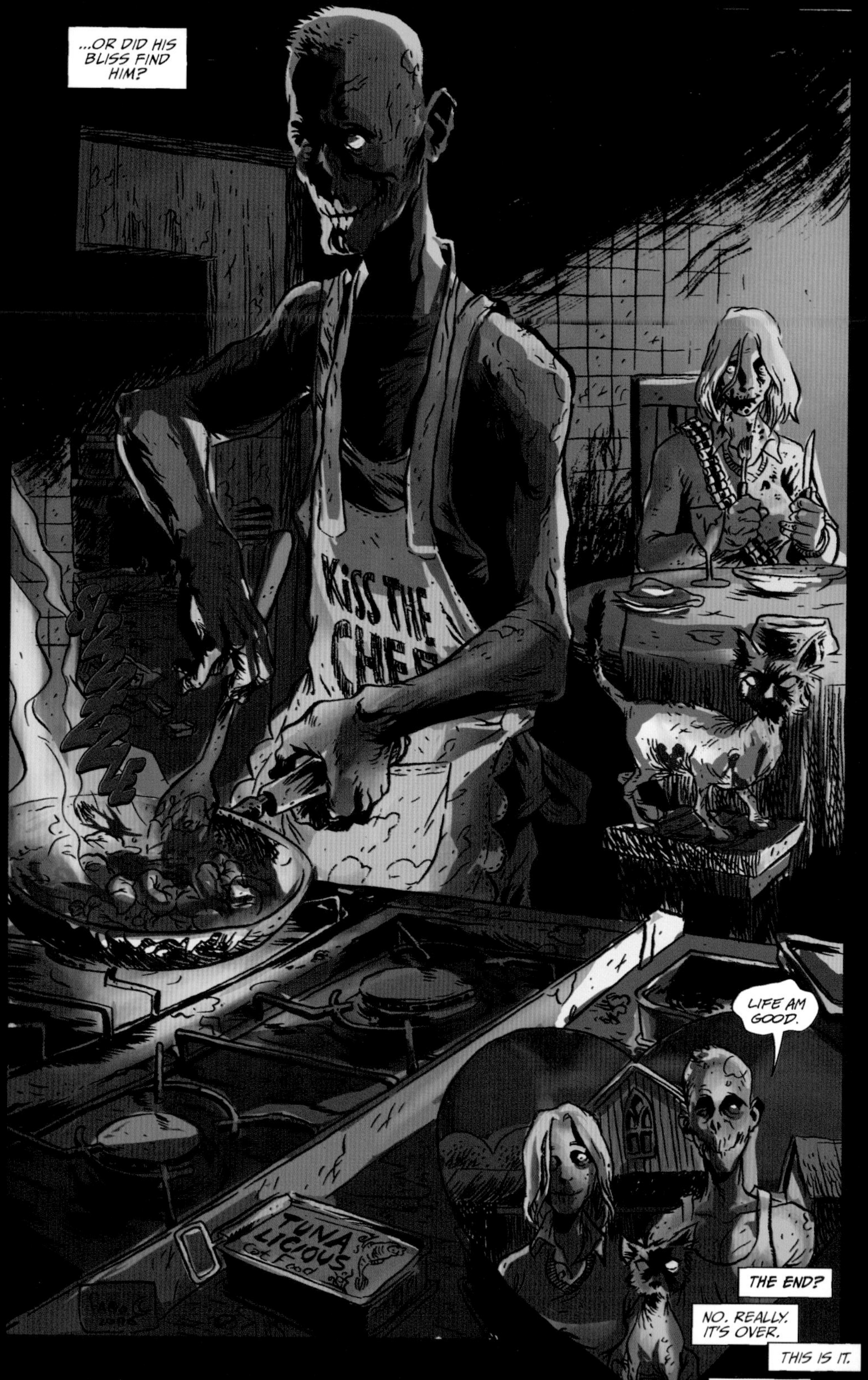
...OR DID HIS BLISS FIND HIM?
KiSS THE
LIFE AM GOOD.
TUNA LICIOUS Cat Food
THE END?
NO. REALLY. IT'S OVER.
THIS IS IT.
...OR IS IT?

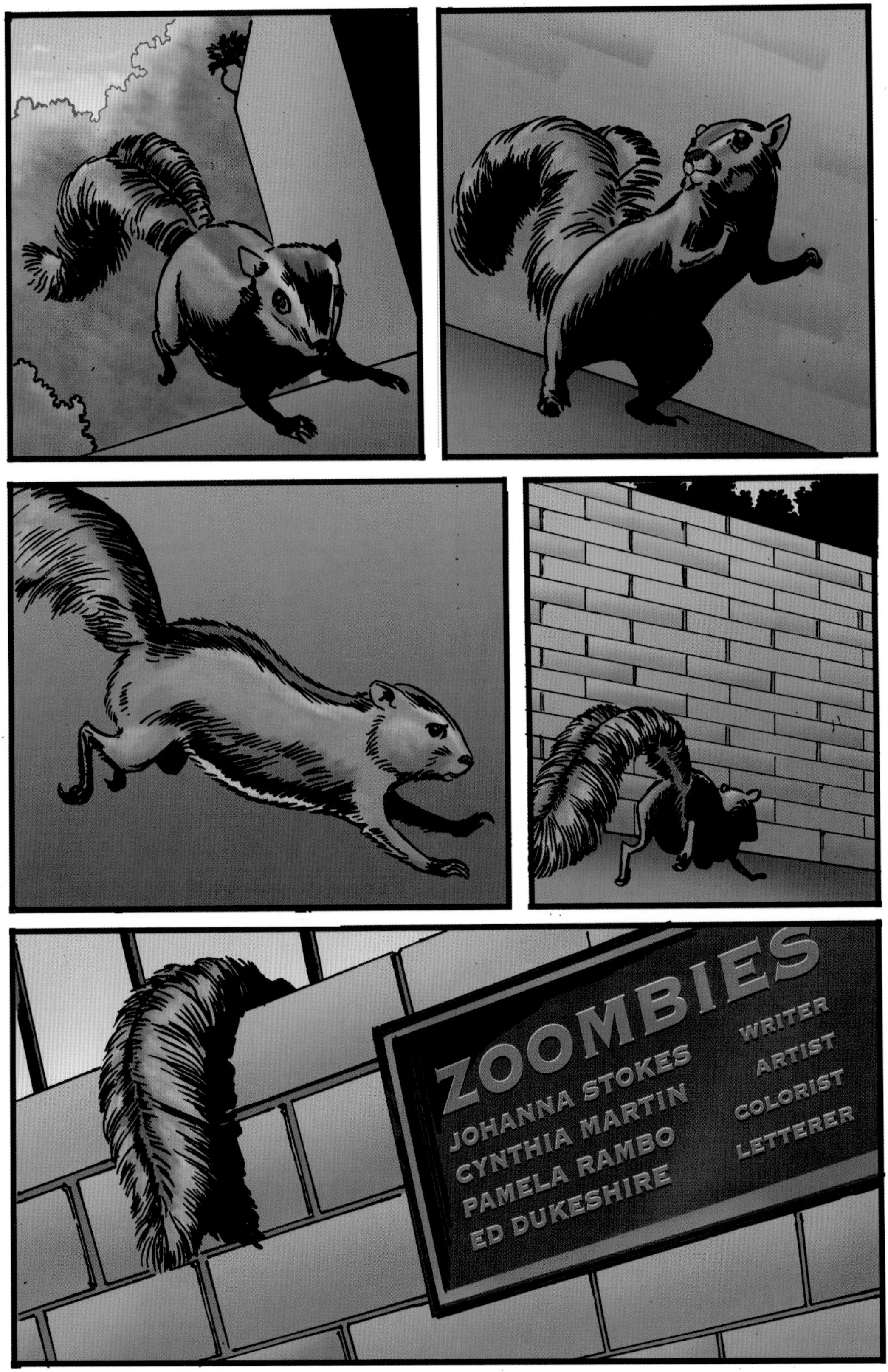
ZOOMBIES
JOHANNA STOKES WRITER
CYNTHIA MARTIN ARTIST
PAMELA RAMBO COLORIST
ED DUKESHIRE LETTERER

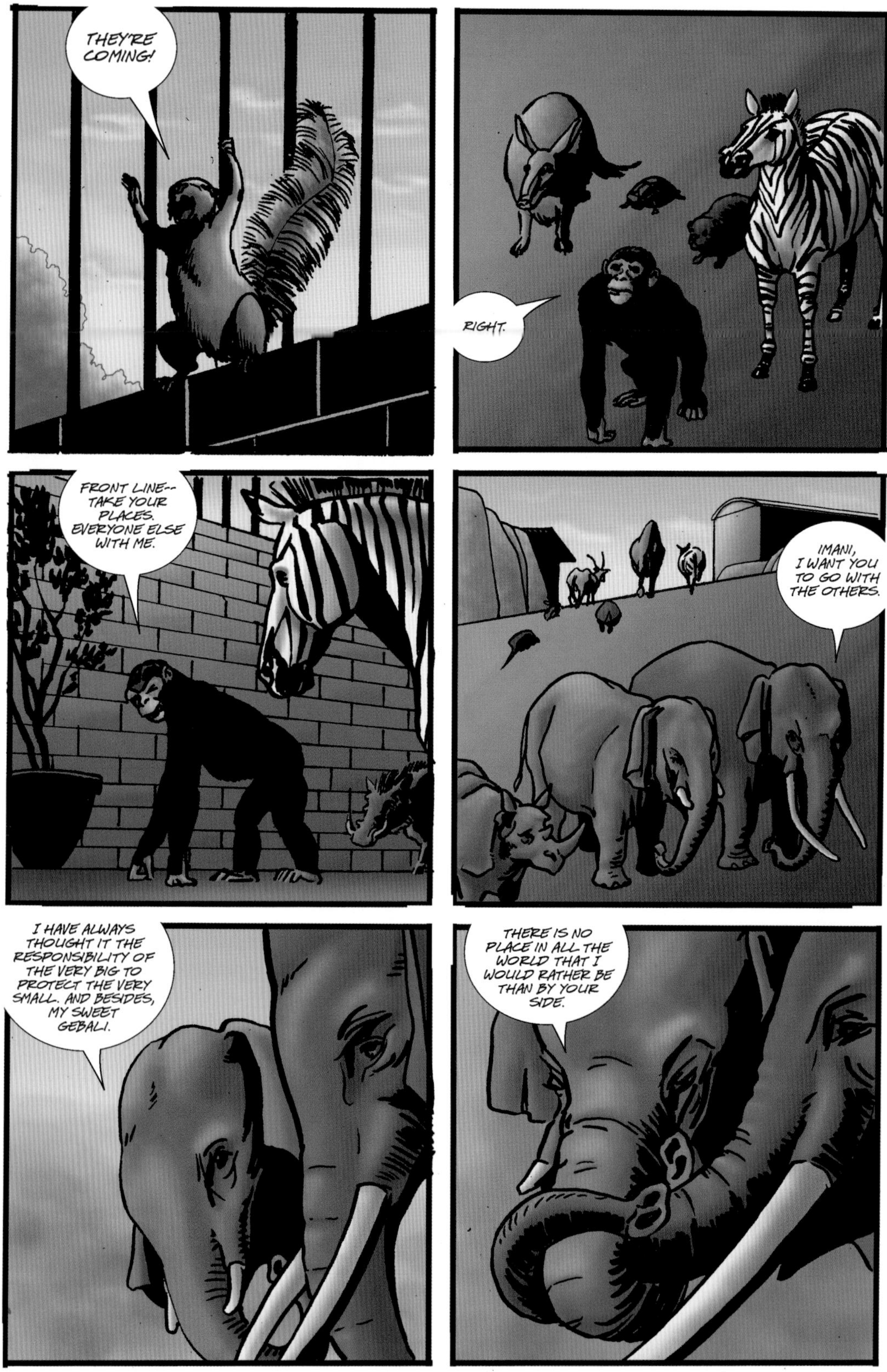
THEY'RE COMING!
RIGHT.
FRONT LINE-- TAKE YOUR PLACES. EVERYONE ELSE WITH ME.
IMANI, I WANT YOU TO GO WITH THE OTHERS.
I HAVE ALWAYS THOUGHT IT THE RESPONSIBILITY OF THE VERY BIG TO PROTECT THE VERY SMALL. AND BESIDES, MY SWEET GEBALI.
THERE IS NO PLACE IN ALL THE WORLD THAT I WOULD RATHER BE THAN BY YOUR SIDE.

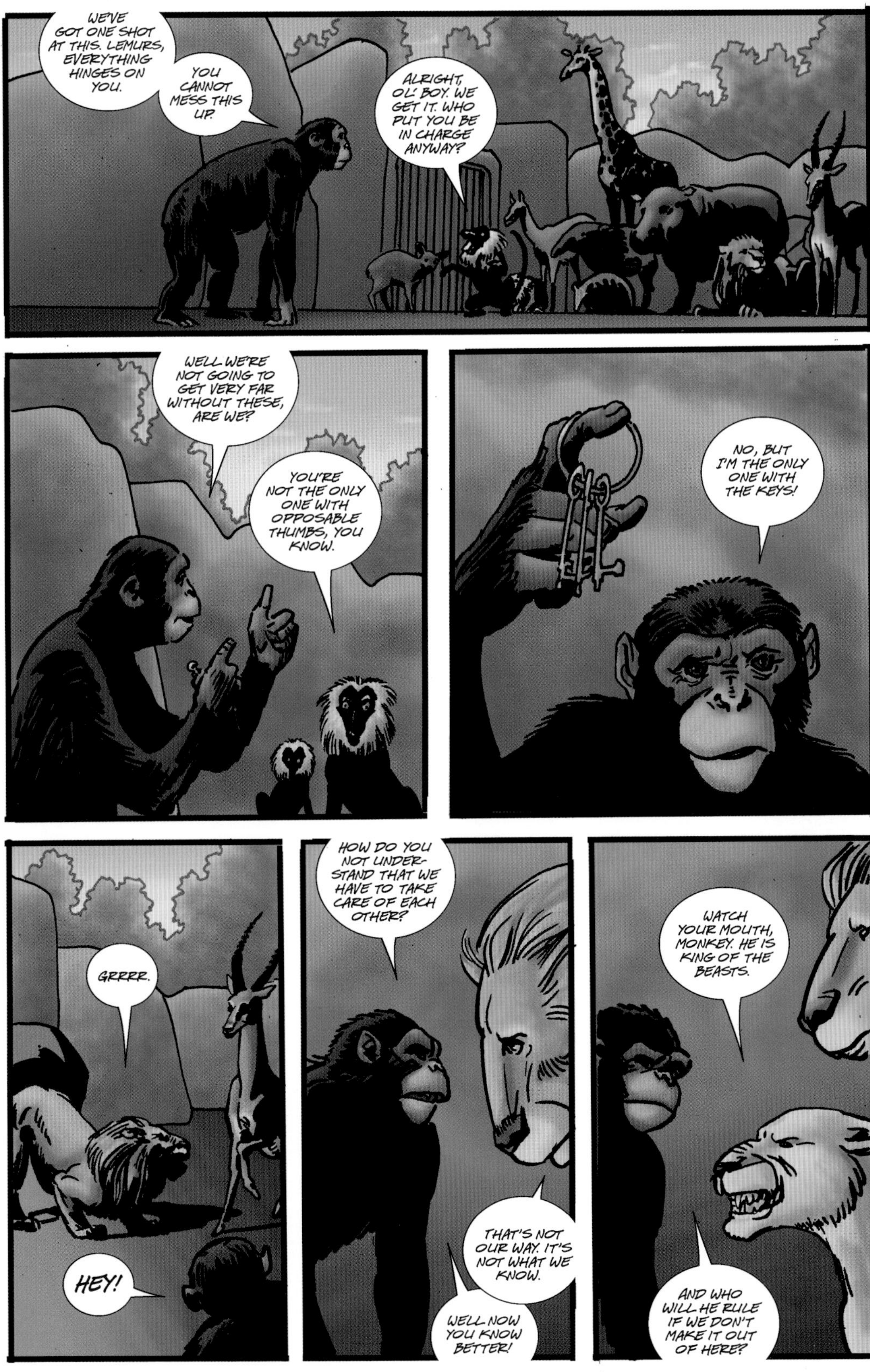
WE'VE GOT ONE SHOT AT THIS. LEMURS, EVERYTHING HINGES ON YOU.
YOU CANNOT MESS THIS UP.
ALRIGHT, OL' BOY. WE GET IT. WHO PUT YOU BE IN CHARGE ANYWAY?
WELL WE'RE NOT GOING TO GET VERY FAR WITHOUT THESE, ARE WE?
YOU'RE NOT THE ONLY ONE WITH OPPOSABLE THUMBS, YOU KNOW.
NO, BUT I'M THE ONLY ONE WITH THE KEYS!
GRRRR.
HEY!
HOW DO YOU NOT UNDER-STAND THAT WE HAVE TO TAKE CARE OF EACH OTHER?
THAT'S NOT OUR WAY. IT'S NOT WHAT WE KNOW.
WELL NOW YOU KNOW BETTER!
WATCH YOUR MOUTH, MONKEY. HE IS KING OF THE BEASTS.
AND WHO WILL HE RULE IF WE DON'T MAKE IT OUT OF HERE?

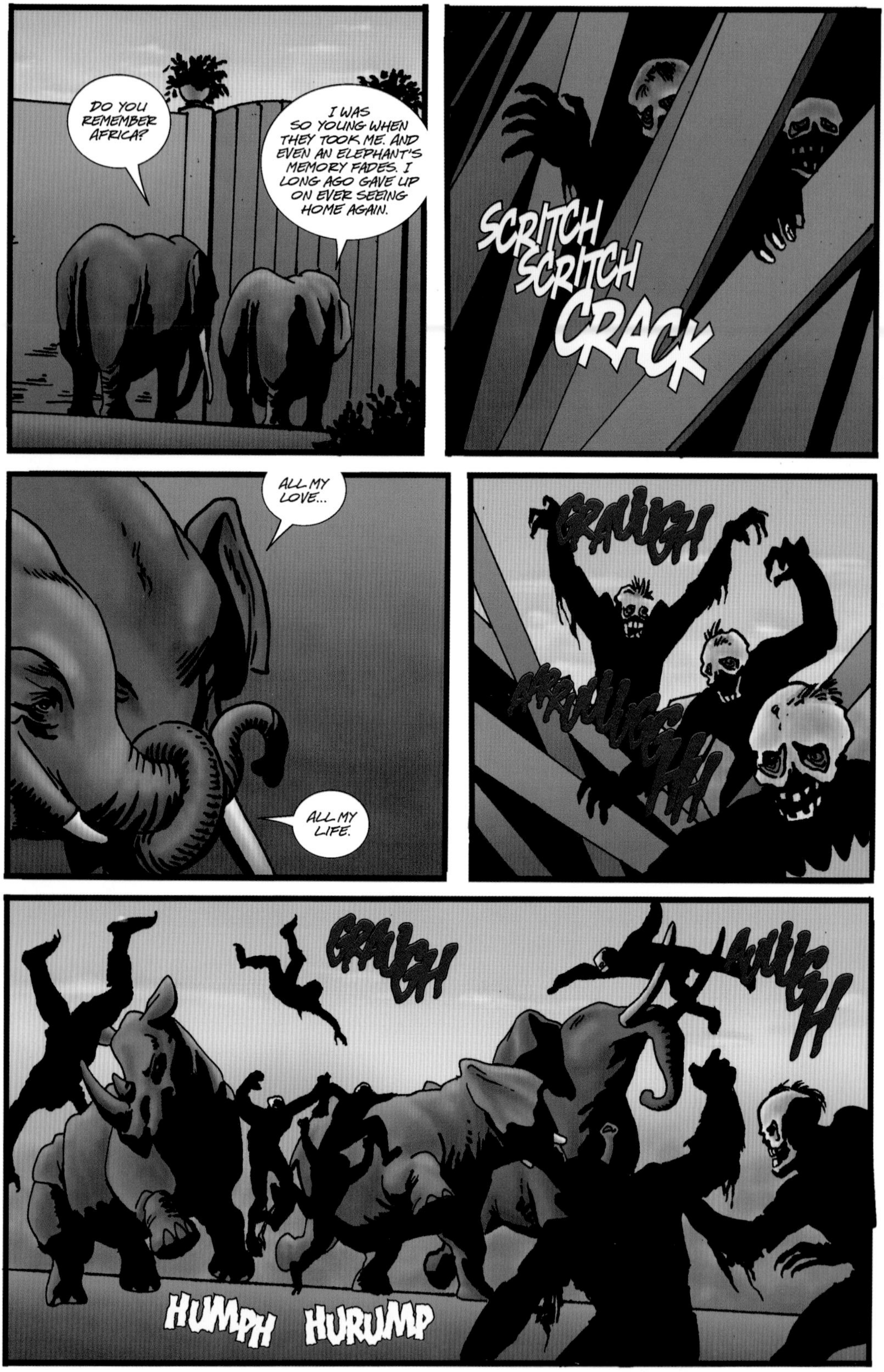
DO YOU REMEMBER AFRICA?
I WAS SO YOUNG WHEN THEY TOOK ME. AND EVEN AN ELEPHANT'S MEMORY FADES. I LONG AGO GAVE UP ON EVER SEEING HOME AGAIN.
SCRITCH SCRITCH CRACK
ALL MY LOVE...
ALL MY LIFE.
GRAUGH
GRAUGH
HUMPH HURUMP

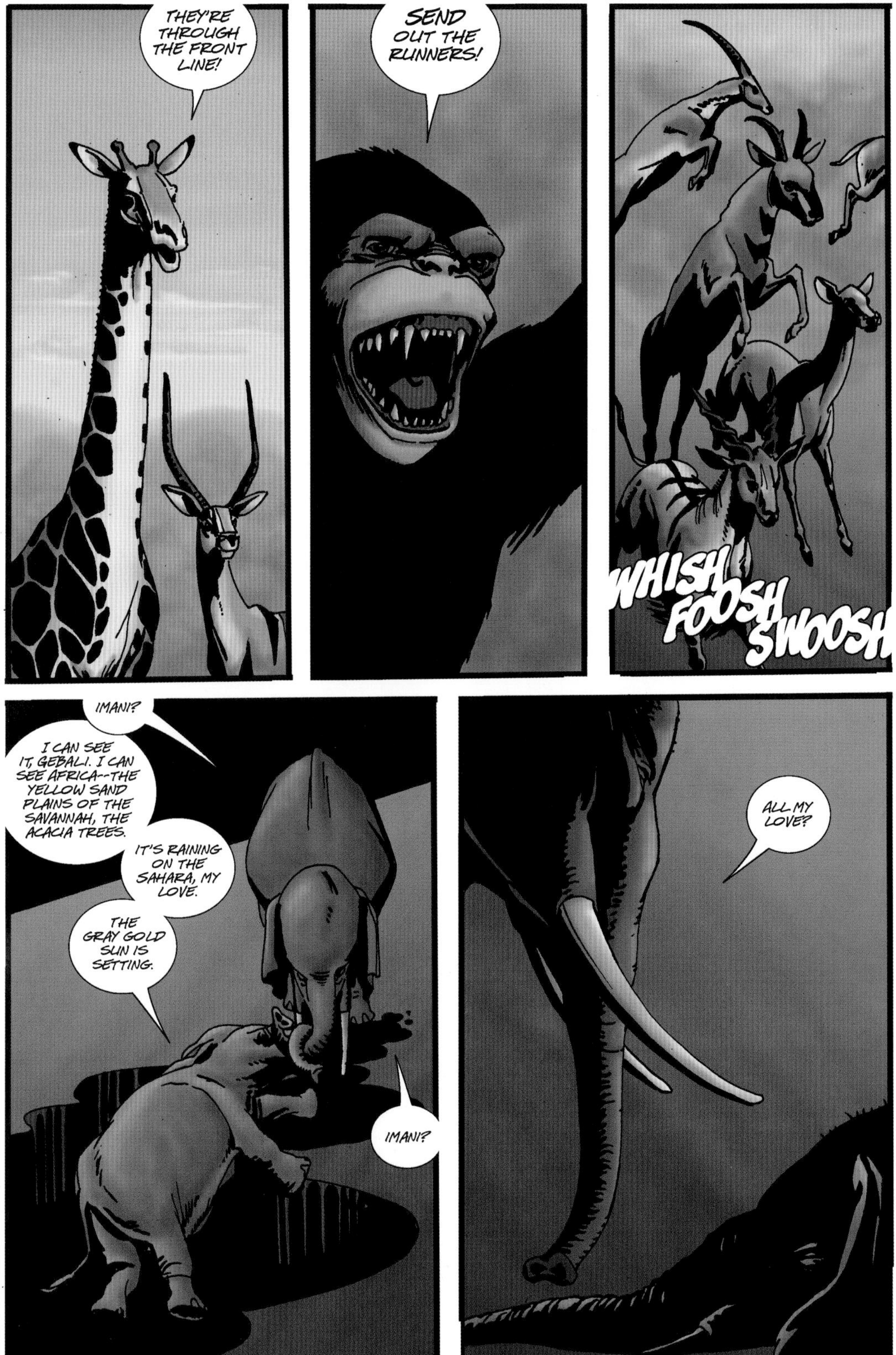
THEY'RE THROUGH THE FRONT LINE!
SEND OUT THE RUNNERS!
WHISH
FOOSH
SWOOSH
IMANI?
I CAN SEE IT, GEBALI. I CAN SEE AFRICA--THE YELLOW SAND PLAINS OF THE SAVANNAH, THE ACACIA TREES.
IT'S RAINING ON THE SAHARA, MY LOVE.
THE GRAY GOLD SUN IS SETTING.
IMANI?
ALL MY LOVE?

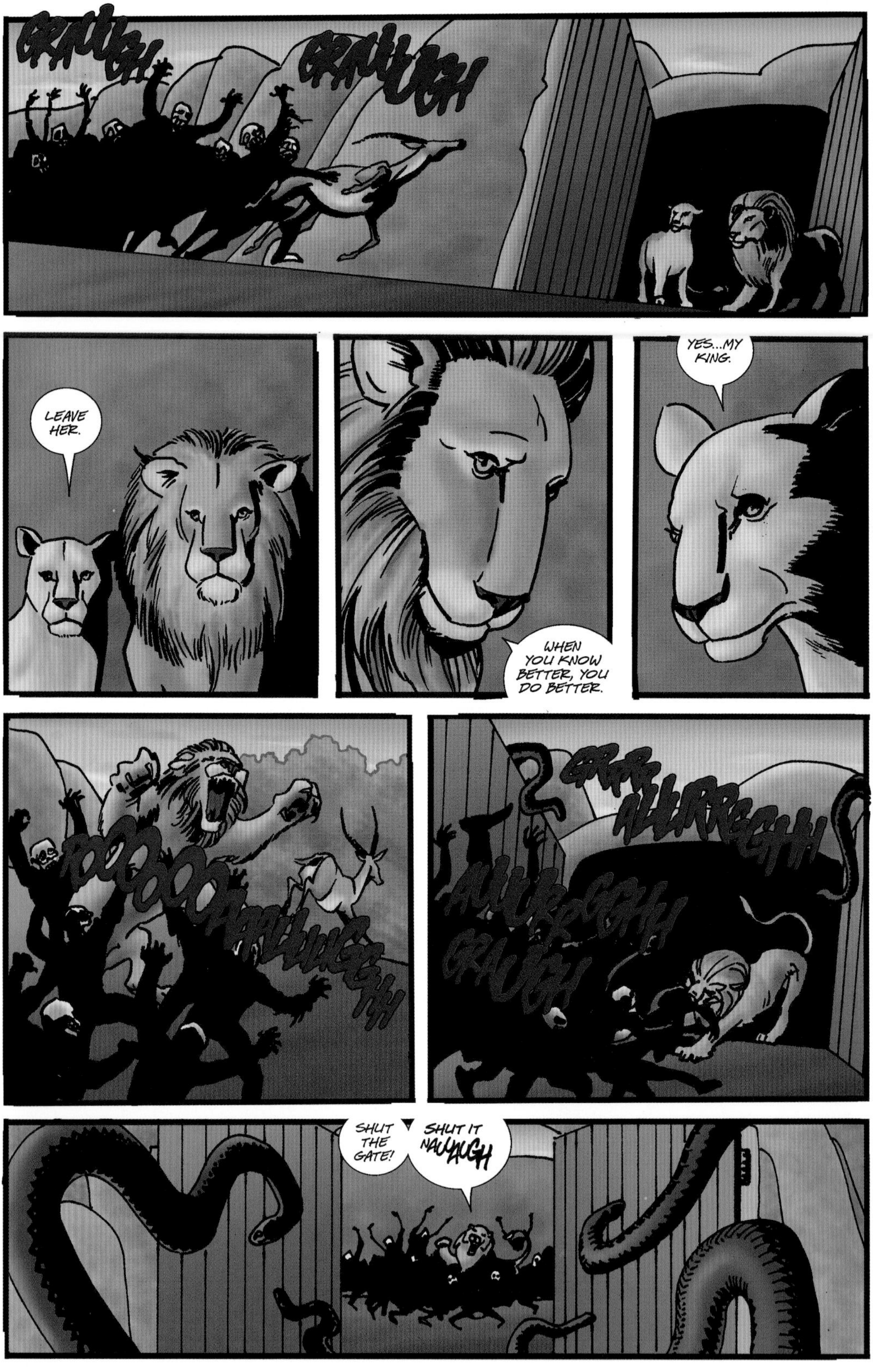
LEAVE HER.
WHEN YOU KNOW BETTER, YOU DO BETTER.
YES...MY KING.
SHUT THE GATE!
SHUT IT NAUAUGH

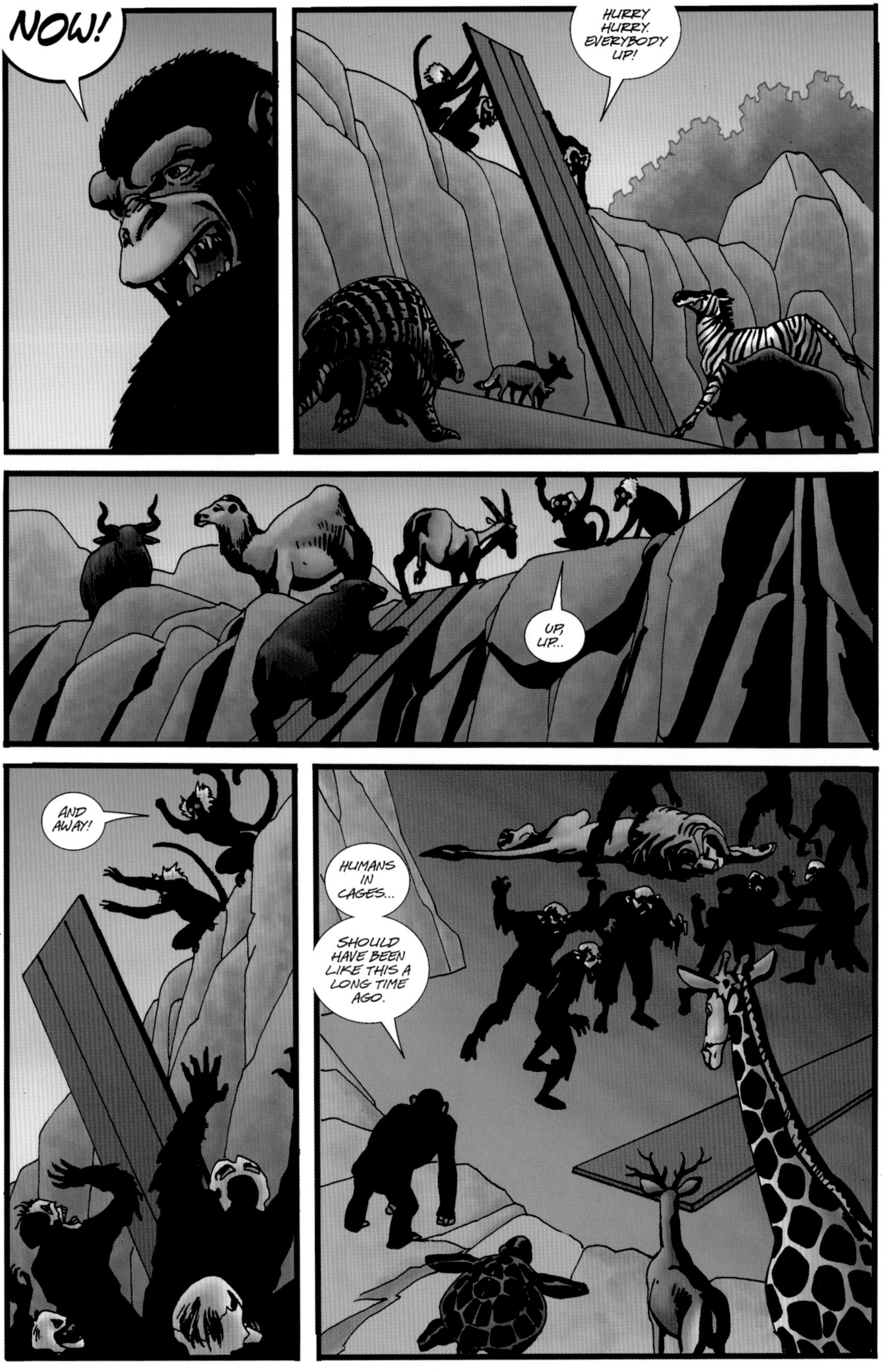
NOW!
HURRY HURRY. EVERYBODY UP!
UP, UP...
AND AWAY!
HUMANS IN CAGES...
SHOULD HAVE BEEN LIKE THIS A LONG TIME AGO.

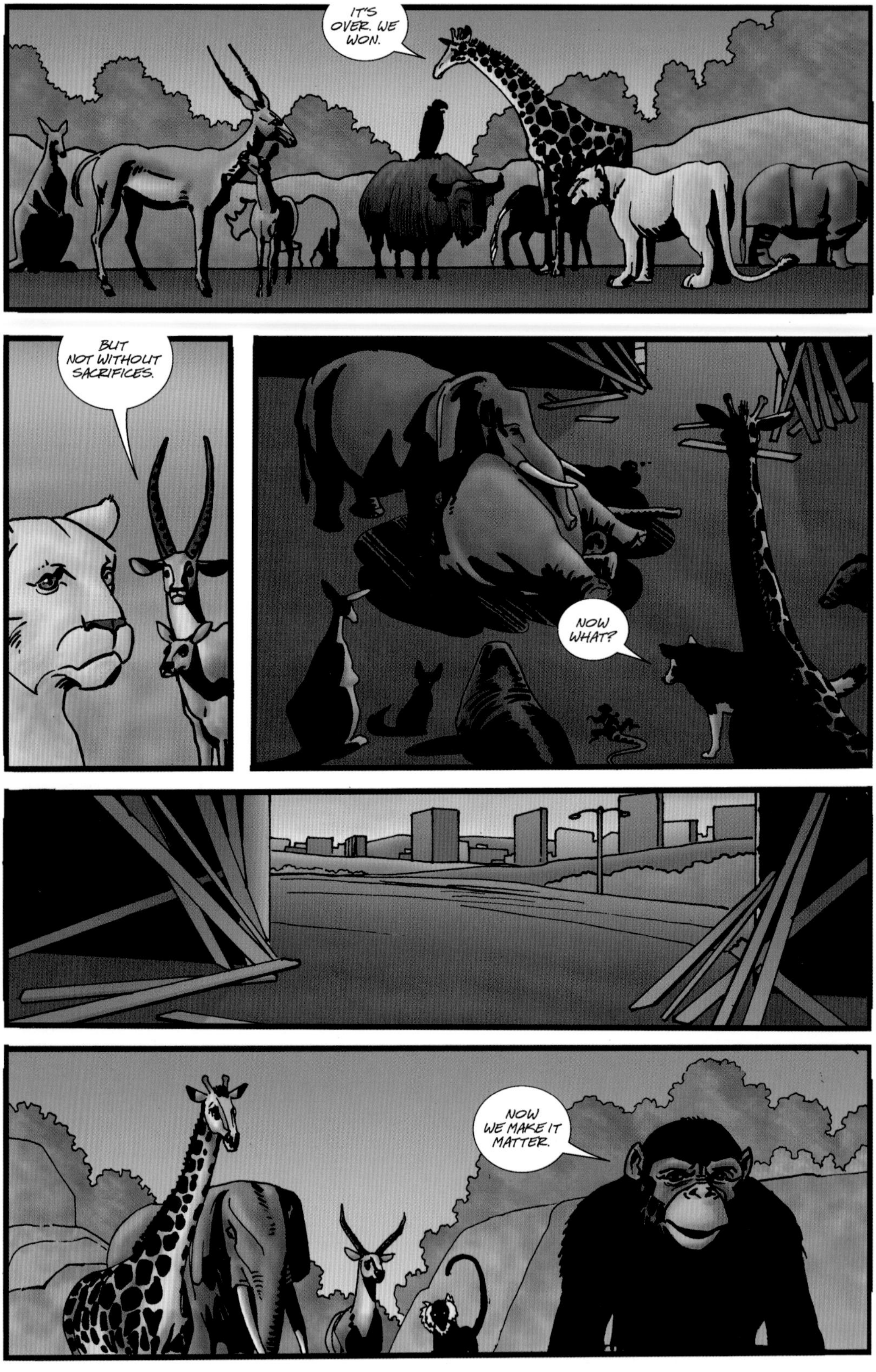
IT'S OVER. WE WON.
BUT NOT WITHOUT SACRIFICES.
NOW WHAT?
NOW WE MAKE IT MATTER.

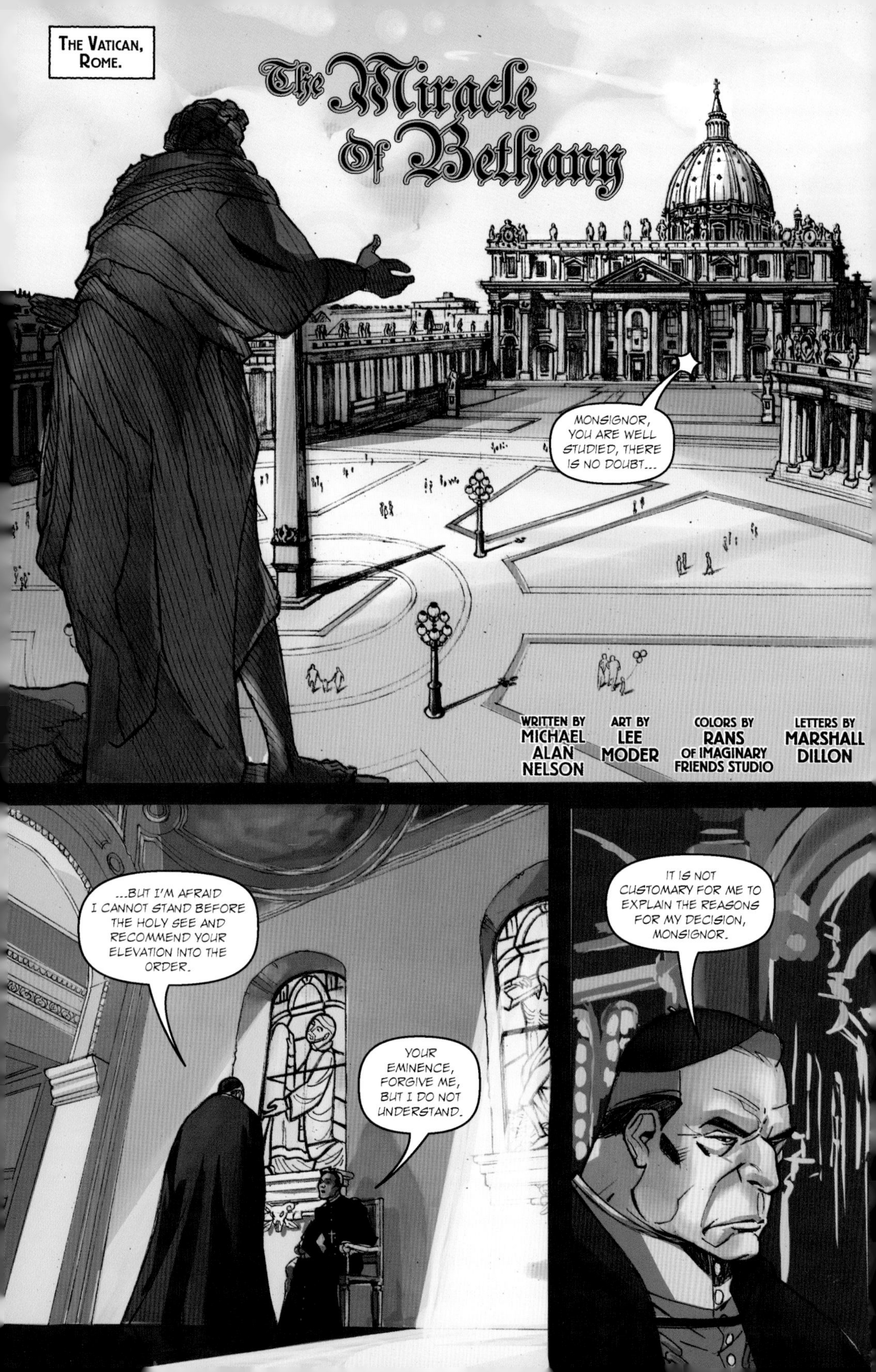
THE VATICAN, ROME.
The Miracle of Bethany
MONSIGNOR, YOU ARE WELL STUDIED, THERE IS NO DOUBT...
WRITTEN BY MICHAEL ALAN NELSON
ART BY LEE MODER
COLORS BY RANS OF IMAGINARY FRIENDS STUDIO
LETTERS BY MARSHALL DILLON
...BUT I'M AFRAID I CANNOT STAND BEFORE THE HOLY SEE AND RECOMMEND YOUR ELEVATION INTO THE ORDER.
YOUR EMINENCE, FORGIVE ME, BUT I DO NOT UNDERSTAND.
IT IS NOT CUSTOMARY FOR ME TO EXPLAIN THE REASONS FOR MY DECISION, MONSIGNOR.

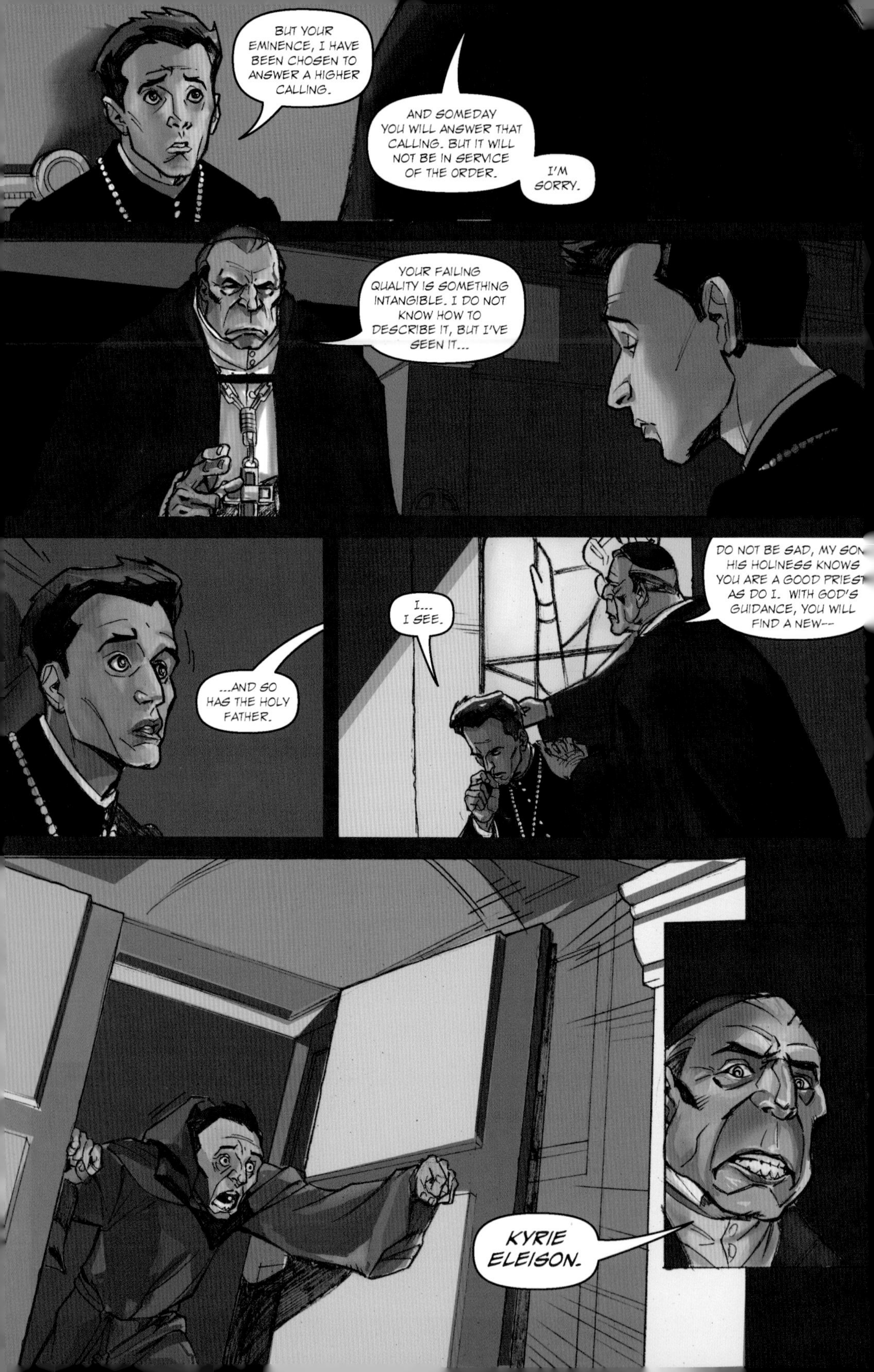
BUT YOUR EMINENCE, I HAVE BEEN CHOSEN TO ANSWER A HIGHER CALLING.
AND SOMEDAY YOU WILL ANSWER THAT CALLING. BUT IT WILL NOT BE IN SERVICE OF THE ORDER.
I'M SORRY.
YOUR FAILING QUALITY IS SOMETHING INTANGIBLE. I DO NOT KNOW HOW TO DESCRIBE IT, BUT I'VE SEEN IT...
...AND SO HAS THE HOLY FATHER.
I... I SEE.
DO NOT BE SAD, MY SON HIS HOLINESS KNOWS YOU ARE A GOOD PRIEST AS DO I. WITH GOD'S GUIDANCE, YOU WILL FIND A NEW--
KYRIE ELEISON.

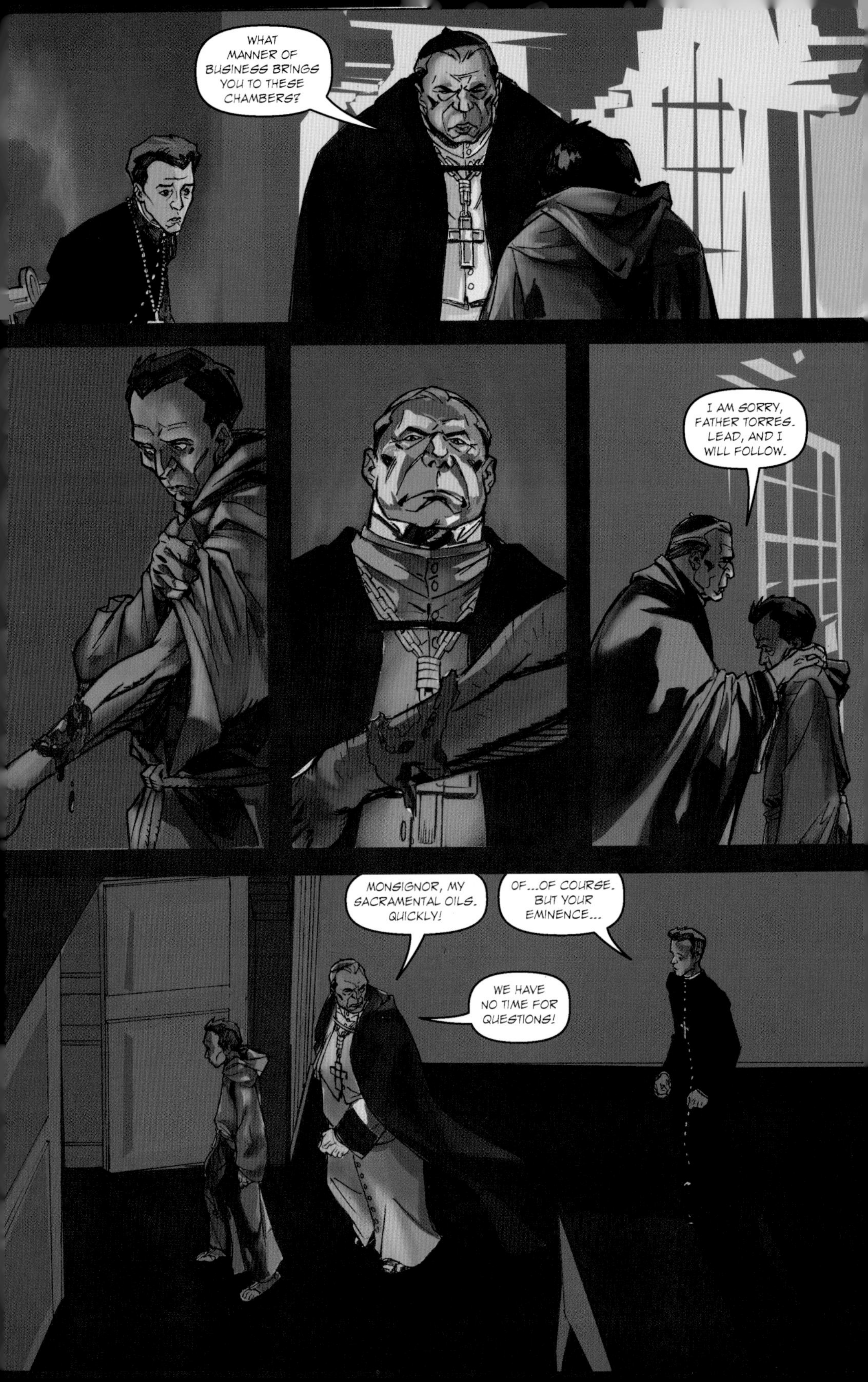
WHAT MANNER OF BUSINESS BRINGS YOU TO THESE CHAMBERS?
I AM SORRY, FATHER TORRES. LEAD, AND I WILL FOLLOW.
MONSIGNOR, MY SACRAMENTAL OILS. QUICKLY!
OF...OF COURSE. BUT YOUR EMINENCE...
WE HAVE NO TIME FOR QUESTIONS!

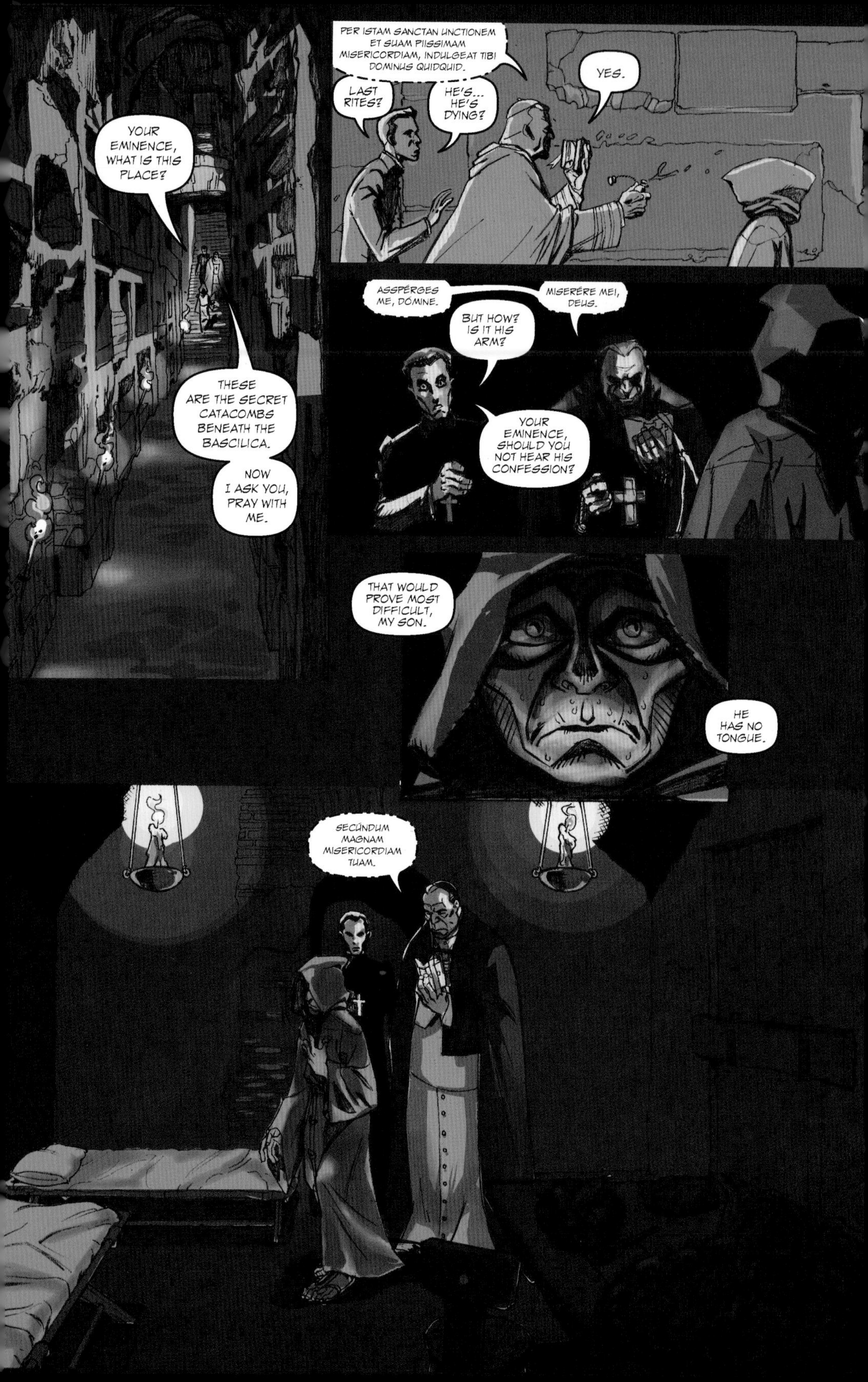
YOUR EMINENCE, WHAT IS THIS PLACE?
THESE ARE THE SECRET CATACOMBS BENEATH THE BASCILICA.
NOW I ASK YOU, PRAY WITH ME.
PER ISTAM SANCTAN UNCTIONEM ET SUAM PIISSIMAM MISERICORDIAM, INDULGEAT TIBI DOMINUS QUIDQUID.
LAST RITES?
HE'S... HE'S DYING?
YES.
ASSPÉRGES ME, DÓMINE.
MISERÉRE MEI, DEUS.
BUT HOW? IS IT HIS ARM?
YOUR EMINENCE, SHOULD YOU NOT HEAR HIS CONFESSION?
THAT WOULD PROVE MOST DIFFICULT, MY SON.
HE HAS NO TONGUE.
SECÚNDUM MAGNAM MISERICORDIAM TUAM.

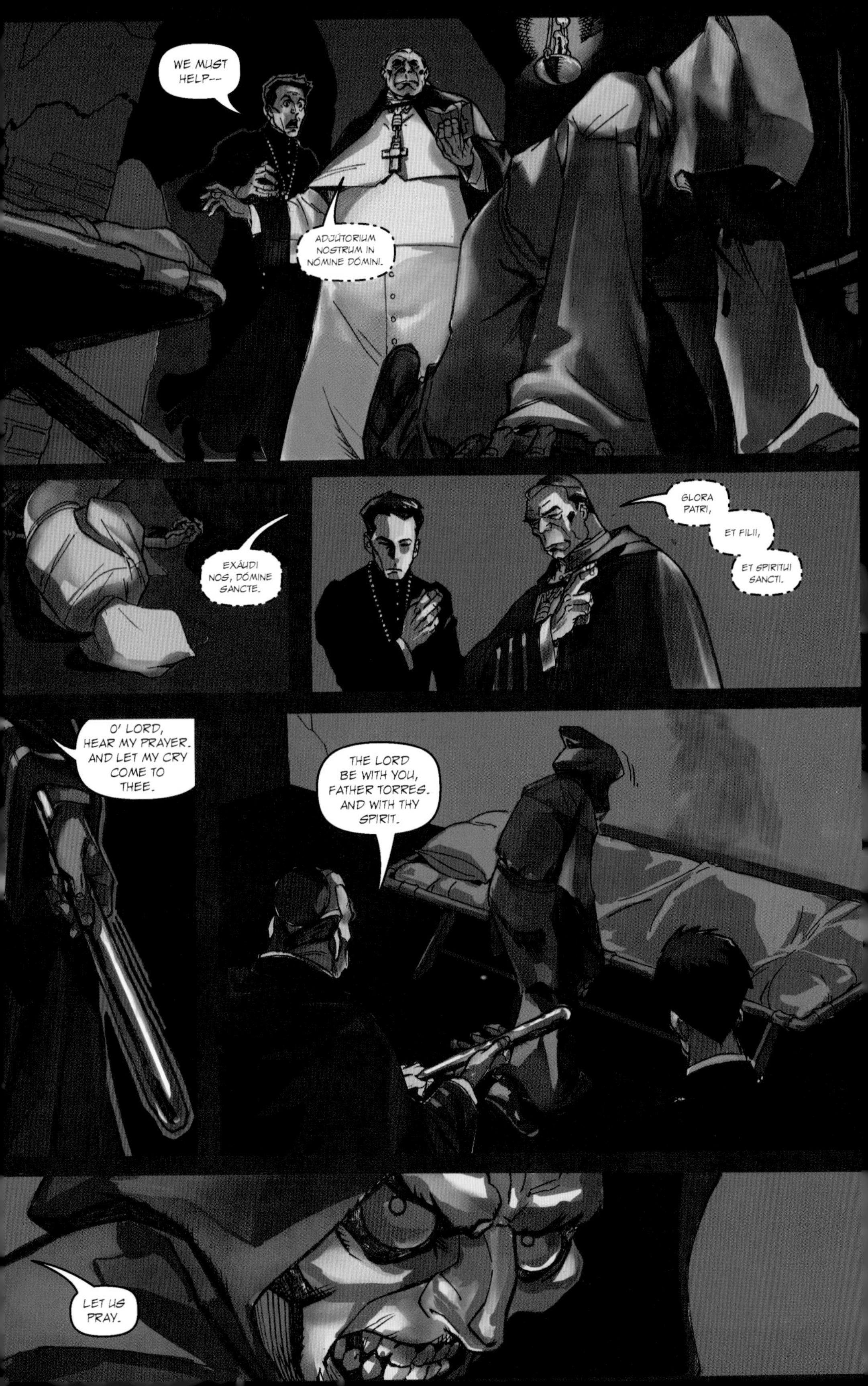
WE MUST HELP--
ADJÚTORIUM NOSTRUM IN NÓMINE DÓMINI.
EXÁUDI NOS, DÓMINE SANCTE.
GLORA PATRI,
ET FILII,
ET SPIRITUI SANCTI.
O' LORD, HEAR MY PRAYER. AND LET MY CRY COME TO THEE.
THE LORD BE WITH YOU, FATHER TORRES. AND WITH THY SPIRIT.
LET US PRAY.

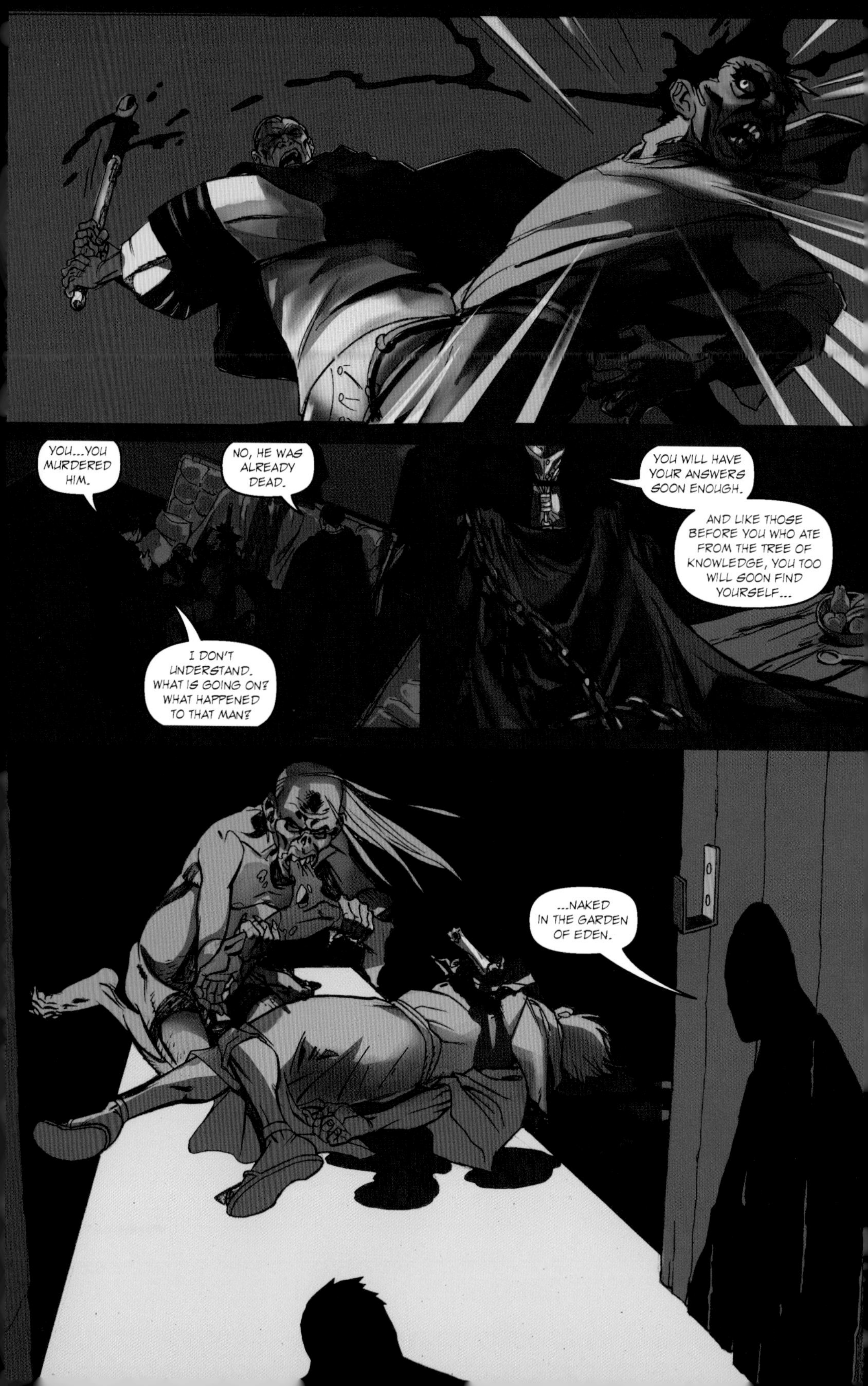
YOU...YOU MURDERED HIM.
NO, HE WAS ALREADY DEAD.
I DON'T UNDERSTAND. WHAT IS GOING ON? WHAT HAPPENED TO THAT MAN?
YOU WILL HAVE YOUR ANSWERS SOON ENOUGH.
AND LIKE THOSE BEFORE YOU WHO ATE FROM THE TREE OF KNOWLEDGE, YOU TOO WILL SOON FIND YOURSELF...
...NAKED IN THE GARDEN OF EDEN.

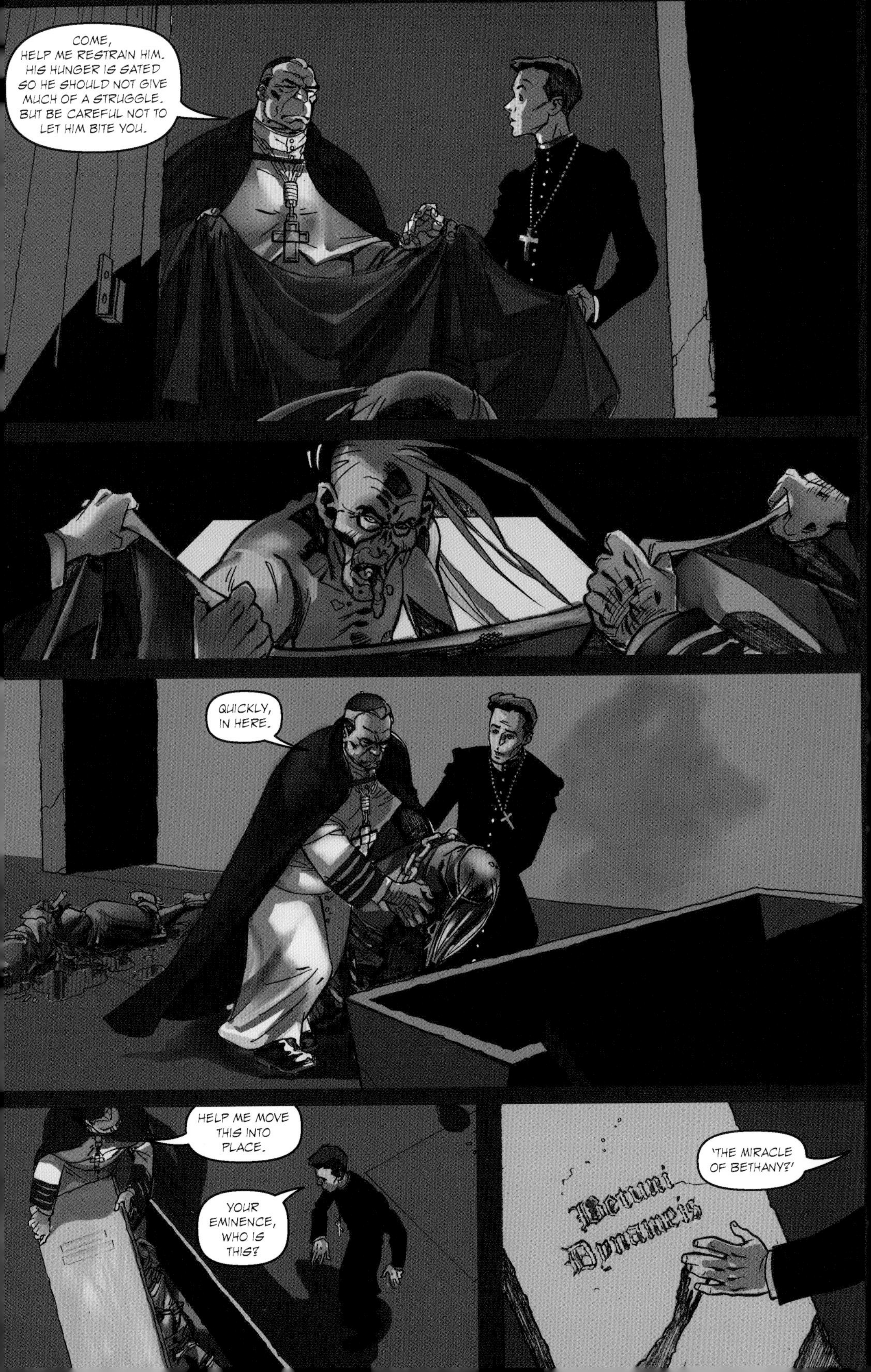
COME, HELP ME RESTRAIN HIM. HIS HUNGER IS SATED SO HE SHOULD NOT GIVE MUCH OF A STRUGGLE. BUT BE CAREFUL NOT TO LET HIM BITE YOU.
QUICKLY, IN HERE.
HELP ME MOVE THIS INTO PLACE.
YOUR EMINENCE, WHO IS THIS?
Betuni Dynameis
'THE MIRACLE OF BETHANY?'

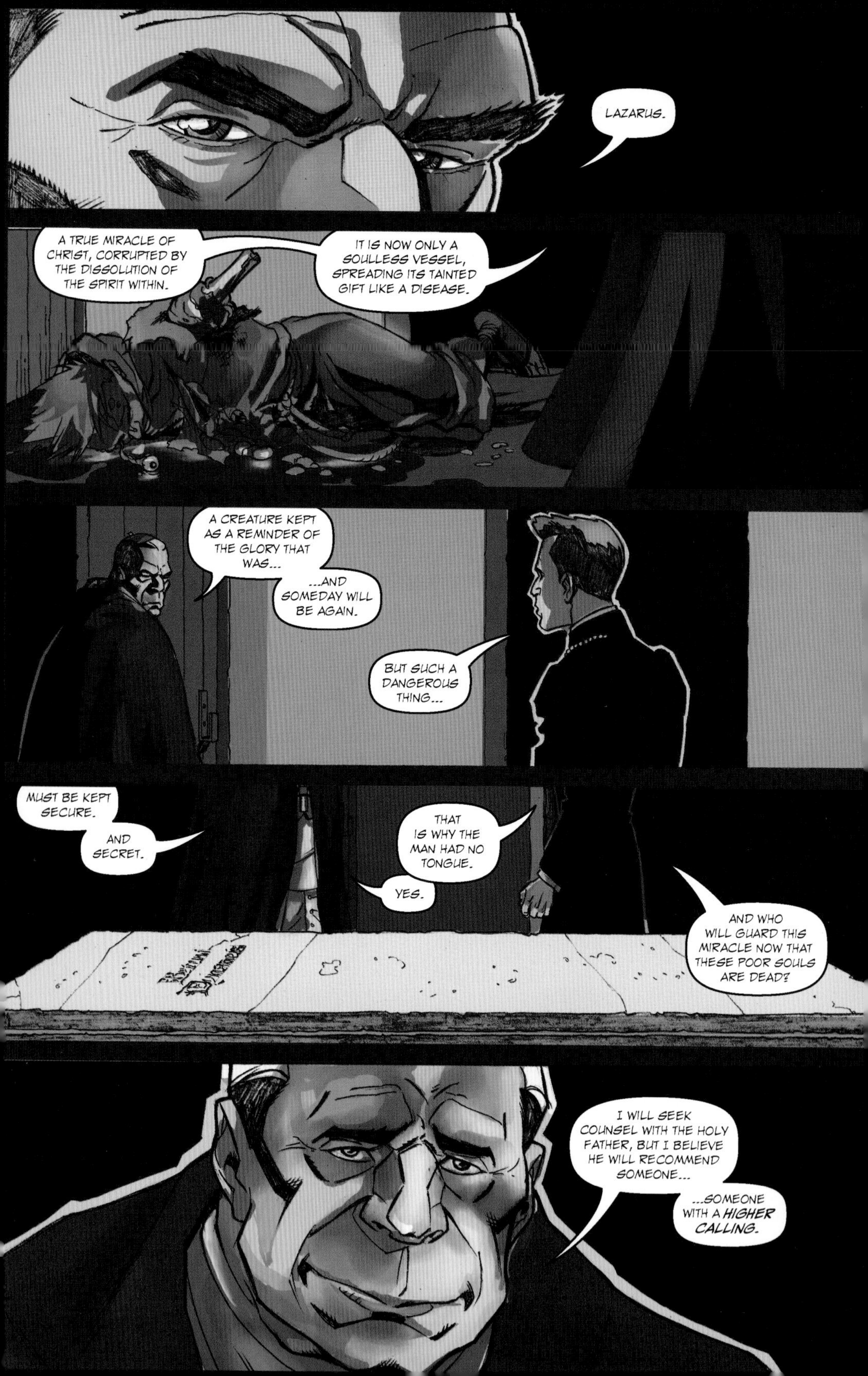
LAZARUS.
A TRUE MIRACLE OF CHRIST, CORRUPTED BY THE DISSOLUTION OF THE SPIRIT WITHIN.
IT IS NOW ONLY A SOULLESS VESSEL, SPREADING ITS TAINTED GIFT LIKE A DISEASE.
A CREATURE KEPT AS A REMINDER OF THE GLORY THAT WAS...
...AND SOMEDAY WILL BE AGAIN.
BUT SUCH A DANGEROUS THING...
MUST BE KEPT SECURE.
AND SECRET.
THAT IS WHY THE MAN HAD NO TONGUE.
YES.
AND WHO WILL GUARD THIS MIRACLE NOW THAT THESE POOR SOULS ARE DEAD?
I WILL SEEK COUNSEL WITH THE HOLY FATHER, BUT I BELIEVE HE WILL RECOMMEND SOMEONE...
...SOMEONE WITH A *HIGHER CALLING*.

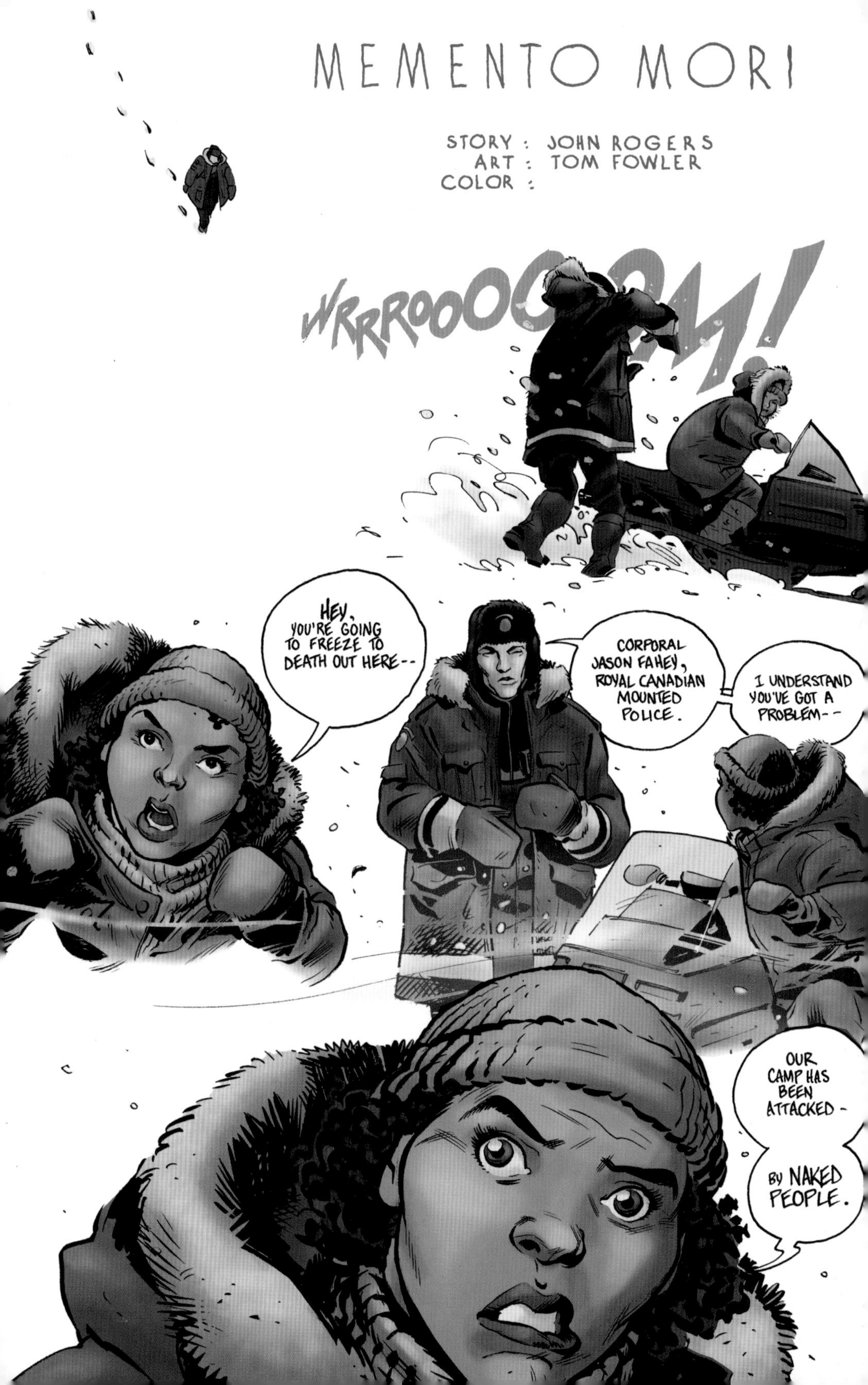
MEMENTO MORI
STORY : JOHN ROGERS
ART : TOM FOWLER
COLOR :
WRRROOOOOOM!
HEY, YOU'RE GOING TO FREEZE TO DEATH OUT HERE--
CORPORAL JASON FAHEY, ROYAL CANADIAN MOUNTED POLICE.
I UNDERSTAND YOU'VE GOT A PROBLEM--
OUR CAMP HAS BEEN ATTACKED -
BY NAKED PEOPLE.

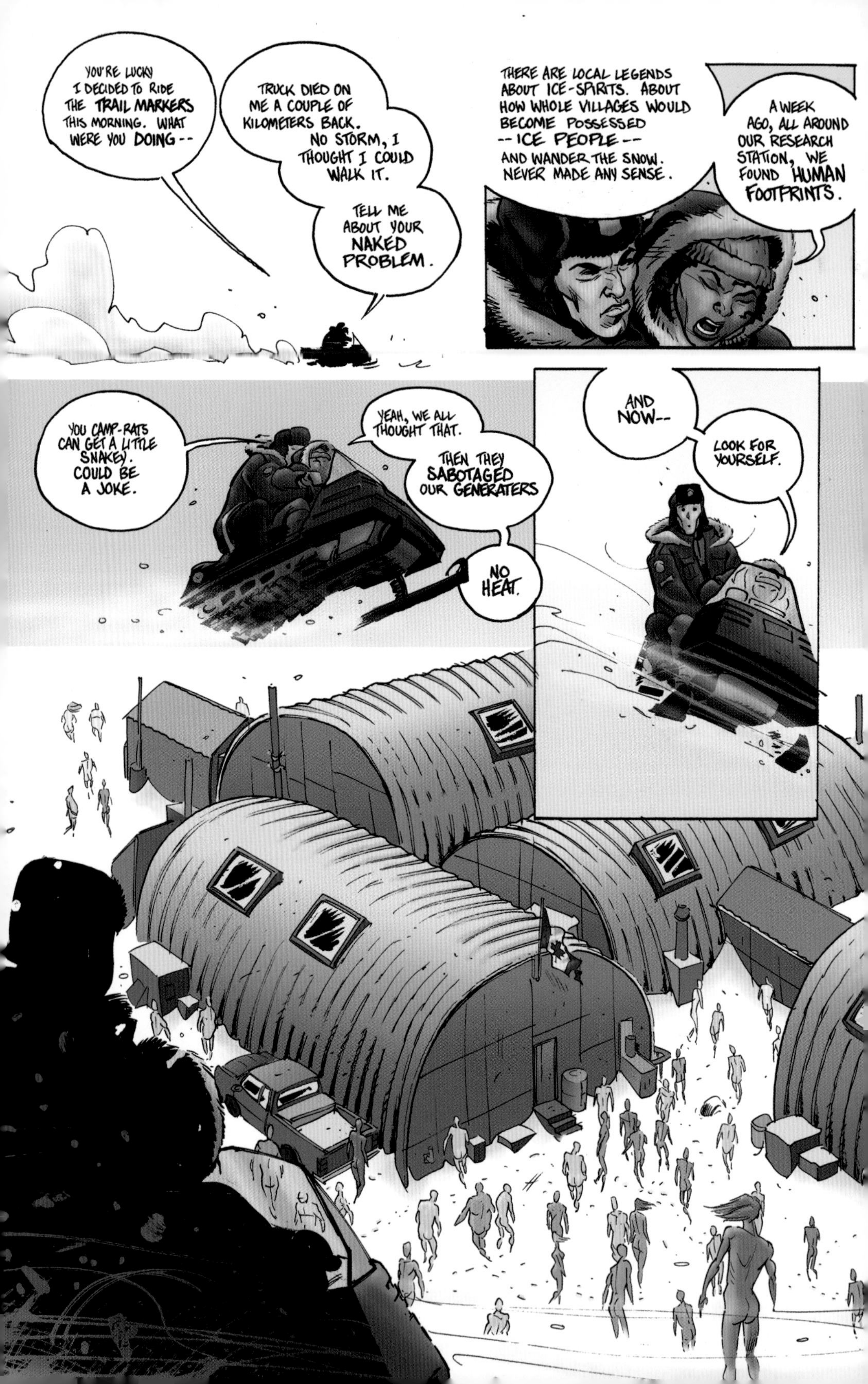

YOU'RE LUCKY I DECIDED TO RIDE THE TRAIL MARKERS THIS MORNING. WHAT WERE YOU DOING--
TRUCK DIED ON ME A COUPLE OF KILOMETERS BACK.
NO STORM, I THOUGHT I COULD WALK IT.
TELL ME ABOUT YOUR NAKED PROBLEM.
THERE ARE LOCAL LEGENDS ABOUT ICE-SPIRITS. ABOUT HOW WHOLE VILLAGES WOULD BECOME POSSESSED --ICE PEOPLE-- AND WANDER THE SNOW. NEVER MADE ANY SENSE.
A WEEK AGO, ALL AROUND OUR RESEARCH STATION, WE FOUND HUMAN FOOTPRINTS.
YOU CAMP-RATS CAN GET A LITTLE SNAKEY. COULD BE A JOKE.
YEAH, WE ALL THOUGHT THAT.
THEN THEY SABOTAGED OUR GENERATERS
NO HEAT.
AND NOW--
LOOK FOR YOURSELF.

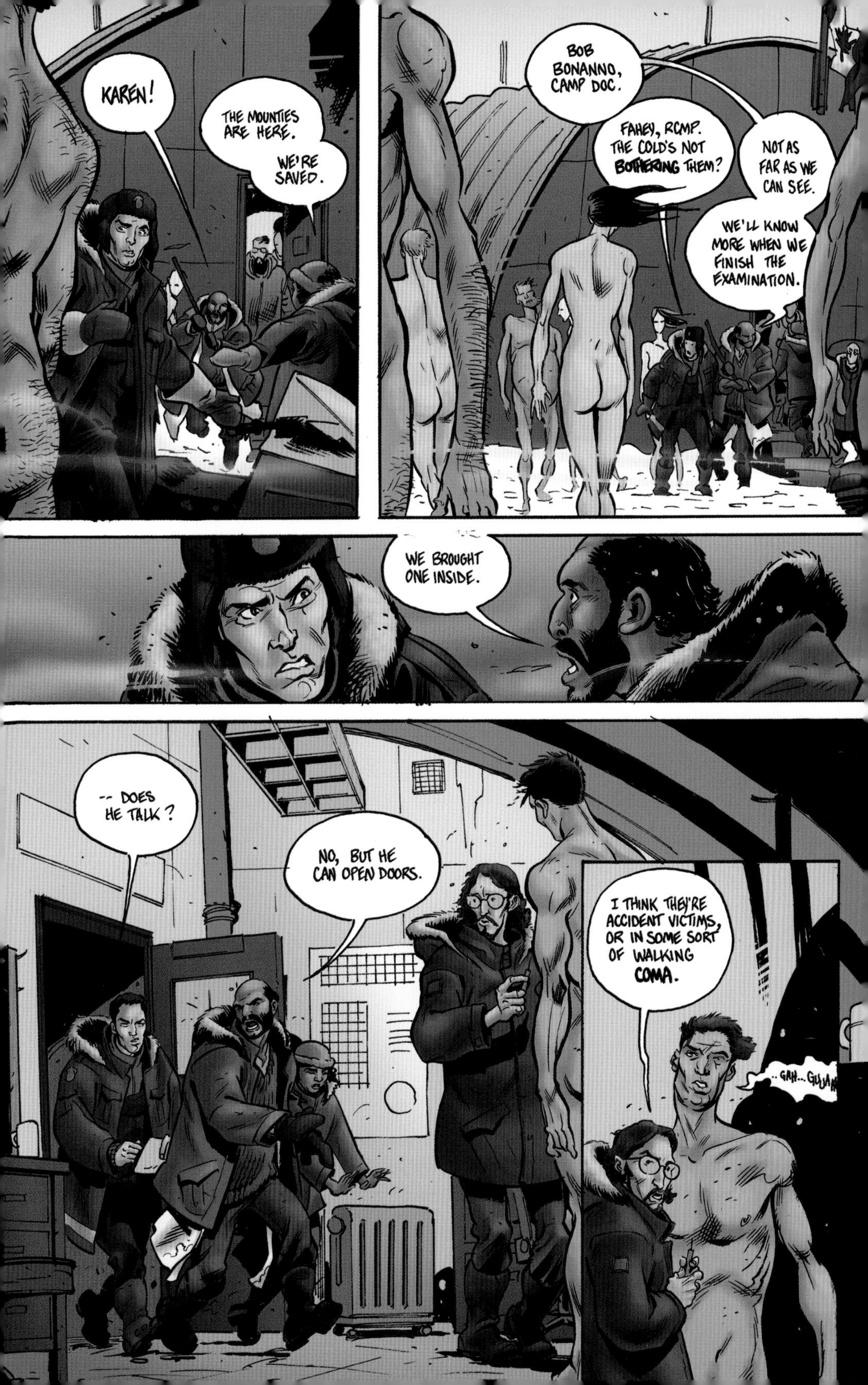
KAREN!
THE MOUNTIES ARE HERE.
WE'RE SAVED.
BOB BONANNO, CAMP DOC.
FAHEY, RCMP. THE COLD'S NOT BOTHERING THEM?
NOT AS FAR AS WE CAN SEE.
WE'LL KNOW MORE WHEN WE FINISH THE EXAMINATION.
WE BROUGHT ONE INSIDE.
-- DOES HE TALK?
NO, BUT HE CAN OPEN DOORS.
I THINK THEY'RE ACCIDENT VICTIMS, OR IN SOME SORT OF WALKING COMA.
.. GAH... GUUA

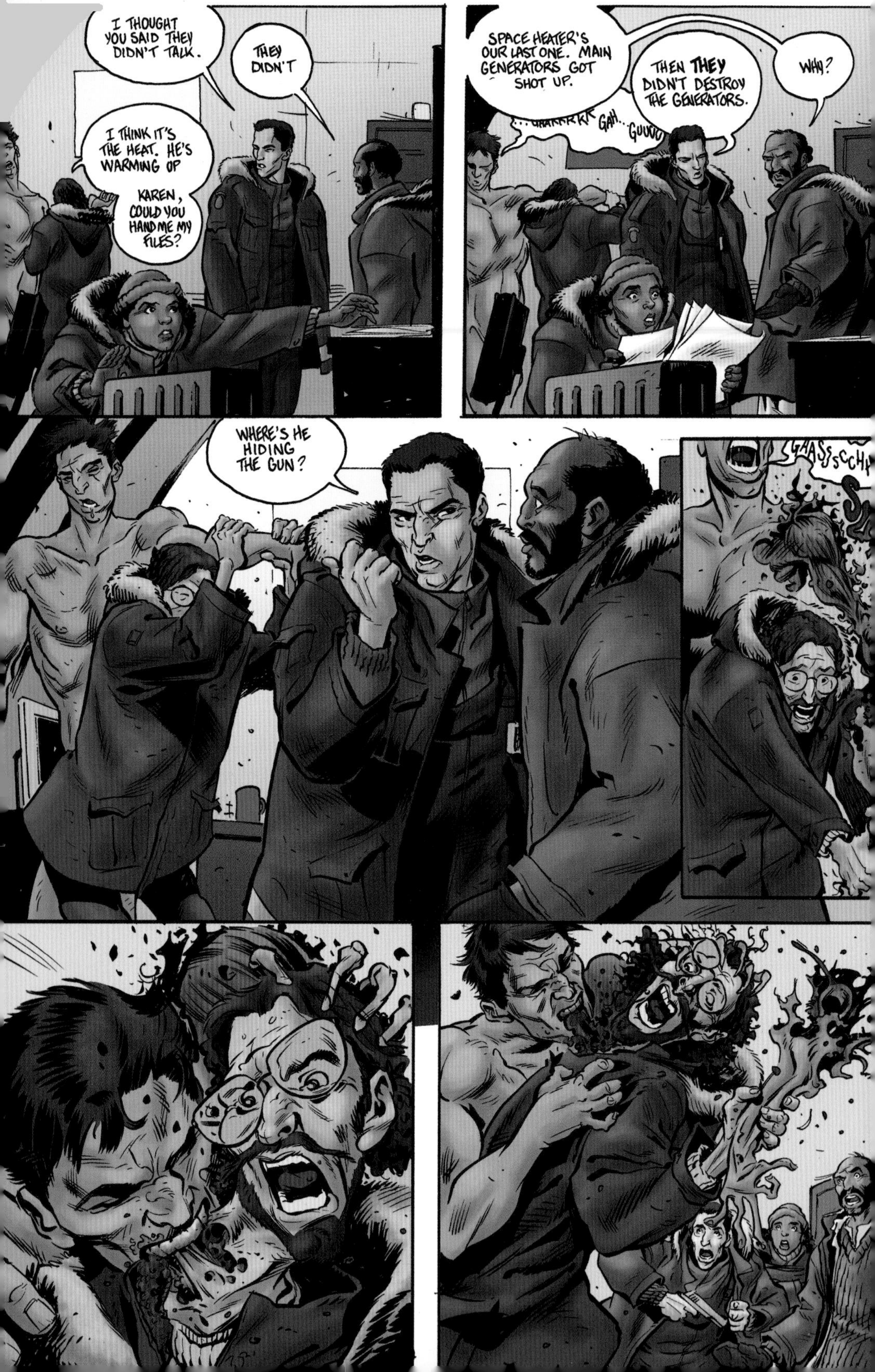
I THOUGHT YOU SAID THEY DIDN'T TALK.
THEY DIDN'T
I THINK IT'S THE HEAT. HE'S WARMING UP
KAREN, COULD YOU HAND ME MY FILES?
SPACE HEATER'S OUR LAST ONE. MAIN GENERATORS GOT SHOT UP.
THEN THEY DIDN'T DESTROY THE GENERATORS.
WHY?
GAH...GUUUU
WHERE'S HE HIDING THE GUN?
GHASSSCCH

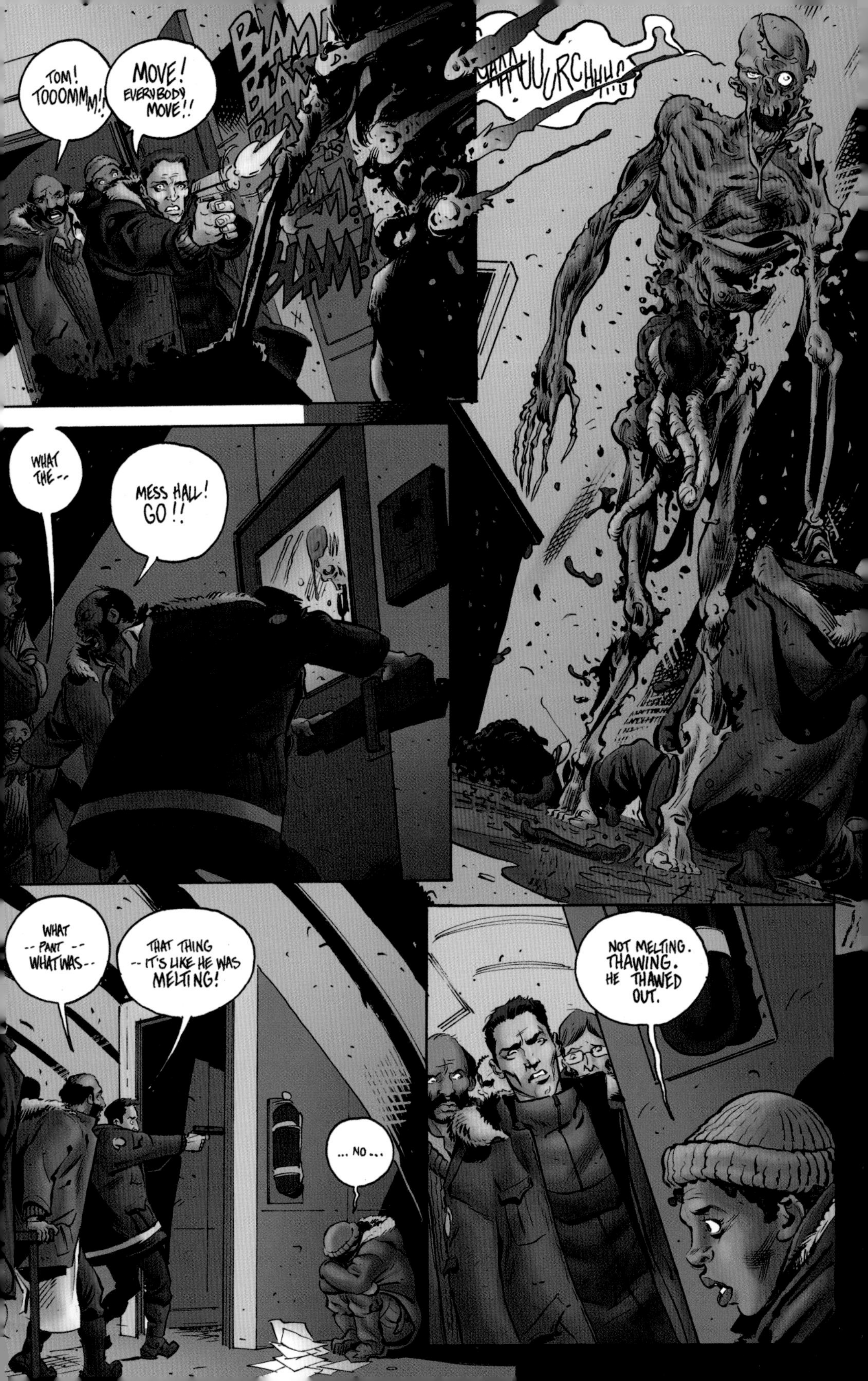
TOM! TOOOMMM!!
MOVE! EVERYBODY MOVE!!
BLAM! BLAM! BLAM!
BLAM!
GAAAAUUURCHHHG
WHAT THE--
MESS HALL! GO!!
WHAT --PANT-- WHAT WAS--
THAT THING --IT'S LIKE HE WAS MELTING!
...NO...
NOT MELTING. THAWING. HE THAWED OUT.

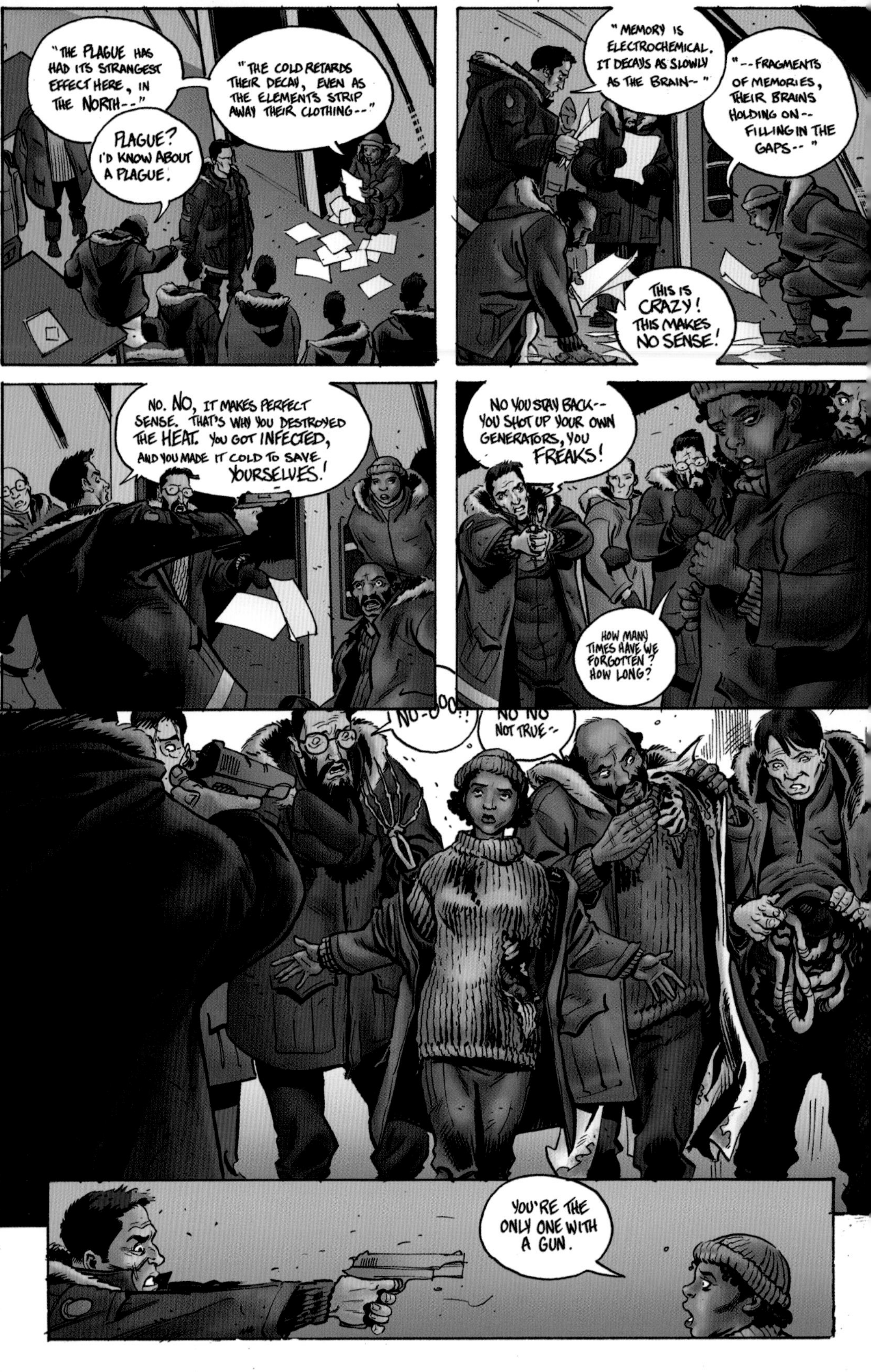
"THE PLAGUE HAS HAD ITS STRANGEST EFFECT HERE, IN THE NORTH--"
PLAGUE? I'D KNOW ABOUT A PLAGUE.
"THE COLD RETARDS THEIR DECAY, EVEN AS THE ELEMENTS STRIP AWAY THEIR CLOTHING--"
"MEMORY IS ELECTROCHEMICAL. IT DECAYS AS SLOWLY AS THE BRAIN--"
"--FRAGMENTS OF MEMORIES, THEIR BRAINS HOLDING ON-- FILLING IN THE GAPS--"
THIS IS CRAZY! THIS MAKES NO SENSE!
NO. NO, IT MAKES PERFECT SENSE. THAT'S WHY YOU DESTROYED THE HEAT. YOU GOT INFECTED, AND YOU MADE IT COLD TO SAVE YOURSELVES!
NO YOU STAY BACK-- YOU SHOT UP YOUR OWN GENERATORS, YOU FREAKS!
HOW MANY TIMES HAVE WE FORGOTTEN? HOW LONG?
NO-OOO!!
NO NO NOT TRUE--
YOU'RE THE ONLY ONE WITH A GUN.

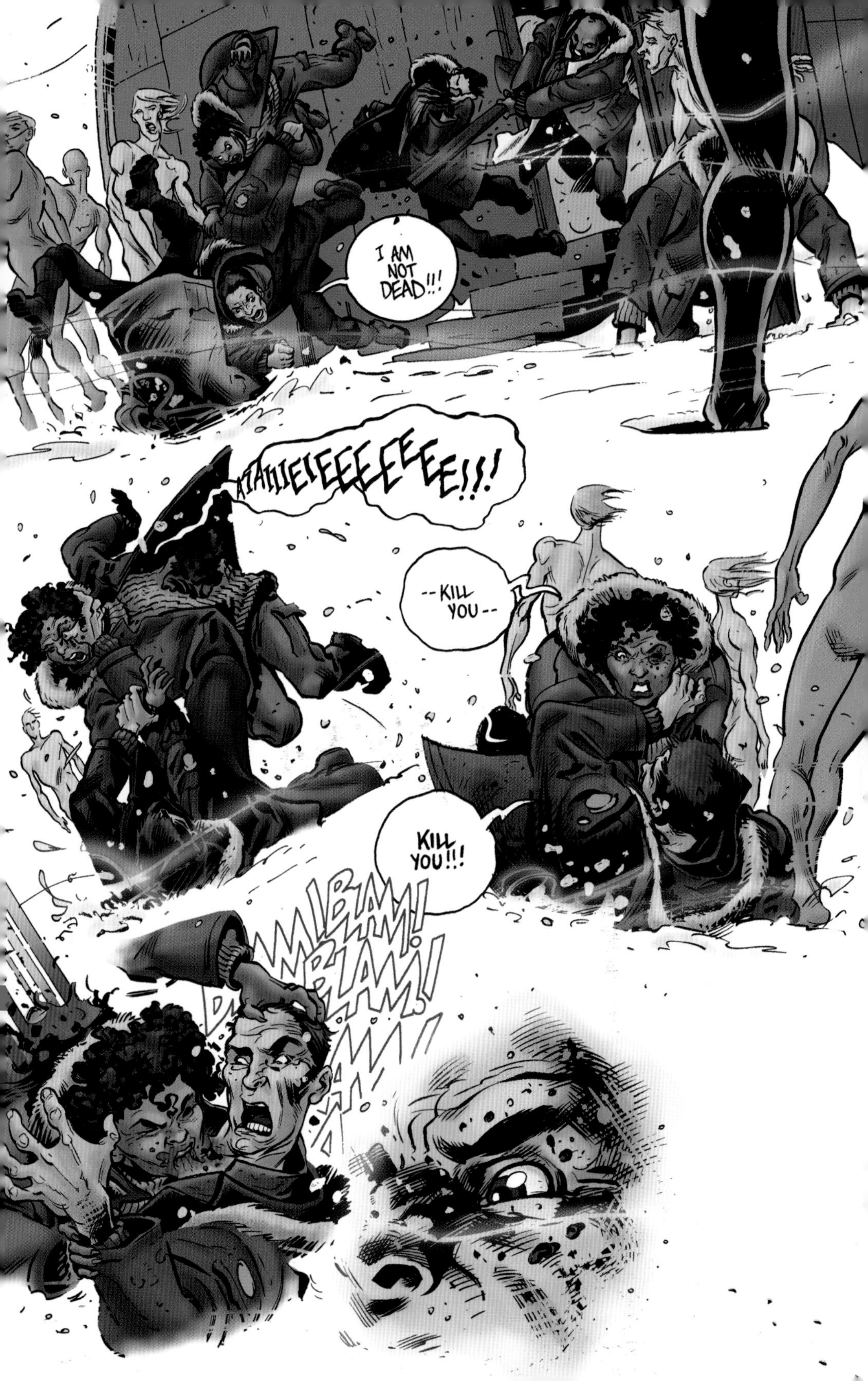
I AM NOT DEAD!!!
AIAIIIEIEEEEEEE!!!
--KILL YOU--
KILL YOU!!!
BLAM! BLAM! BLAM!

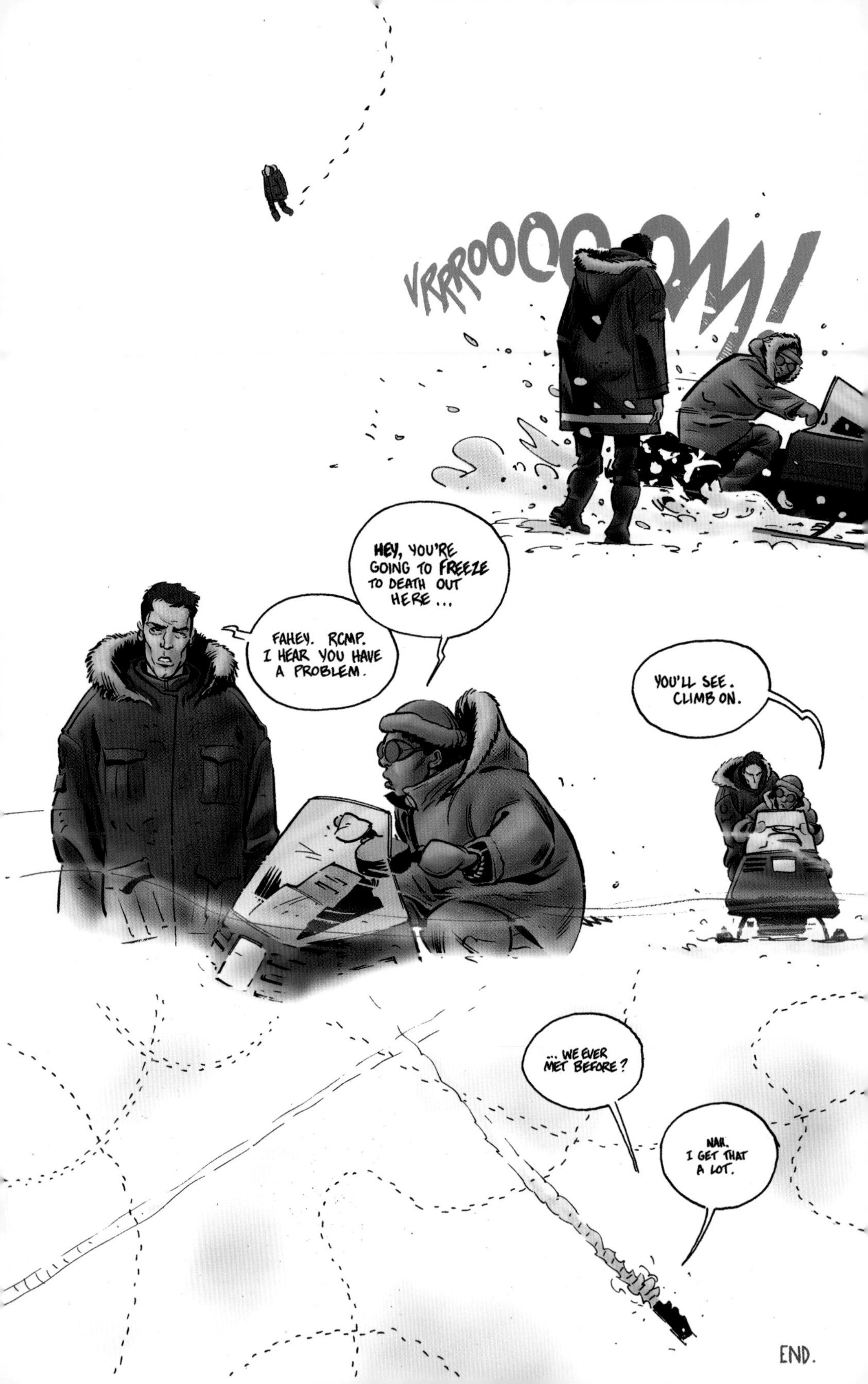
VRRROOOOOOM!
HEY, YOU'RE GOING TO FREEZE TO DEATH OUT HERE...
FAHEY. RCMP. I HEAR YOU HAVE A PROBLEM.
YOU'LL SEE. CLIMB ON.
... WE EVER MET BEFORE?
NAH. I GET THAT A LOT.
END.

RIOT GRRRL

STORY: MIKE NELSON ART: ANDY KUHN COLORS: MATT NELSON

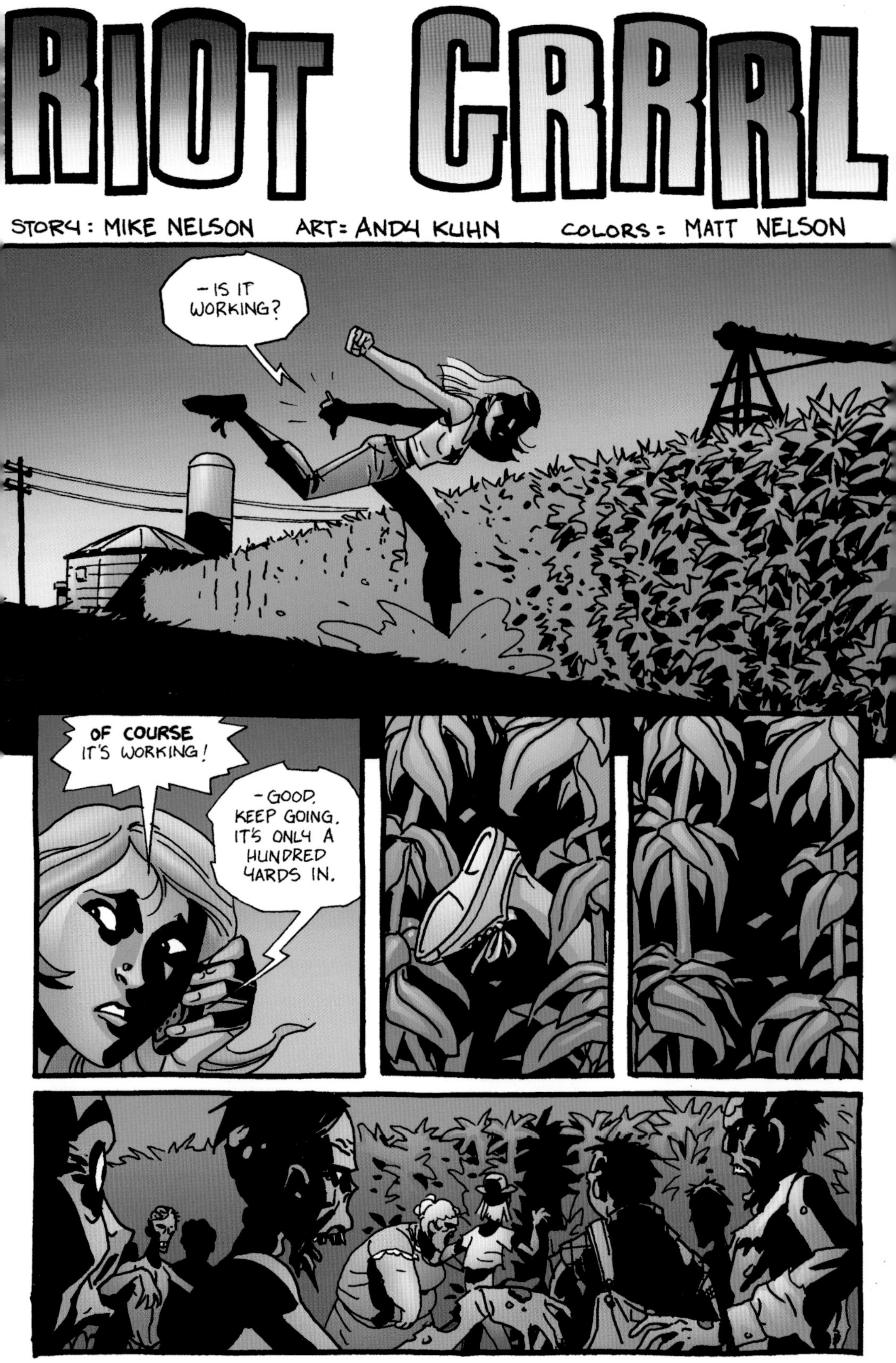

–IS IT WORKING?
OF COURSE IT'S WORKING!
–GOOD. KEEP GOING. IT'S ONLY A HUNDRED YARDS IN.

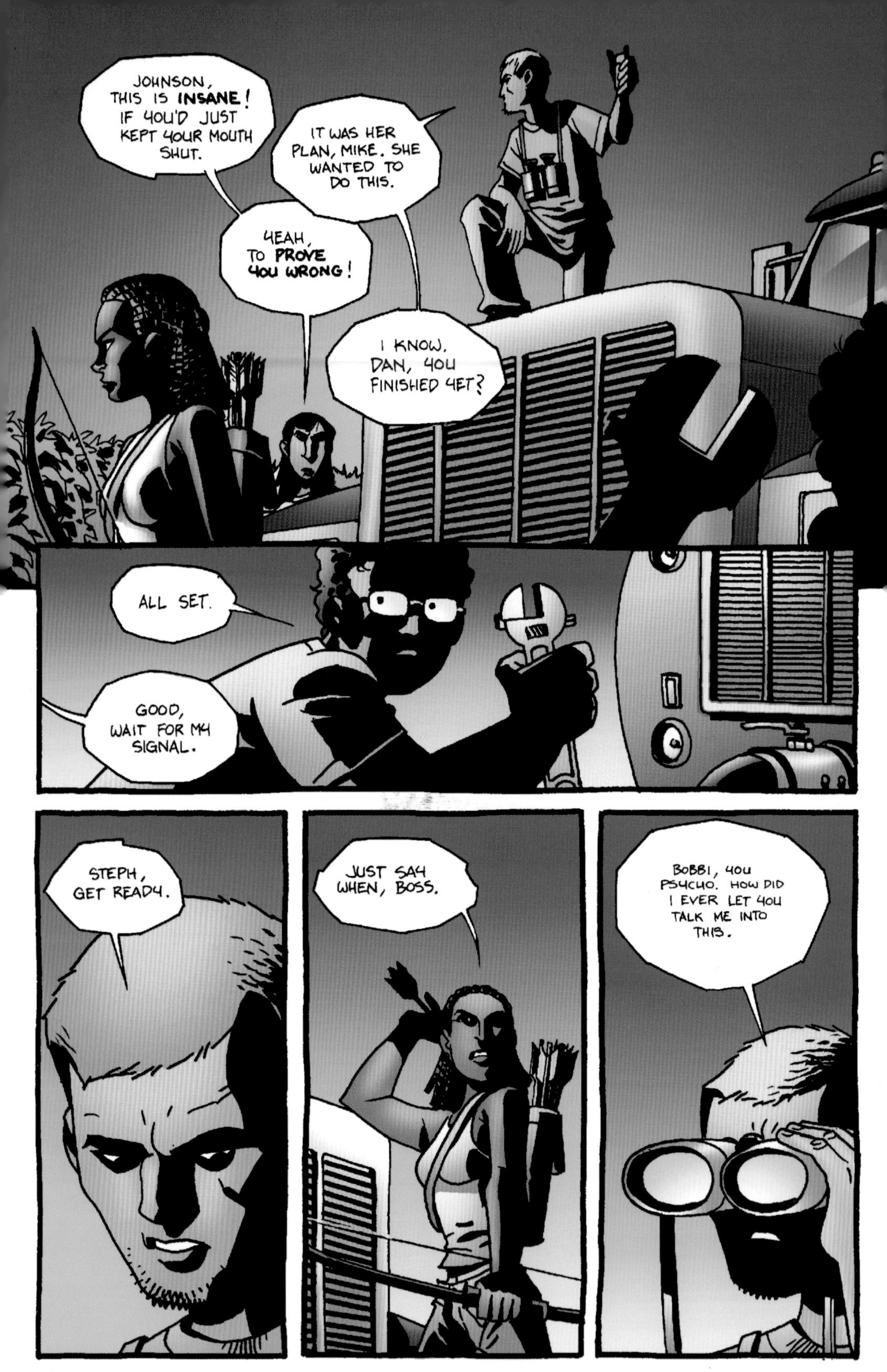
JOHNSON, THIS IS **INSANE**! IF YOU'D JUST KEPT YOUR MOUTH SHUT.
IT WAS HER PLAN, MIKE. SHE WANTED TO DO THIS.
YEAH, TO **PROVE YOU WRONG**!
I KNOW. DAN, YOU FINISHED YET?
ALL SET.
GOOD, WAIT FOR MY SIGNAL.
STEPH, GET READY.
JUST SAY WHEN, BOSS.
BOBBI, YOU PSYCHO. HOW DID I EVER LET YOU TALK ME INTO THIS.

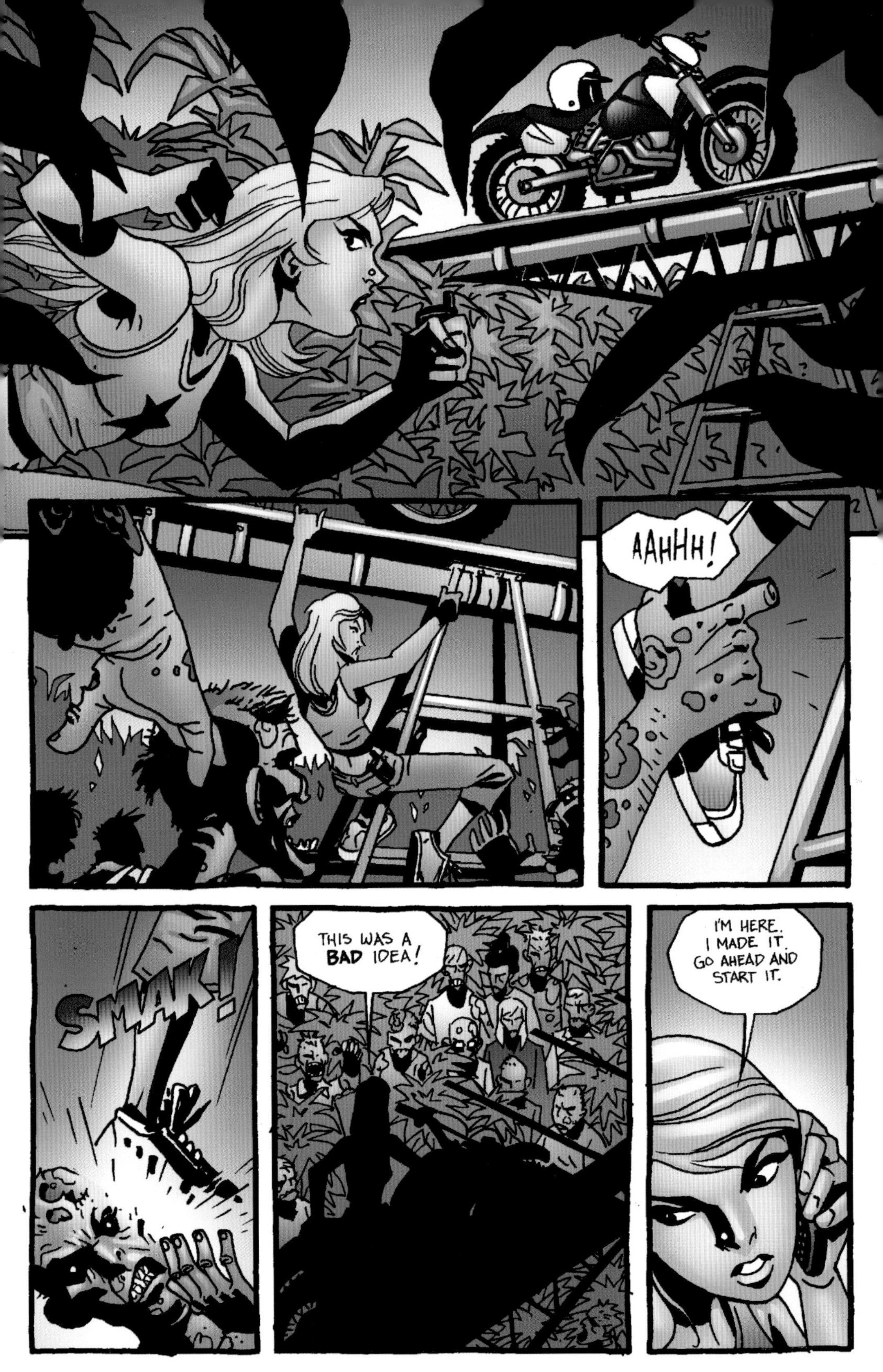
AAHHH!
SMAK!
THIS WAS A **BAD** IDEA!
I'M HERE. I MADE IT. GO AHEAD AND START IT.

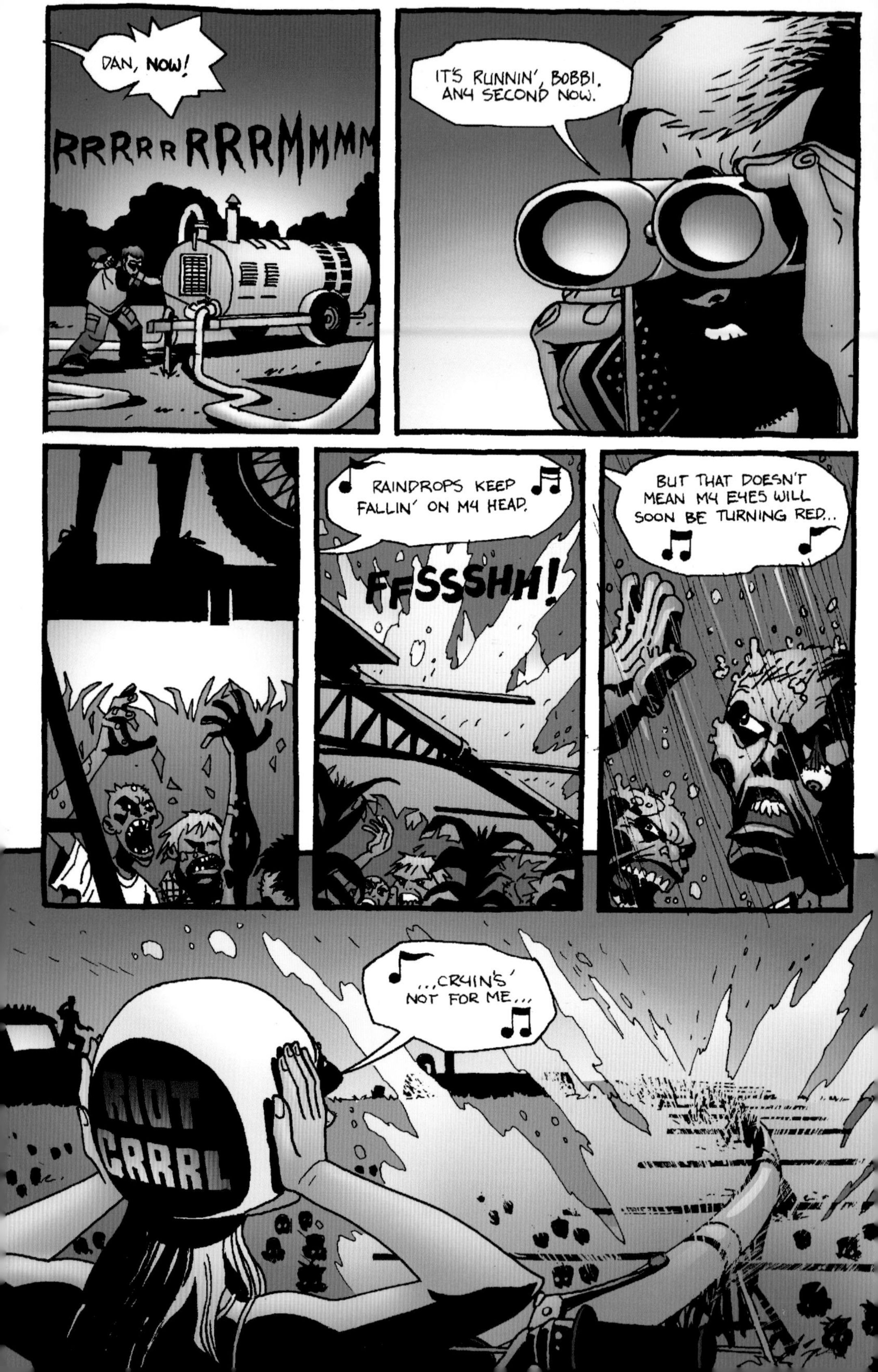
DAN, NOW!
RRRRRRRRMMMM
IT'S RUNNIN', BOBBI. ANY SECOND NOW.
RAINDROPS KEEP FALLIN' ON MY HEAD,
FFSSSHH!
BUT THAT DOESN'T MEAN MY EYES WILL SOON BE TURNING RED...
...CRYIN'S NOT FOR ME...
RIOT GRRRL

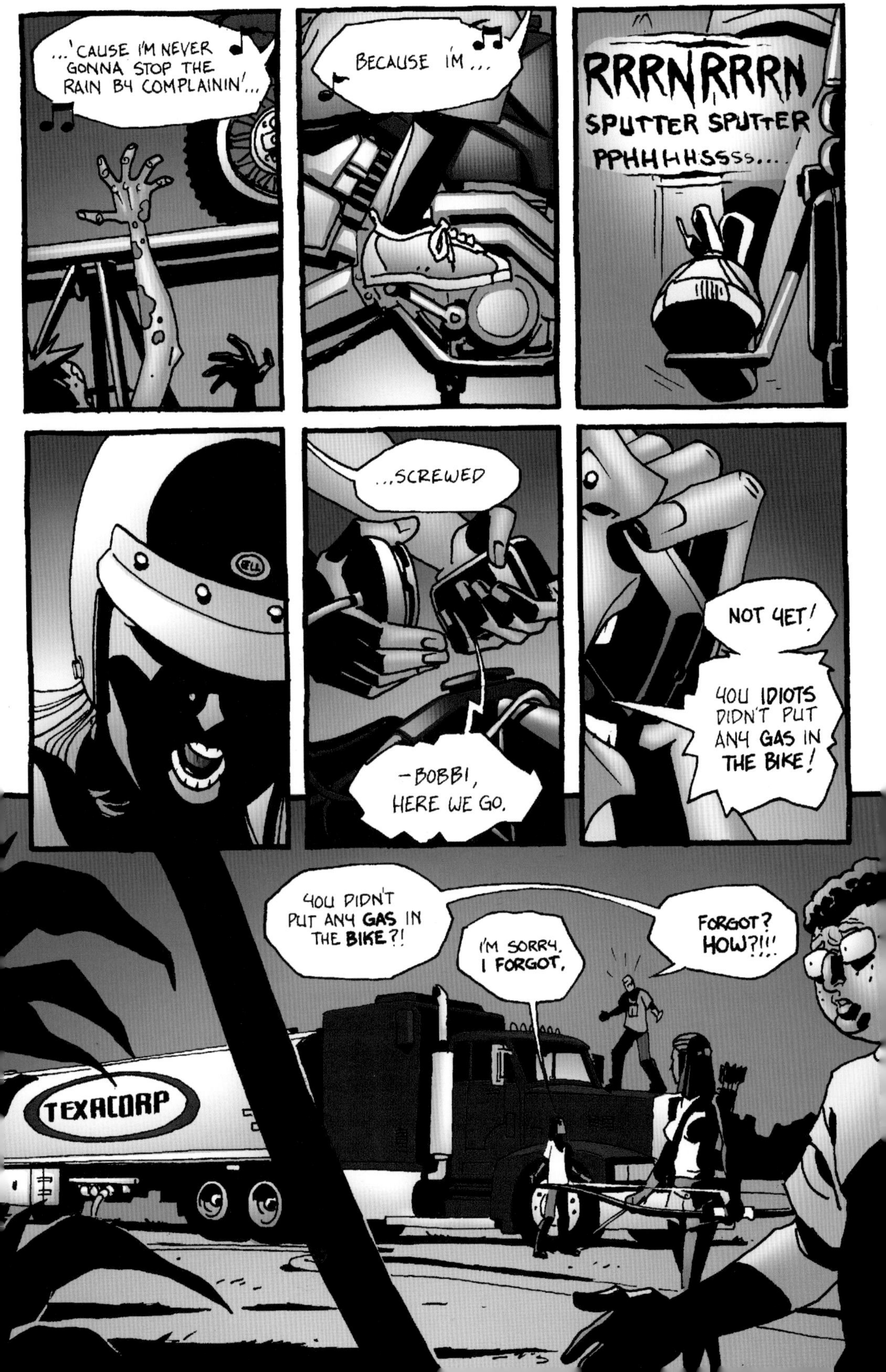
...'CAUSE I'M NEVER GONNA STOP THE RAIN BY COMPLAININ'...
BECAUSE I'M...
RRRNRRRN
SPUTTER SPUTTER
PPHHHHSSsss...
...SCREWED
-BOBBI, HERE WE GO.
NOT YET!
YOU IDIOTS DIDN'T PUT ANY GAS IN THE BIKE!
YOU DIDN'T PUT ANY GAS IN THE BIKE?!
I'M SORRY. I FORGOT.
FORGOT? HOW?!!!
TEXACORP

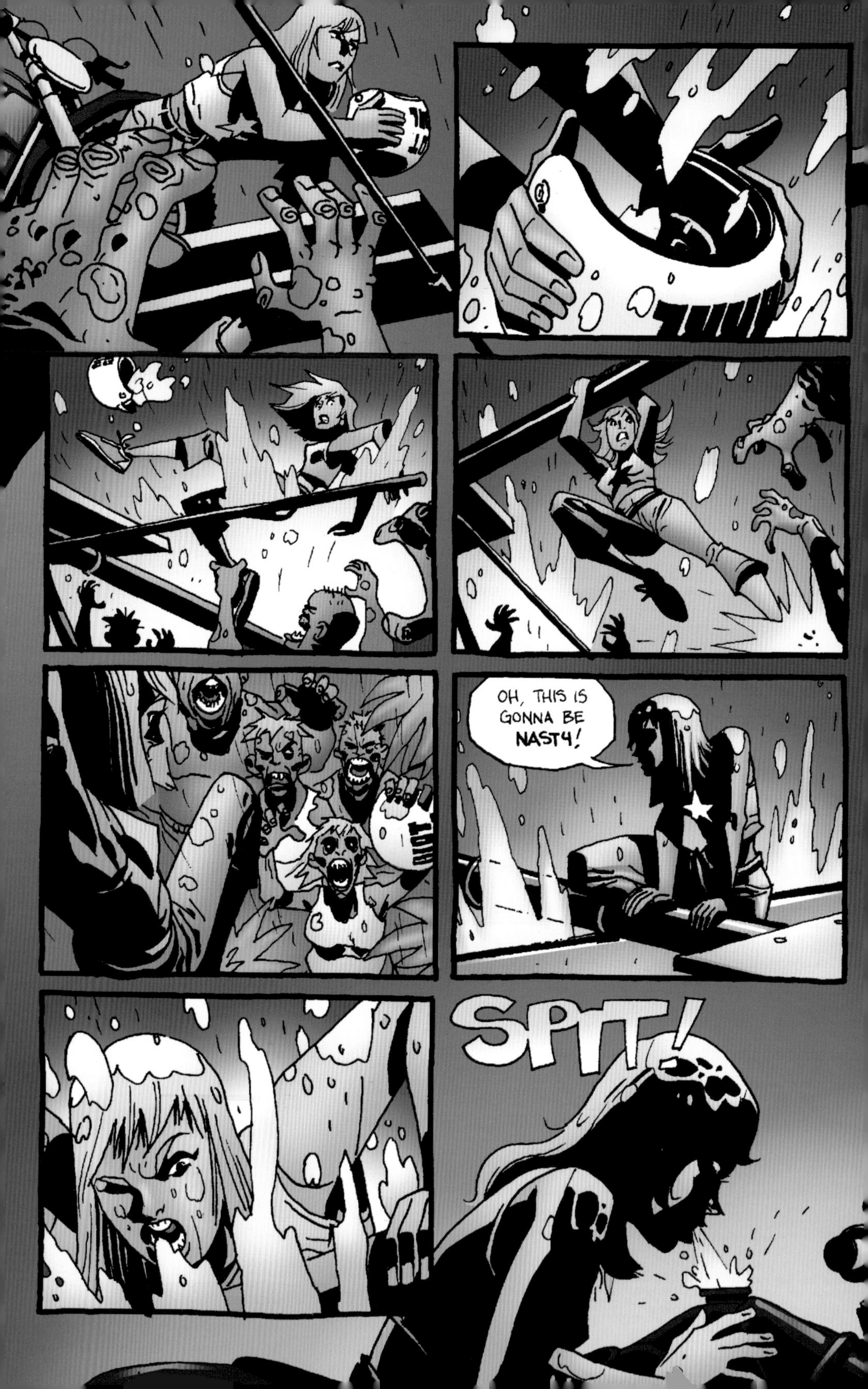
OH, THIS IS GONNA BE NASTY!
SPIT!

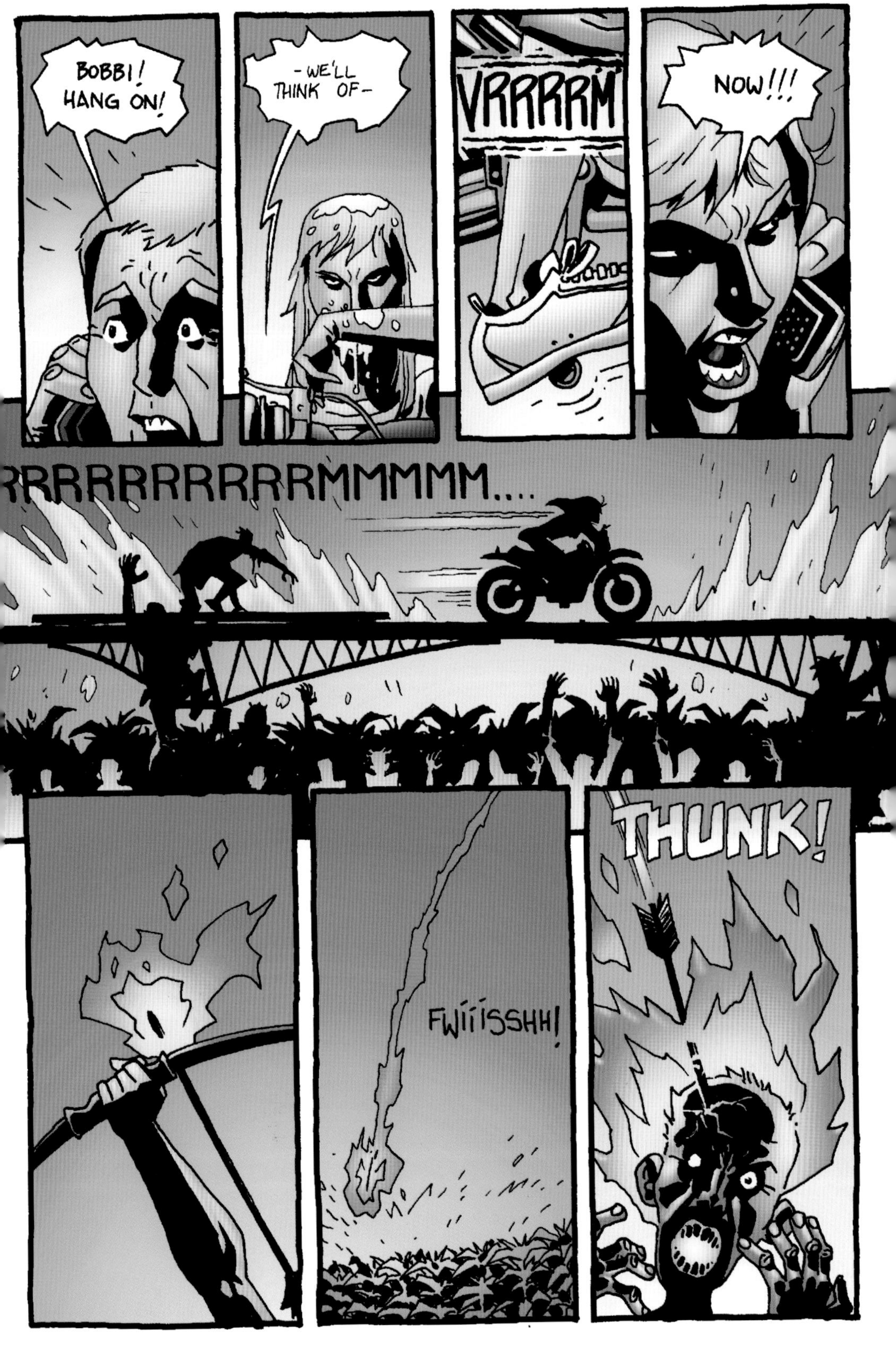
BOBBI! HANG ON!
-WE'LL THINK OF-
VRRRRM
NOW!!!
RRRRRRRRRRRRMMMMM....
FWIIISSHH!
THUNK!

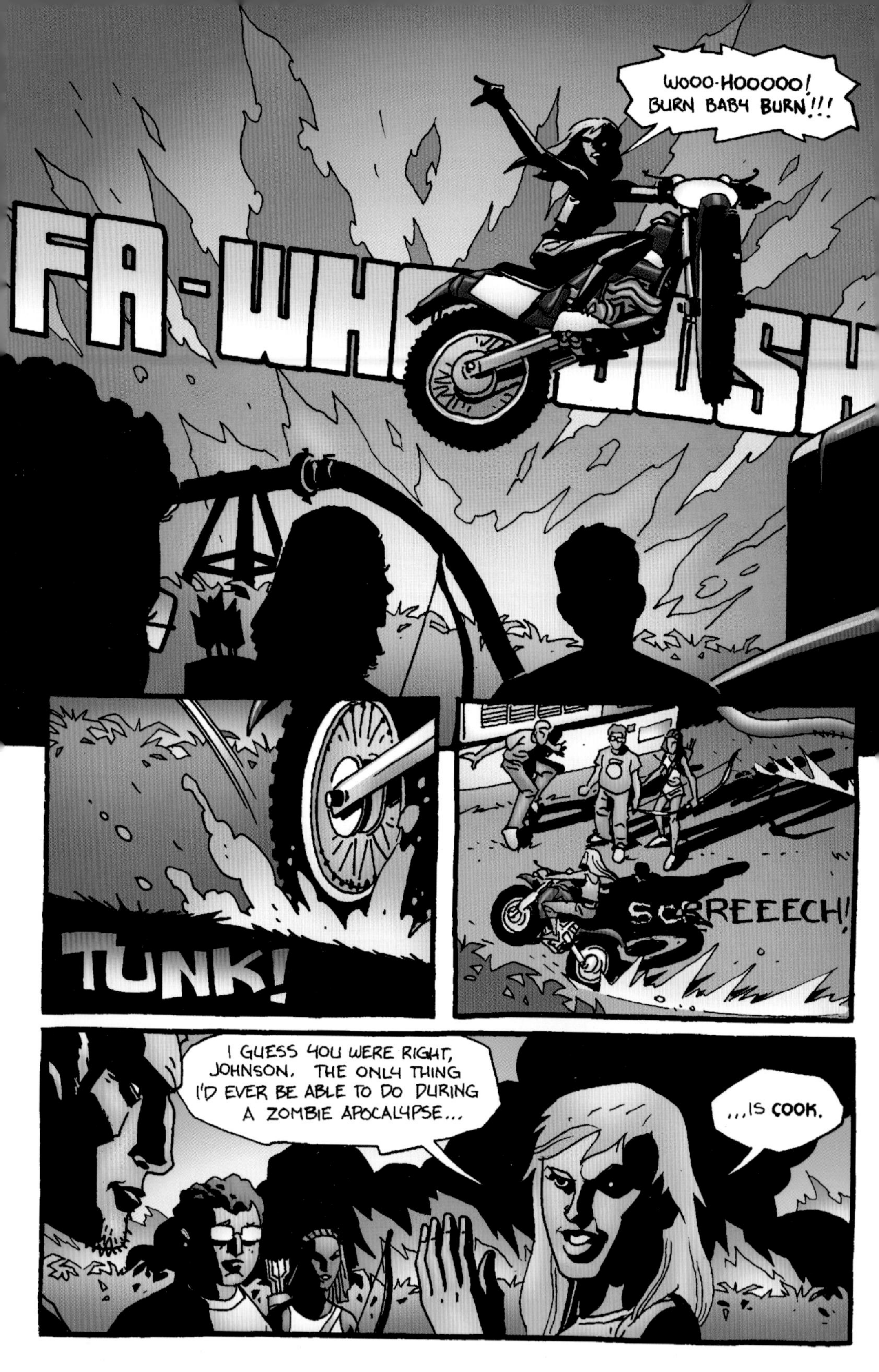
WOOO-HOOOOO! BURN BABY BURN!!!
FA-WHOOSH
TUNK!
SCREEECH!
I GUESS YOU WERE RIGHT, JOHNSON. THE ONLY THING I'D EVER BE ABLE TO DO DURING A ZOMBIE APOCALYPSE...
...IS COOK.

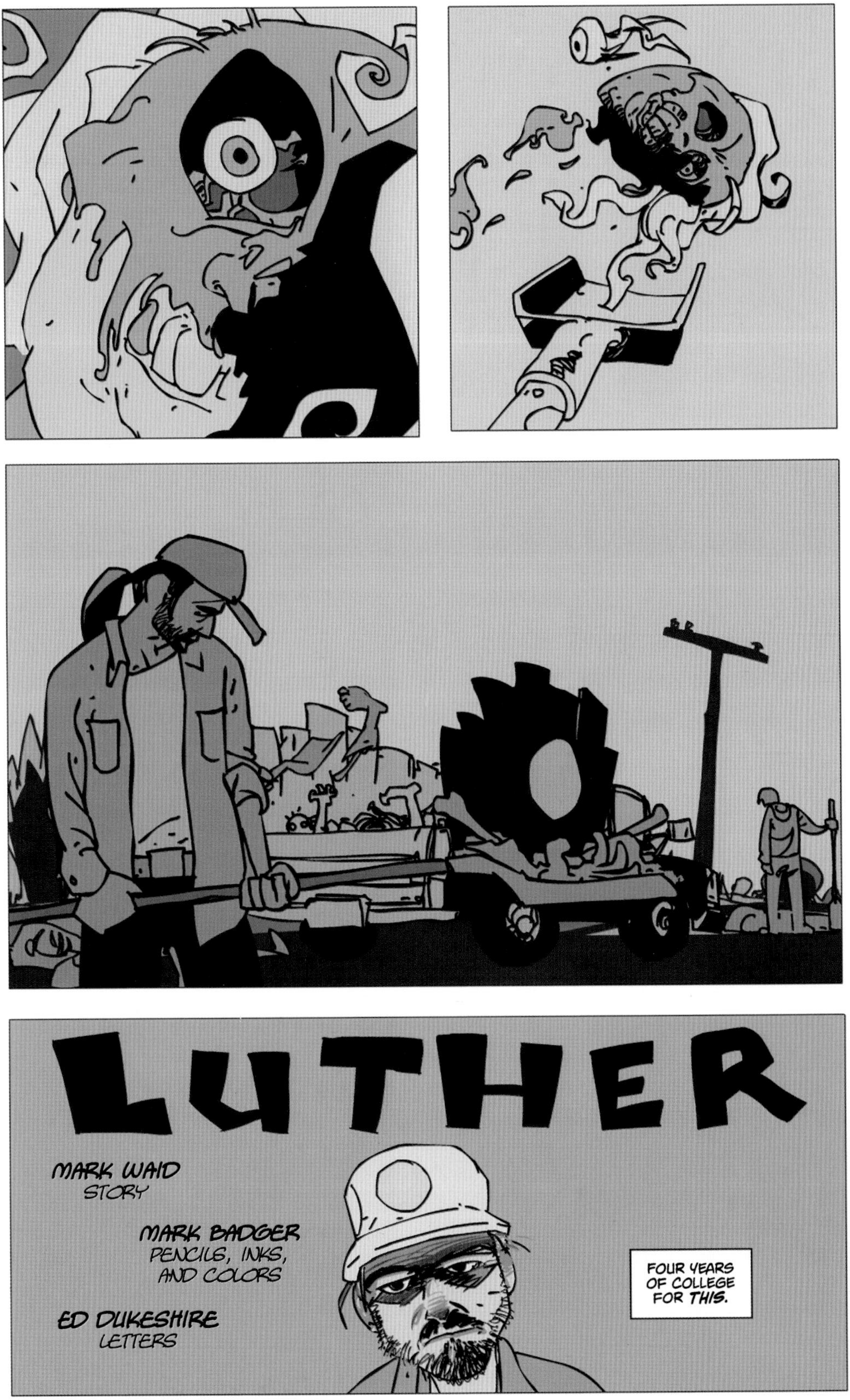
LUTHER
MARK WAID
STORY
MARK BADGER
PENCILS, INKS, AND COLORS
ED DUKESHIRE
LETTERS
FOUR YEARS OF COLLEGE FOR THIS.

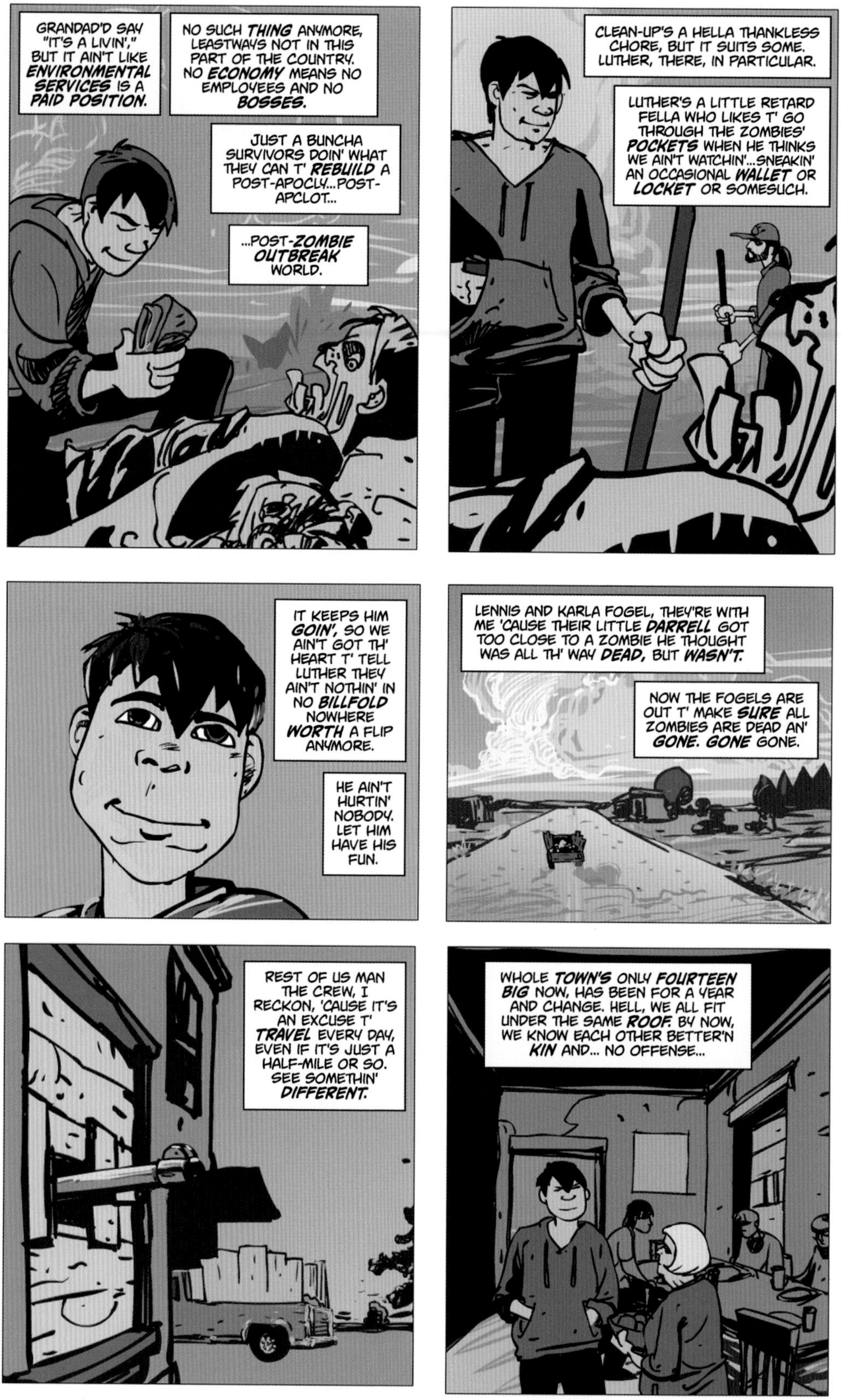
GRANDAD'D SAY "IT'S A LIVIN'," BUT IT AIN'T LIKE ENVIRONMENTAL SERVICES IS A PAID POSITION.
NO SUCH THING ANYMORE, LEASTWAYS NOT IN THIS PART OF THE COUNTRY. NO ECONOMY MEANS NO EMPLOYEES AND NO BOSSES.
JUST A BUNCHA SURVIVORS DOIN' WHAT THEY CAN T' REBUILD A POST-APOCLY...POST-APCLOT...
...POST-ZOMBIE OUTBREAK WORLD.
CLEAN-UP'S A HELLA THANKLESS CHORE, BUT IT SUITS SOME. LUTHER, THERE, IN PARTICULAR.
LUTHER'S A LITTLE RETARD FELLA WHO LIKES T' GO THROUGH THE ZOMBIES' POCKETS WHEN HE THINKS WE AIN'T WATCHIN'...SNEAKIN' AN OCCASIONAL WALLET OR LOCKET OR SOMESUCH.
IT KEEPS HIM GOIN', SO WE AIN'T GOT TH' HEART T' TELL LUTHER THEY AIN'T NOTHIN' IN NO BILLFOLD NOWHERE WORTH A FLIP ANYMORE.
HE AIN'T HURTIN' NOBODY. LET HIM HAVE HIS FUN.
LENNIS AND KARLA FOGEL, THEY'RE WITH ME 'CAUSE THEIR LITTLE DARRELL GOT TOO CLOSE TO A ZOMBIE HE THOUGHT WAS ALL TH' WAY DEAD, BUT WASN'T.
NOW THE FOGELS ARE OUT T' MAKE SURE ALL ZOMBIES ARE DEAD AN' GONE. GONE GONE.
REST OF US MAN THE CREW, I RECKON, 'CAUSE IT'S AN EXCUSE T' TRAVEL EVERY DAY, EVEN IF IT'S JUST A HALF-MILE OR SO. SEE SOMETHIN' DIFFERENT.
WHOLE TOWN'S ONLY FOURTEEN BIG NOW, HAS BEEN FOR A YEAR AND CHANGE. HELL, WE ALL FIT UNDER THE SAME ROOF. BY NOW, WE KNOW EACH OTHER BETTER'N KIN AND... NO OFFENSE...

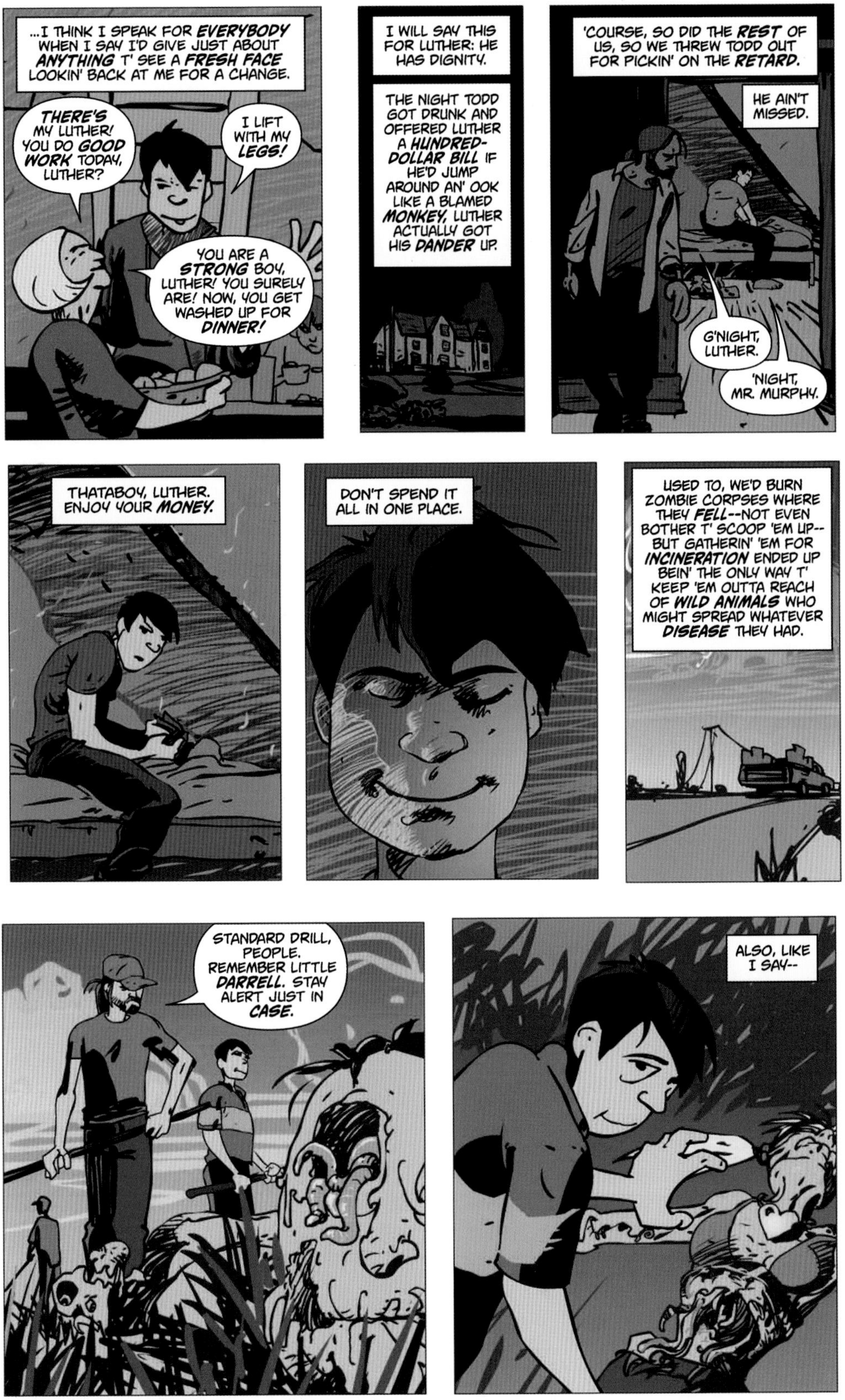
...I THINK I SPEAK FOR EVERYBODY WHEN I SAY I'D GIVE JUST ABOUT ANYTHING T' SEE A FRESH FACE LOOKIN' BACK AT ME FOR A CHANGE.
THERE'S MY LUTHER! YOU DO GOOD WORK TODAY, LUTHER?
I LIFT WITH MY LEGS!
YOU ARE A STRONG BOY, LUTHER! YOU SURELY ARE! NOW, YOU GET WASHED UP FOR DINNER!
I WILL SAY THIS FOR LUTHER: HE HAS DIGNITY.
THE NIGHT TODD GOT DRUNK AND OFFERED LUTHER A HUNDRED-DOLLAR BILL IF HE'D JUMP AROUND AN' OOK LIKE A BLAMED MONKEY, LUTHER ACTUALLY GOT HIS DANDER UP.
'COURSE, SO DID THE REST OF US, SO WE THREW TODD OUT FOR PICKIN' ON THE RETARD.
HE AIN'T MISSED.
G'NIGHT, LUTHER.
'NIGHT, MR. MURPHY.
THATABOY, LUTHER. ENJOY YOUR MONEY.
DON'T SPEND IT ALL IN ONE PLACE.
USED TO, WE'D BURN ZOMBIE CORPSES WHERE THEY FELL--NOT EVEN BOTHER T' SCOOP 'EM UP--BUT GATHERIN' 'EM FOR INCINERATION ENDED UP BEIN' THE ONLY WAY T' KEEP 'EM OUTTA REACH OF WILD ANIMALS WHO MIGHT SPREAD WHATEVER DISEASE THEY HAD.
STANDARD DRILL, PEOPLE. REMEMBER LITTLE DARRELL. STAY ALERT JUST IN CASE.
ALSO, LIKE I SAY--

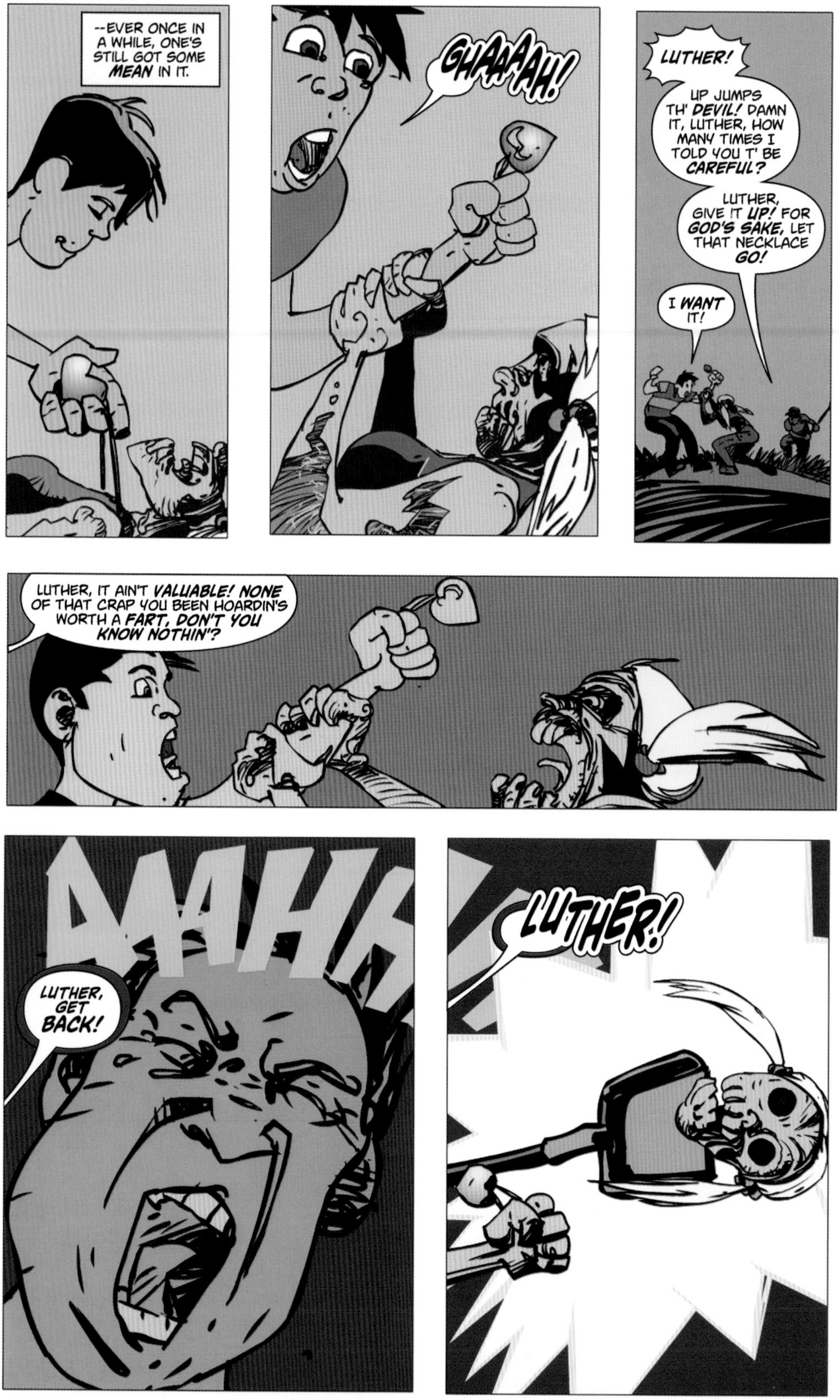
--EVER ONCE IN A WHILE, ONE'S STILL GOT SOME MEAN IN IT.
GHAAAAAH!
LUTHER!
UP JUMPS TH' DEVIL! DAMN IT, LUTHER, HOW MANY TIMES I TOLD YOU T' BE CAREFUL?
LUTHER, GIVE IT UP! FOR GOD'S SAKE, LET THAT NECKLACE GO!
I WANT IT!
LUTHER, IT AIN'T VALUABLE! NONE OF THAT CRAP YOU BEEN HOARDIN'S WORTH A FART, DON'T YOU KNOW NOTHIN'?
AAAHH
LUTHER, GET BACK!
LUTHER!

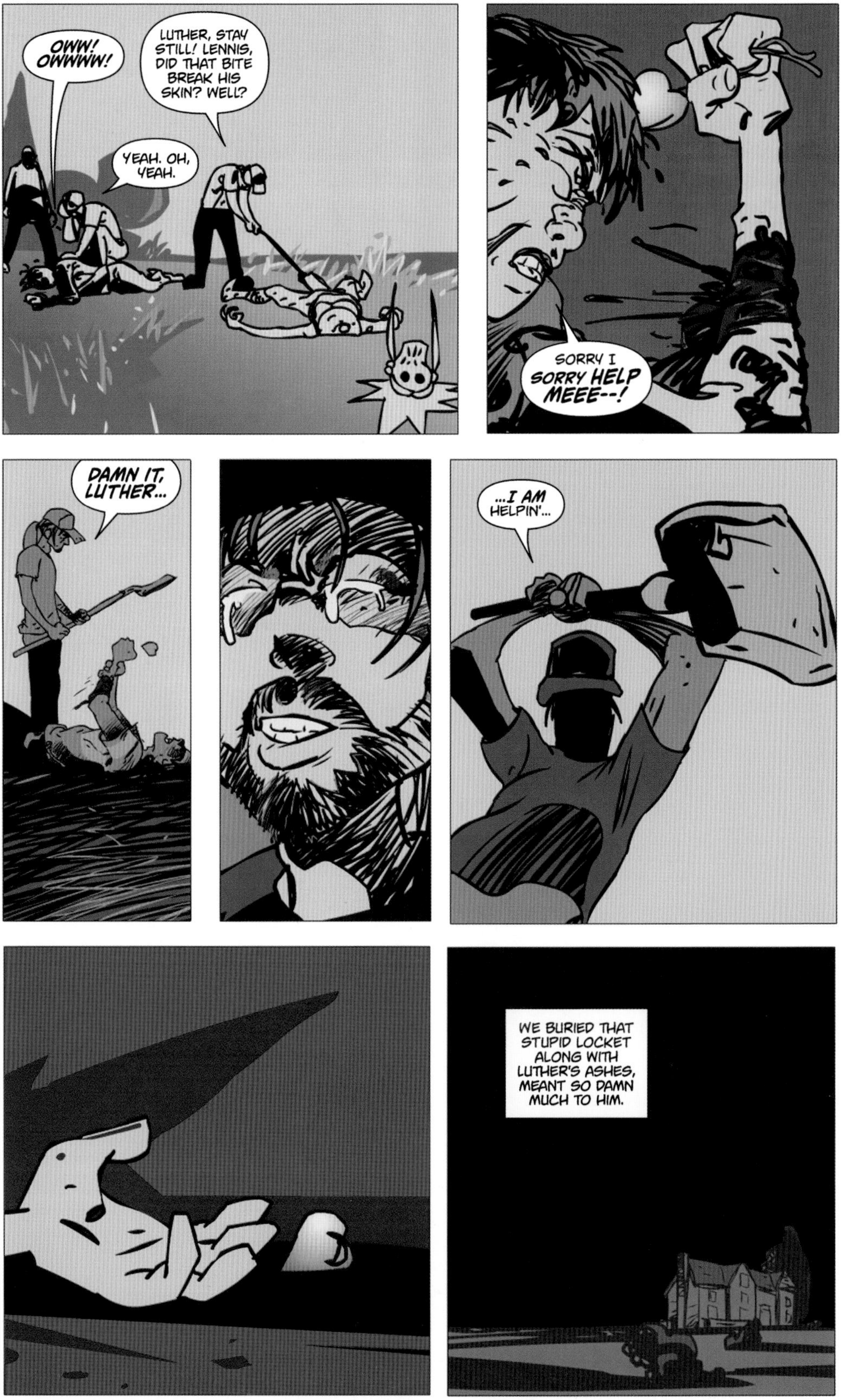
OWW! OWWWW!
LUTHER, STAY STILL! LENNIS, DID THAT BITE BREAK HIS SKIN? WELL?
YEAH. OH, YEAH.
SORRY I SORRY HELP MEEE--!
DAMN IT, LUTHER...
...I AM HELPIN'...
WE BURIED THAT STUPID LOCKET ALONG WITH LUTHER'S ASHES, MEANT SO DAMN MUCH TO HIM.

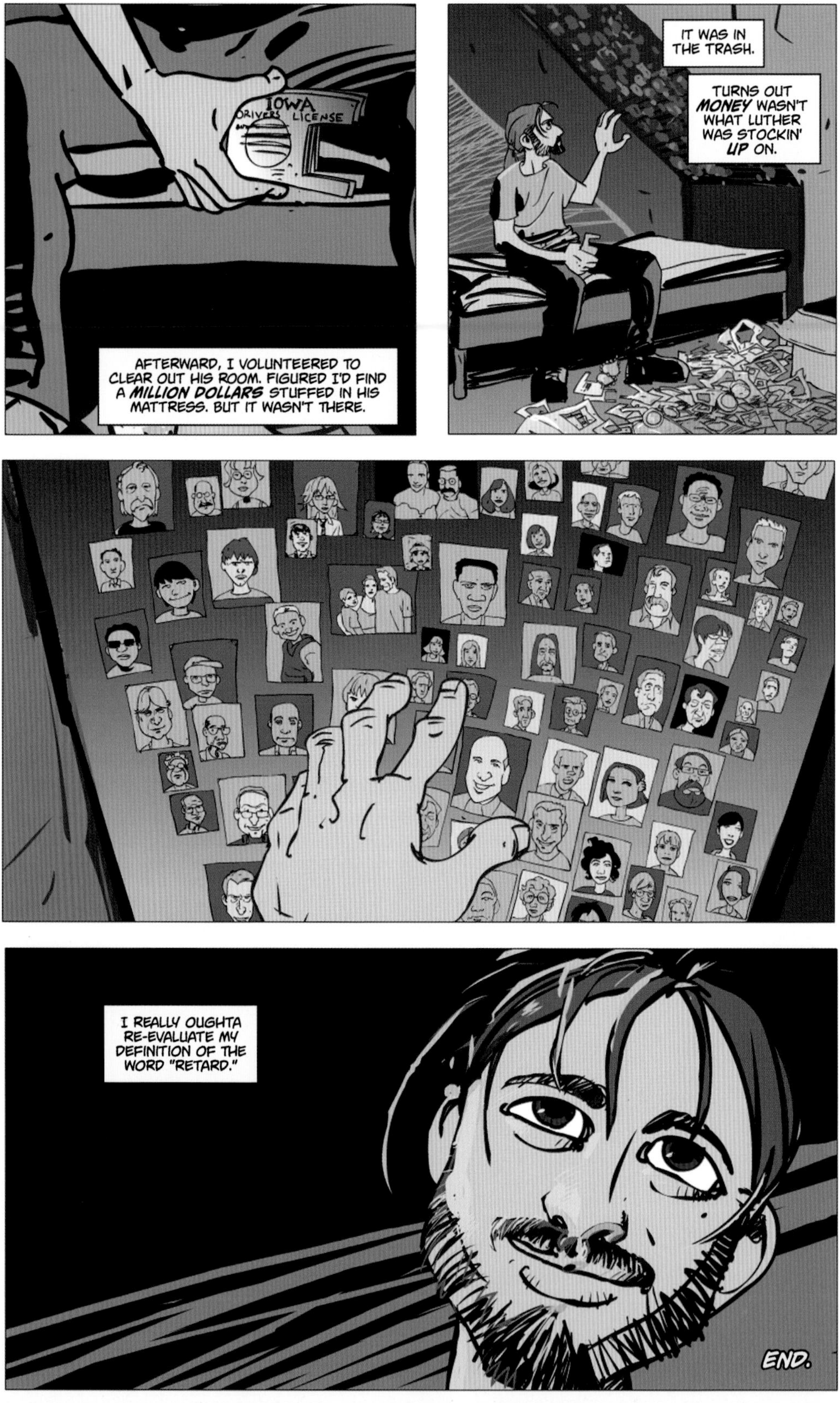
IOWA DRIVERS LICENSE
AFTERWARD, I VOLUNTEERED TO CLEAR OUT HIS ROOM. FIGURED I'D FIND A MILLION DOLLARS STUFFED IN HIS MATTRESS. BUT IT WASN'T THERE.
IT WAS IN THE TRASH.
TURNS OUT MONEY WASN'T WHAT LUTHER WAS STOCKIN' UP ON.
I REALLY OUGHTA RE-EVALUATE MY DEFINITION OF THE WORD "RETARD."
END.

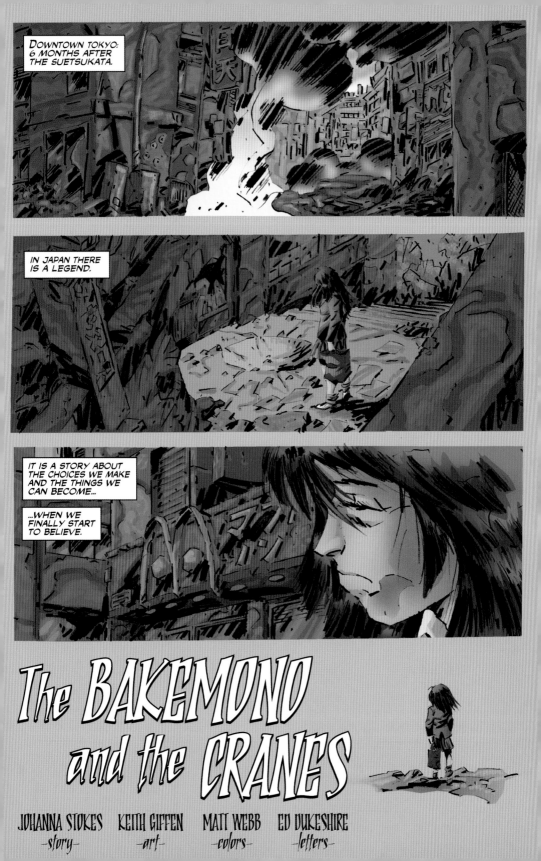

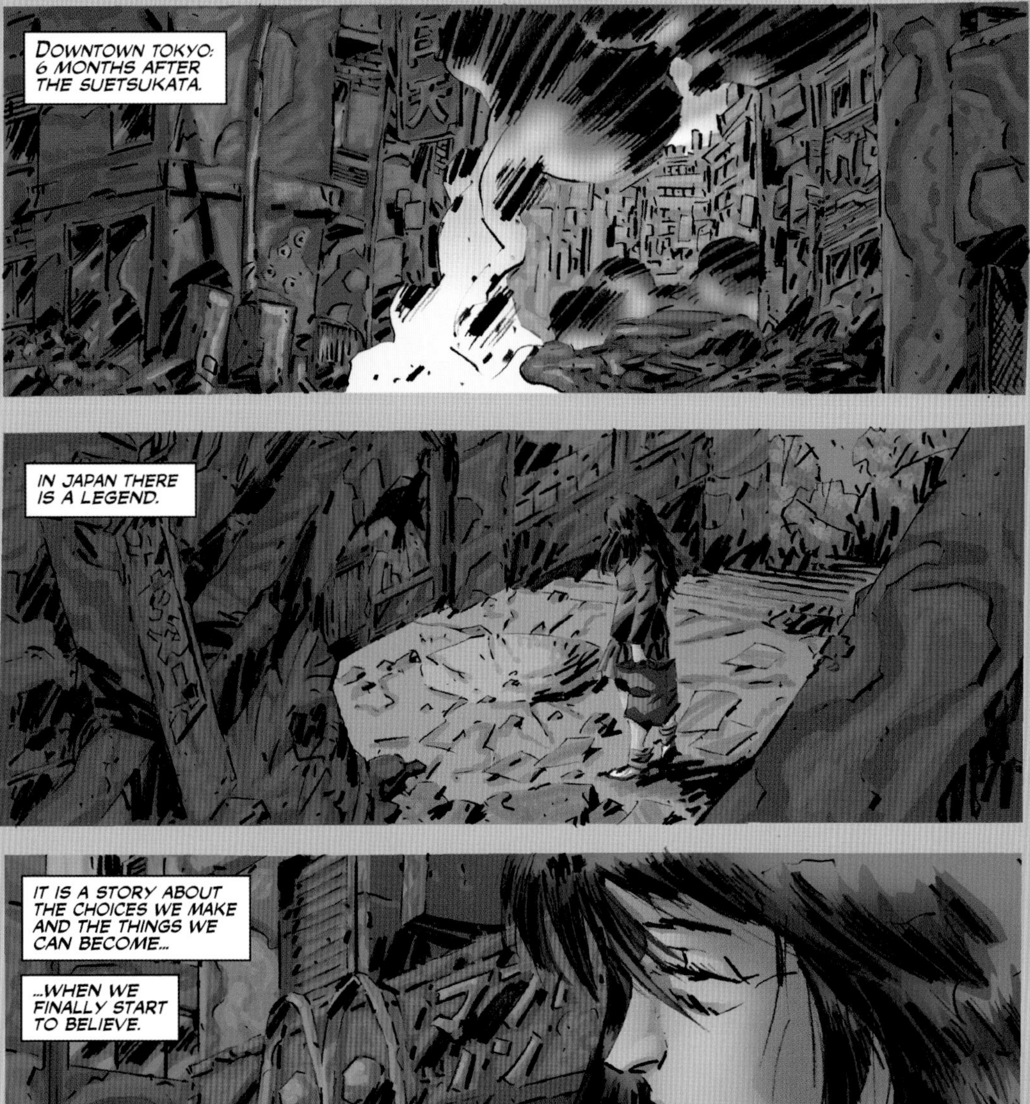
DOWNTOWN TOKYO: 6 MONTHS AFTER THE SUETSUKATA.
IN JAPAN THERE IS A LEGEND.
IT IS A STORY ABOUT THE CHOICES WE MAKE AND THE THINGS WE CAN BECOME...
...WHEN WE FINALLY START TO BELIEVE.

The BAKEMONO and the CRANES

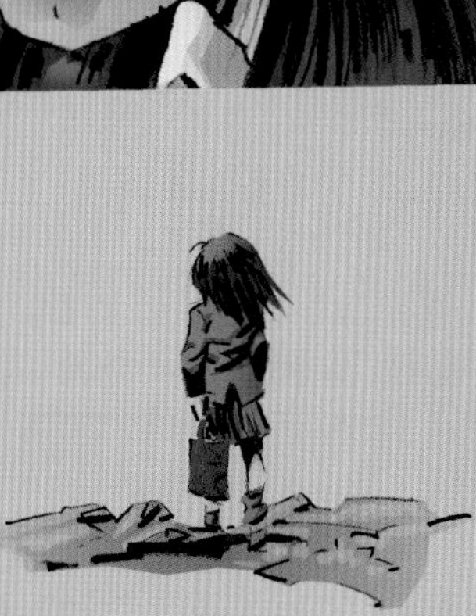

JOHANNA STOKES -story- KEITH GIFFEN -art- MATT WEBB -colors- ED DUKESHIRE -letters-

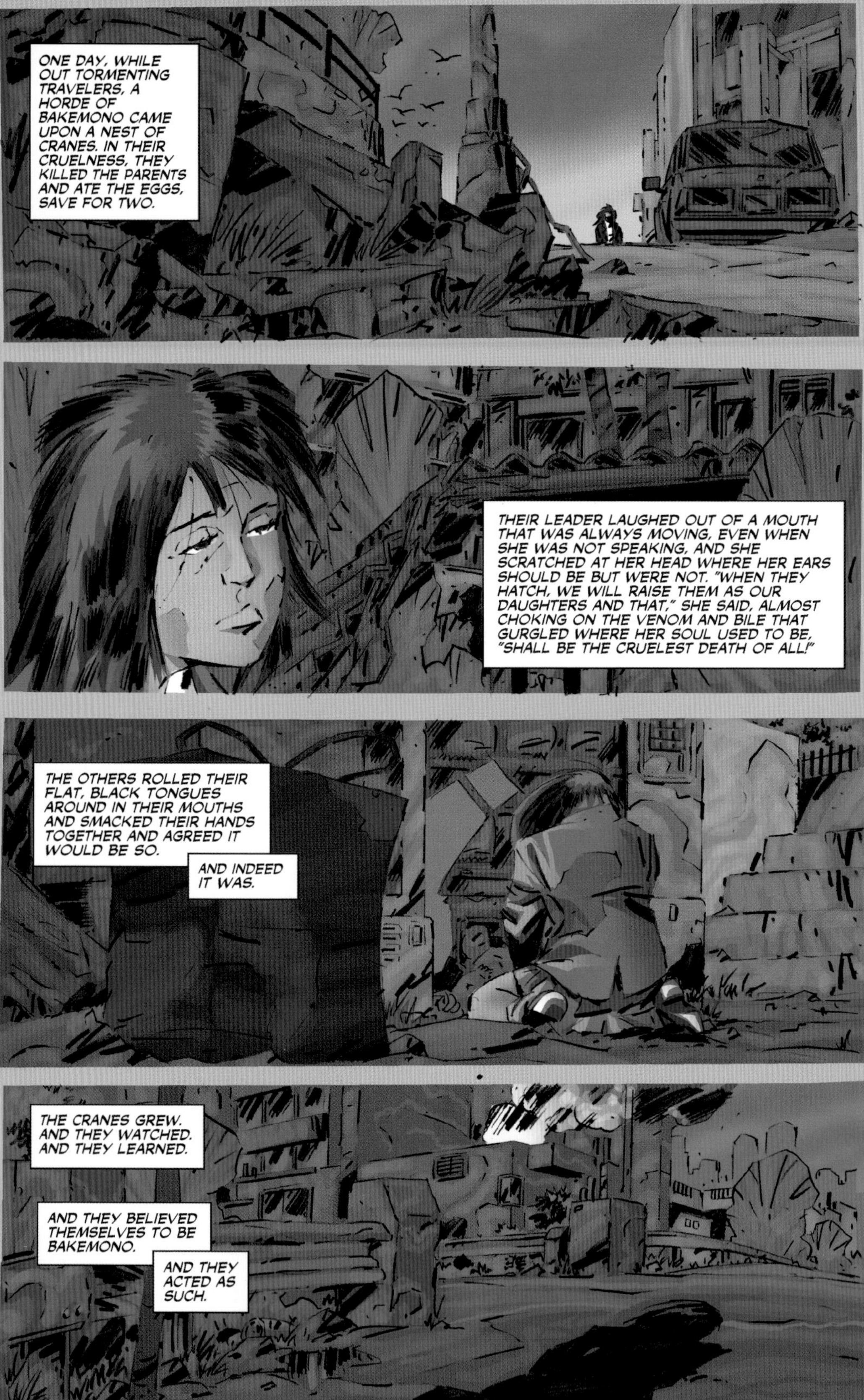
ONE DAY, WHILE OUT TORMENTING TRAVELERS, A HORDE OF BAKEMONO CAME UPON A NEST OF CRANES. IN THEIR CRUELNESS, THEY KILLED THE PARENTS AND ATE THE EGGS, SAVE FOR TWO.
THEIR LEADER LAUGHED OUT OF A MOUTH THAT WAS ALWAYS MOVING, EVEN WHEN SHE WAS NOT SPEAKING, AND SHE SCRATCHED AT HER HEAD WHERE HER EARS SHOULD BE BUT WERE NOT. "WHEN THEY HATCH, WE WILL RAISE THEM AS OUR DAUGHTERS AND THAT," SHE SAID, ALMOST CHOKING ON THE VENOM AND BILE THAT GURGLED WHERE HER SOUL USED TO BE, "SHALL BE THE CRUELEST DEATH OF ALL!"
THE OTHERS ROLLED THEIR FLAT, BLACK TONGUES AROUND IN THEIR MOUTHS AND SMACKED THEIR HANDS TOGETHER AND AGREED IT WOULD BE SO.
AND INDEED IT WAS.
THE CRANES GREW. AND THEY WATCHED. AND THEY LEARNED.
AND THEY BELIEVED THEMSELVES TO BE BAKEMONO.
AND THEY ACTED AS SUCH.

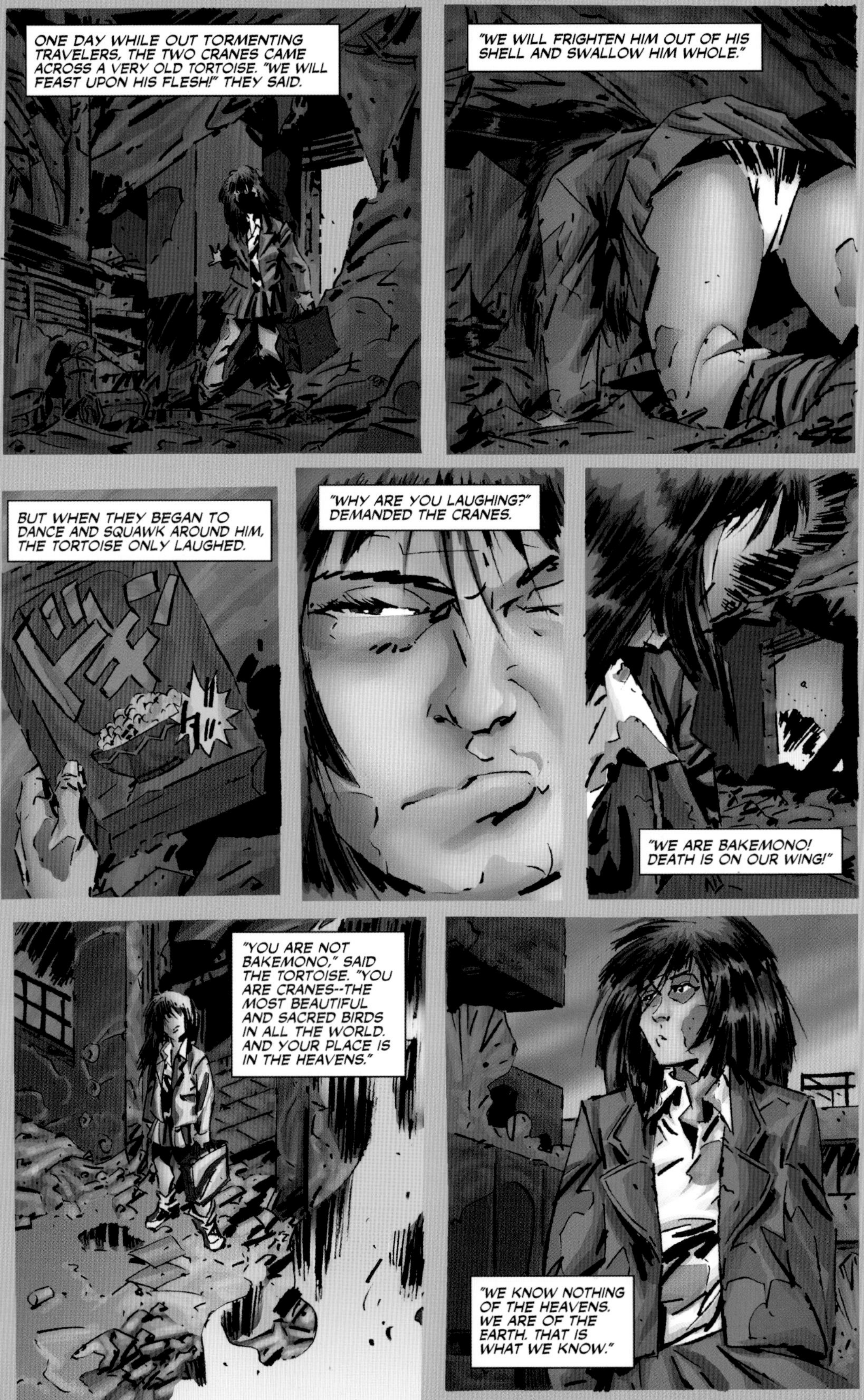
ONE DAY WHILE OUT TORMENTING TRAVELERS, THE TWO CRANES CAME ACROSS A VERY OLD TORTOISE. "WE WILL FEAST UPON HIS FLESH!" THEY SAID.
"WE WILL FRIGHTEN HIM OUT OF HIS SHELL AND SWALLOW HIM WHOLE."
BUT WHEN THEY BEGAN TO DANCE AND SQUAWK AROUND HIM, THE TORTOISE ONLY LAUGHED.
"WHY ARE YOU LAUGHING?" DEMANDED THE CRANES.
"WE ARE BAKEMONO! DEATH IS ON OUR WING!"
"YOU ARE NOT BAKEMONO," SAID THE TORTOISE. "YOU ARE CRANES--THE MOST BEAUTIFUL AND SACRED BIRDS IN ALL THE WORLD. AND YOUR PLACE IS IN THE HEAVENS."
"WE KNOW NOTHING OF THE HEAVENS. WE ARE OF THE EARTH. THAT IS WHAT WE KNOW."

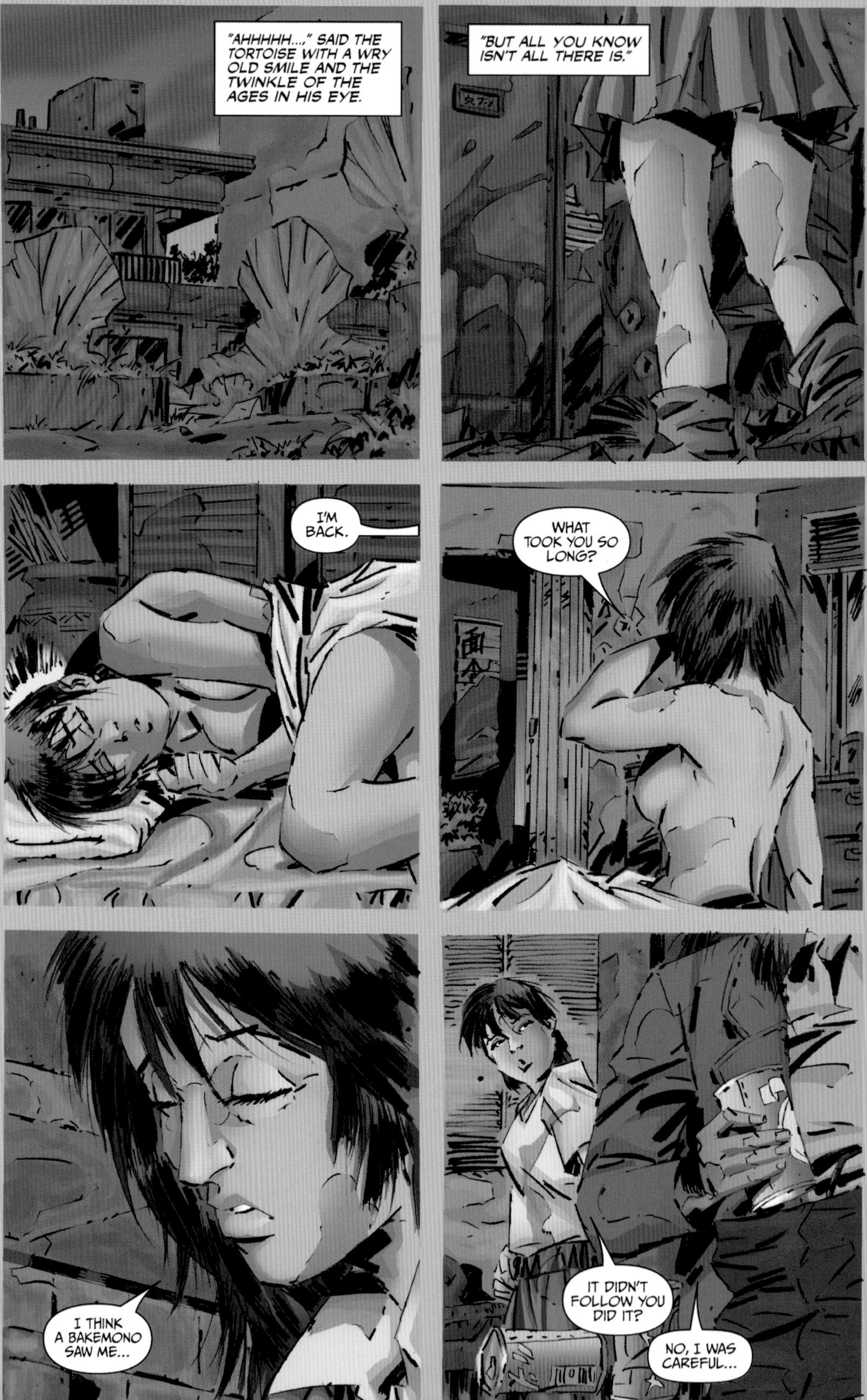
"AHHHHH...," SAID THE TORTOISE WITH A WRY OLD SMILE AND THE TWINKLE OF THE AGES IN HIS EYE.
"BUT ALL YOU KNOW ISN'T ALL THERE IS."
I'M BACK.
WHAT TOOK YOU SO LONG?
I THINK A BAKEMONO SAW ME...
IT DIDN'T FOLLOW YOU DID IT?
NO, I WAS CAREFUL...

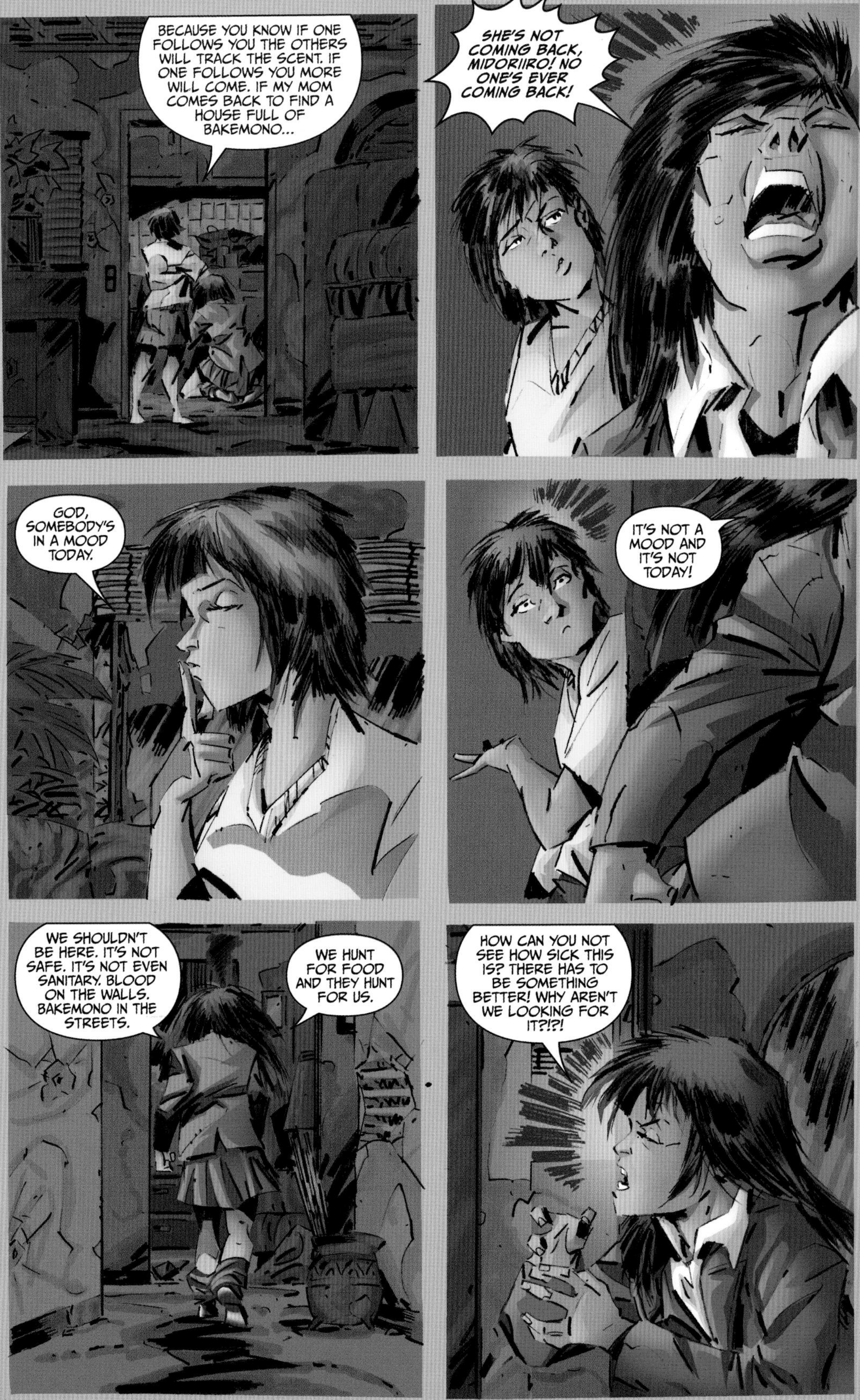
BECAUSE YOU KNOW IF ONE FOLLOWS YOU THE OTHERS WILL TRACK THE SCENT. IF ONE FOLLOWS YOU MORE WILL COME. IF MY MOM COMES BACK TO FIND A HOUSE FULL OF BAKEMONO...
SHE'S NOT COMING BACK, MIDORIIRO! NO ONE'S EVER COMING BACK!
GOD, SOMEBODY'S IN A MOOD TODAY.
IT'S NOT A MOOD AND IT'S NOT TODAY!
WE SHOULDN'T BE HERE. IT'S NOT SAFE. IT'S NOT EVEN SANITARY. BLOOD ON THE WALLS. BAKEMONO IN THE STREETS.
WE HUNT FOR FOOD AND THEY HUNT FOR US.
HOW CAN YOU NOT SEE HOW SICK THIS IS? THERE HAS TO BE SOMETHING BETTER! WHY AREN'T WE LOOKING FOR IT?!?!

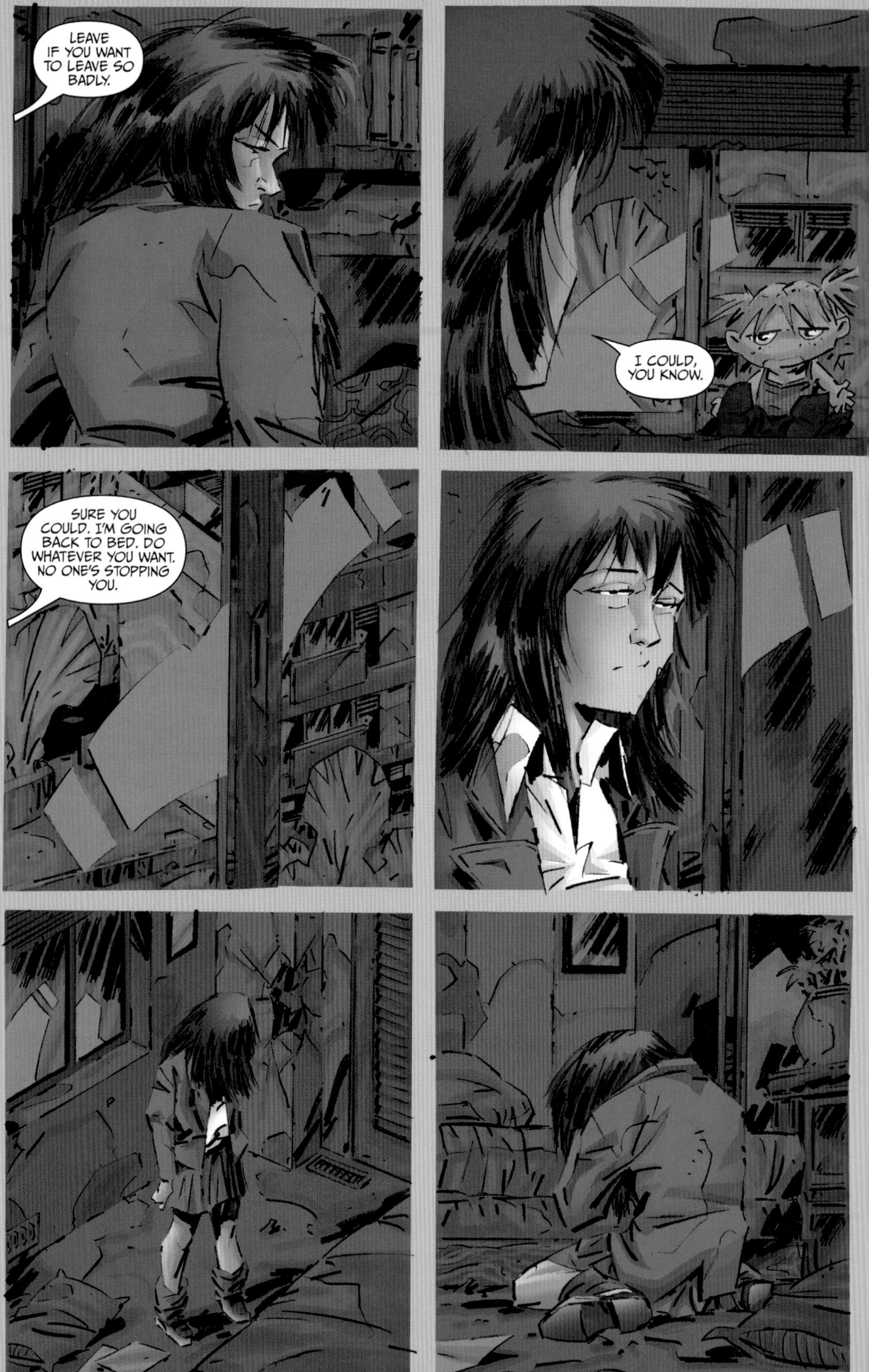
LEAVE IF YOU WANT TO LEAVE SO BADLY.
I COULD, YOU KNOW.
SURE YOU COULD. I'M GOING BACK TO BED. DO WHATEVER YOU WANT. NO ONE'S STOPPING YOU.

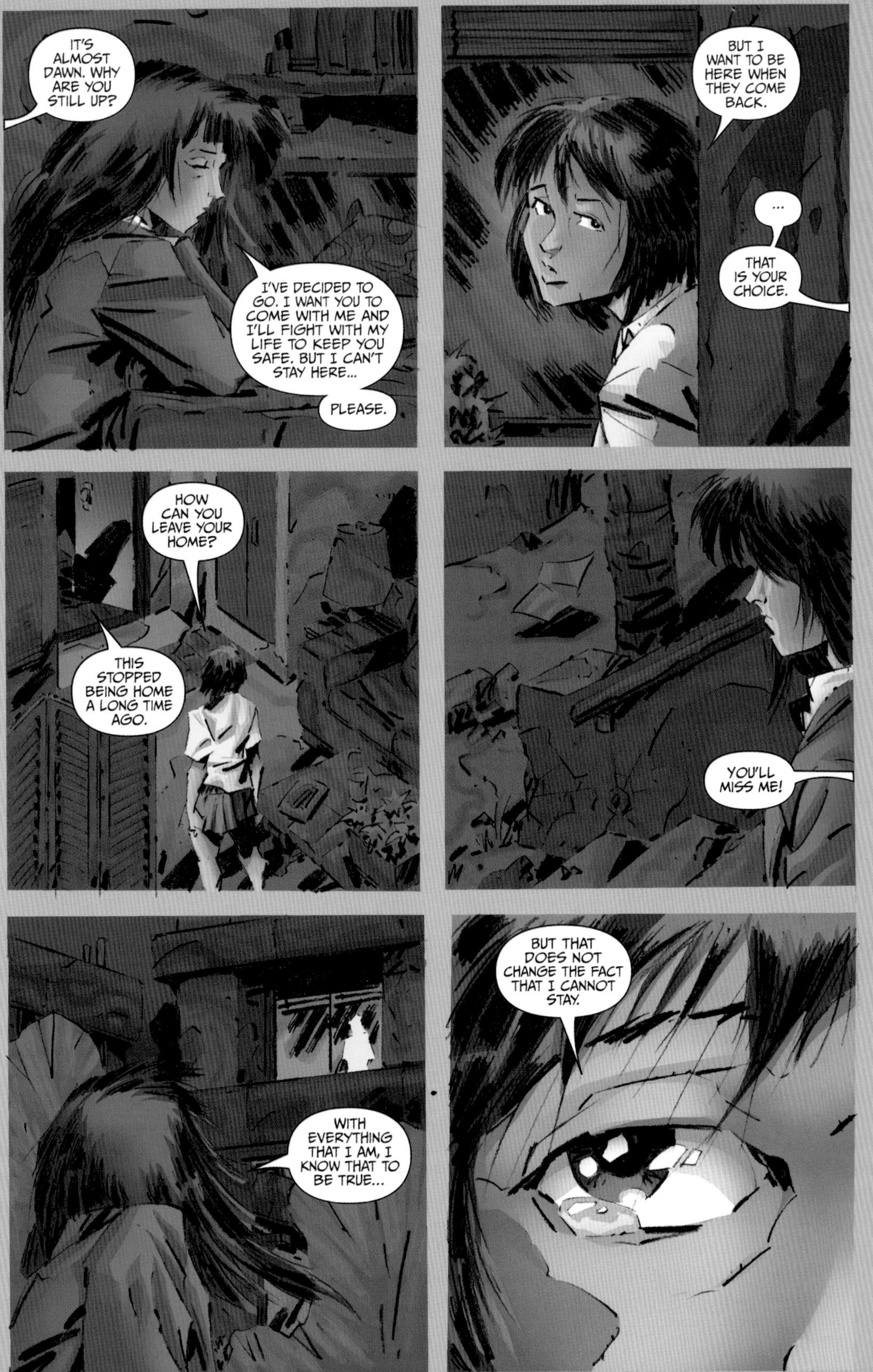
IT'S ALMOST DAWN. WHY ARE YOU STILL UP?
I'VE DECIDED TO GO. I WANT YOU TO COME WITH ME AND I'LL FIGHT WITH MY LIFE TO KEEP YOU SAFE. BUT I CAN'T STAY HERE...
PLEASE.
BUT I WANT TO BE HERE WHEN THEY COME BACK.
...
THAT IS YOUR CHOICE.
HOW CAN YOU LEAVE YOUR HOME?
THIS STOPPED BEING HOME A LONG TIME AGO.
YOU'LL MISS ME!
WITH EVERYTHING THAT I AM, I KNOW THAT TO BE TRUE...
BUT THAT DOES NOT CHANGE THE FACT THAT I CANNOT STAY.

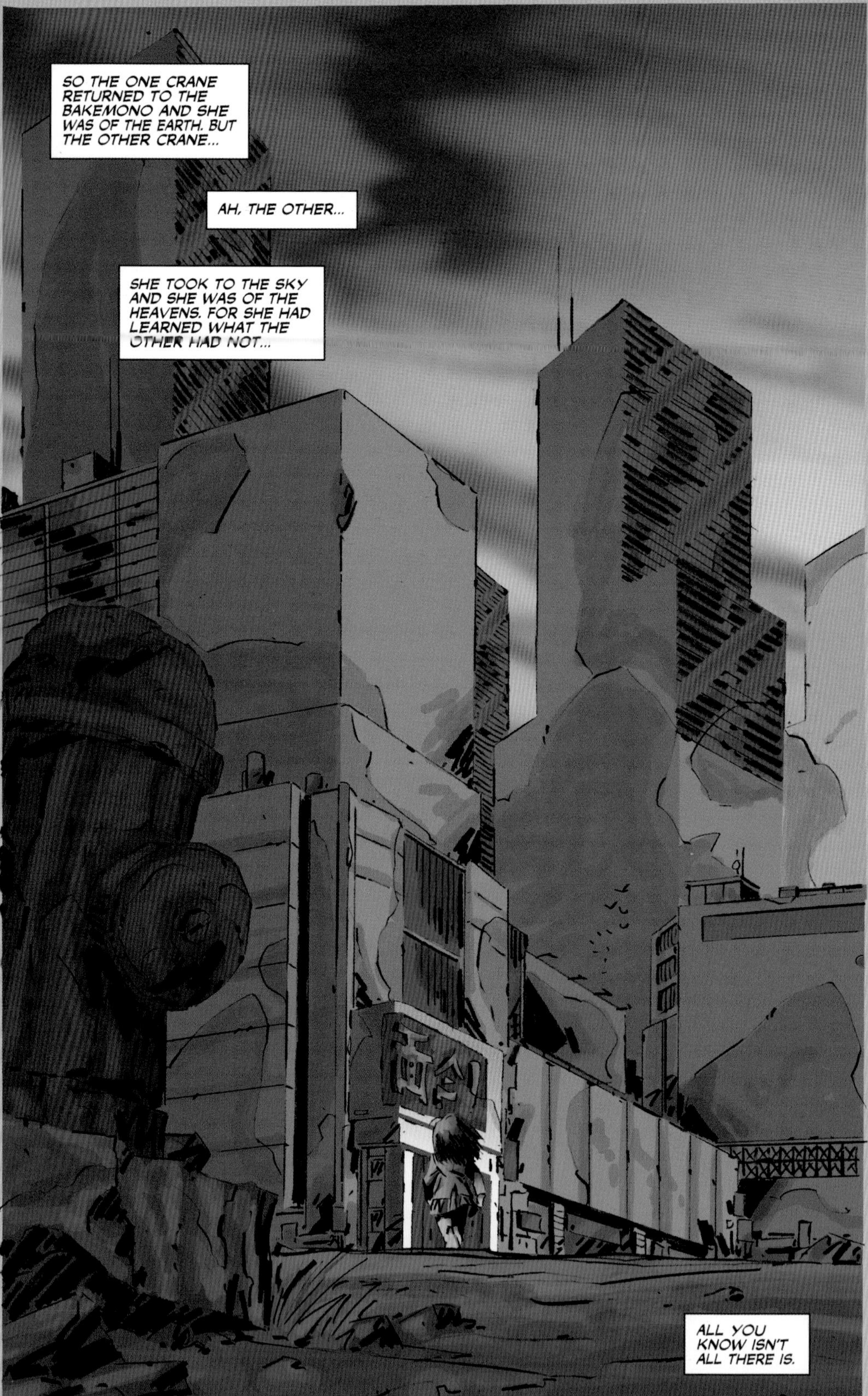

SO THE ONE CRANE RETURNED TO THE BAKEMONO AND SHE WAS OF THE EARTH. BUT THE OTHER CRANE...
AH, THE OTHER...
SHE TOOK TO THE SKY AND SHE WAS OF THE HEAVENS. FOR SHE HAD LEARNED WHAT THE OTHER HAD NOT...
ALL YOU KNOW ISN'T ALL THERE IS.

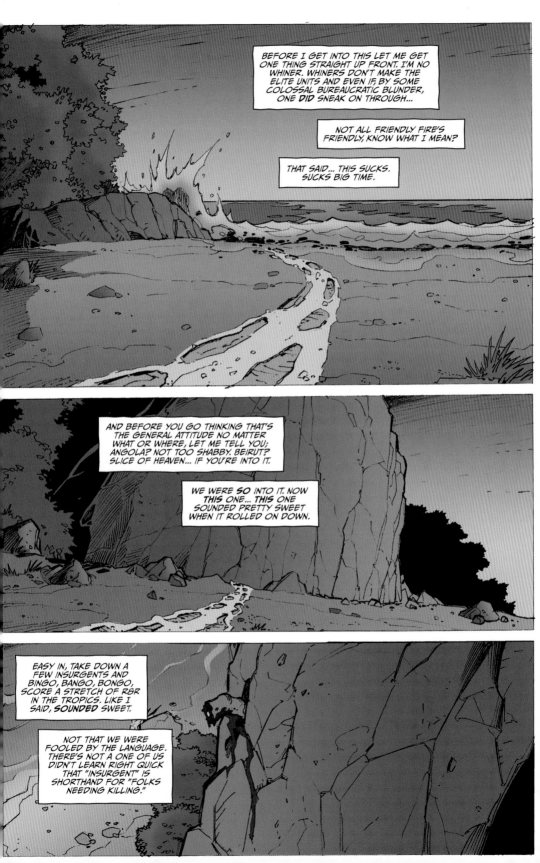

BEFORE I GET INTO THIS LET ME GET ONE THING STRAIGHT UP FRONT. I'M NO WHINER. WHINERS DON'T MAKE THE ELITE UNITS AND EVEN IF, BY SOME COLOSSAL BUREAUCRATIC BLUNDER, ONE *DID* SNEAK ON THROUGH...

NOT ALL FRIENDLY FIRE'S FRIENDLY, KNOW WHAT I MEAN?

THAT SAID... THIS SUCKS. SUCKS BIG TIME.

AND BEFORE YOU GO THINKING THAT'S THE GENERAL ATTITUDE NO MATTER WHAT OR WHERE, LET ME TELL YOU; ANGOLA? NOT TOO SHABBY. BEIRUT? SLICE OF HEAVEN... IF YOU'RE INTO IT.

WE WERE *SO* INTO IT. NOW *THIS* ONE... *THIS* ONE SOUNDED PRETTY SWEET WHEN IT ROLLED ON DOWN.

EASY IN, TAKE DOWN A FEW INSURGENTS AND BINGO, BANGO, BONGO, SCORE A STRETCH OF R&R IN THE TROPICS. LIKE I SAID, *SOUNDED* SWEET.

NOT THAT WE WERE FOOLED BY THE LANGUAGE. THERE'S NOT A ONE OF US DIDN'T LEARN RIGHT QUICK THAT "INSURGENT" IS SHORTHAND FOR "FOLKS NEEDING KILLING."

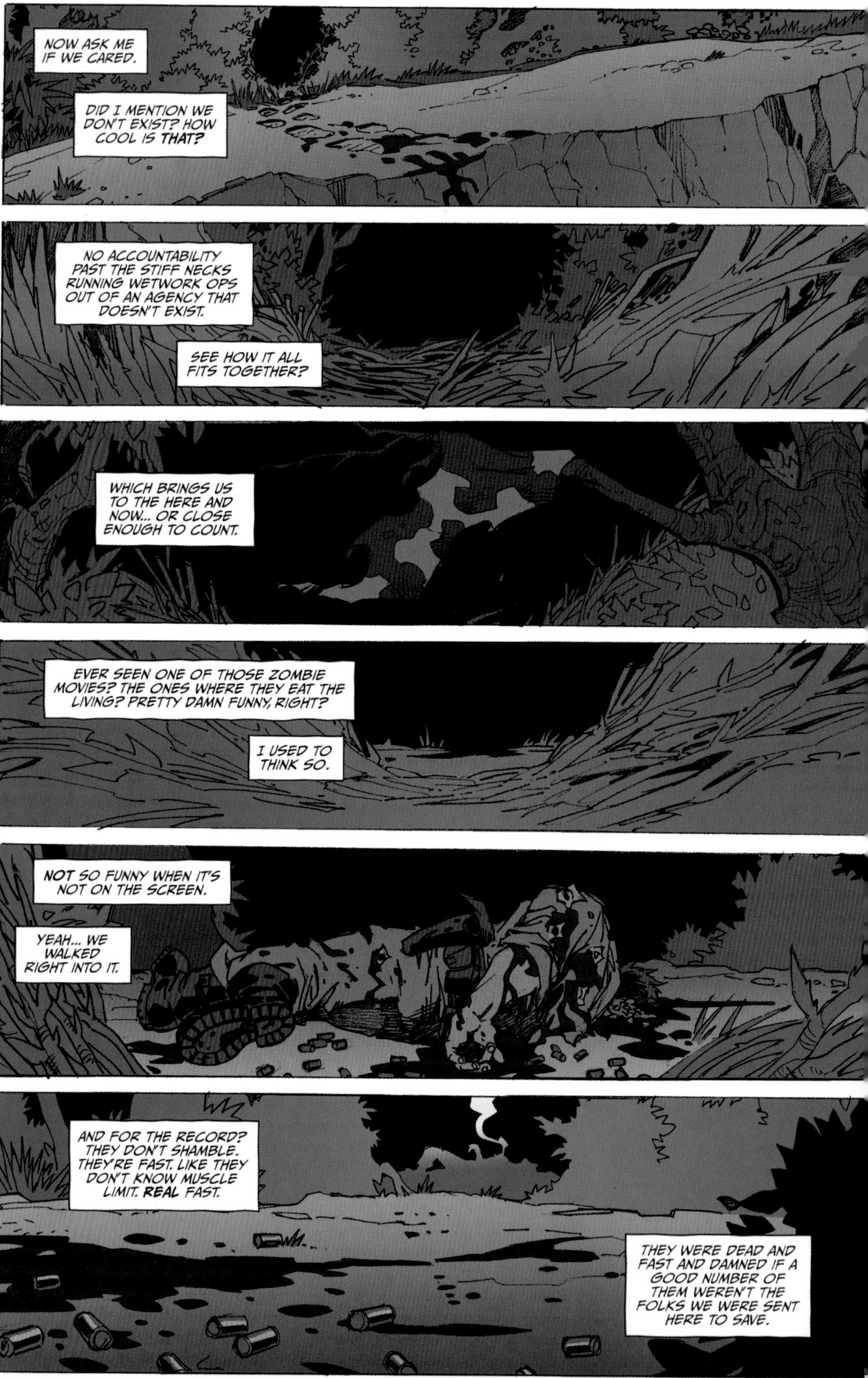
NOW ASK ME IF WE CARED.
DID I MENTION WE DON'T EXIST? HOW COOL IS THAT?
NO ACCOUNTABILITY PAST THE STIFF NECKS RUNNING WETWORK OPS OUT OF AN AGENCY THAT DOESN'T EXIST.
SEE HOW IT ALL FITS TOGETHER?
WHICH BRINGS US TO THE HERE AND NOW... OR CLOSE ENOUGH TO COUNT.
EVER SEEN ONE OF THOSE ZOMBIE MOVIES? THE ONES WHERE THEY EAT THE LIVING? PRETTY DAMN FUNNY, RIGHT?
I USED TO THINK SO.
NOT SO FUNNY WHEN IT'S NOT ON THE SCREEN.
YEAH... WE WALKED RIGHT INTO IT.
AND FOR THE RECORD? THEY DON'T SHAMBLE. THEY'RE FAST. LIKE THEY DON'T KNOW MUSCLE LIMIT. REAL FAST.
THEY WERE DEAD AND FAST AND DAMNED IF A GOOD NUMBER OF THEM WEREN'T THE FOLKS WE WERE SENT HERE TO SAVE.

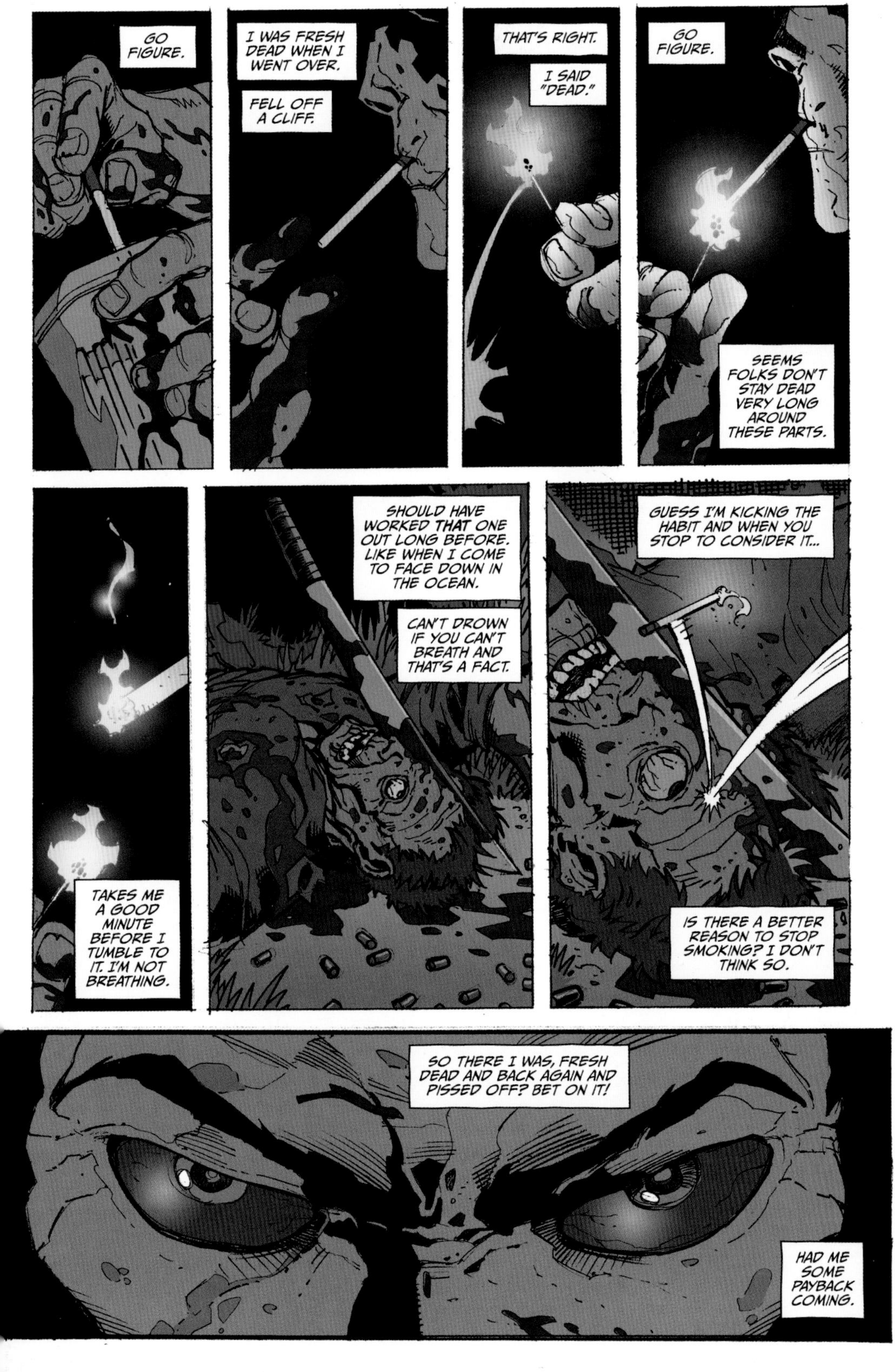
GO FIGURE.
I WAS FRESH DEAD WHEN I WENT OVER.
FELL OFF A CLIFF.
THAT'S RIGHT.
I SAID "DEAD."
GO FIGURE.
SEEMS FOLKS DON'T STAY DEAD VERY LONG AROUND THESE PARTS.
TAKES ME A GOOD MINUTE BEFORE I TUMBLE TO IT. I'M NOT BREATHING.
SHOULD HAVE WORKED THAT ONE OUT LONG BEFORE. LIKE WHEN I COME TO FACE DOWN IN THE OCEAN.
CAN'T DROWN IF YOU CAN'T BREATH AND THAT'S A FACT.
GUESS I'M KICKING THE HABIT AND WHEN YOU STOP TO CONSIDER IT...
IS THERE A BETTER REASON TO STOP SMOKING? I DON'T THINK SO.
SO THERE I WAS, FRESH DEAD AND BACK AGAIN AND PISSED OFF? BET ON IT!
HAD ME SOME PAYBACK COMING.

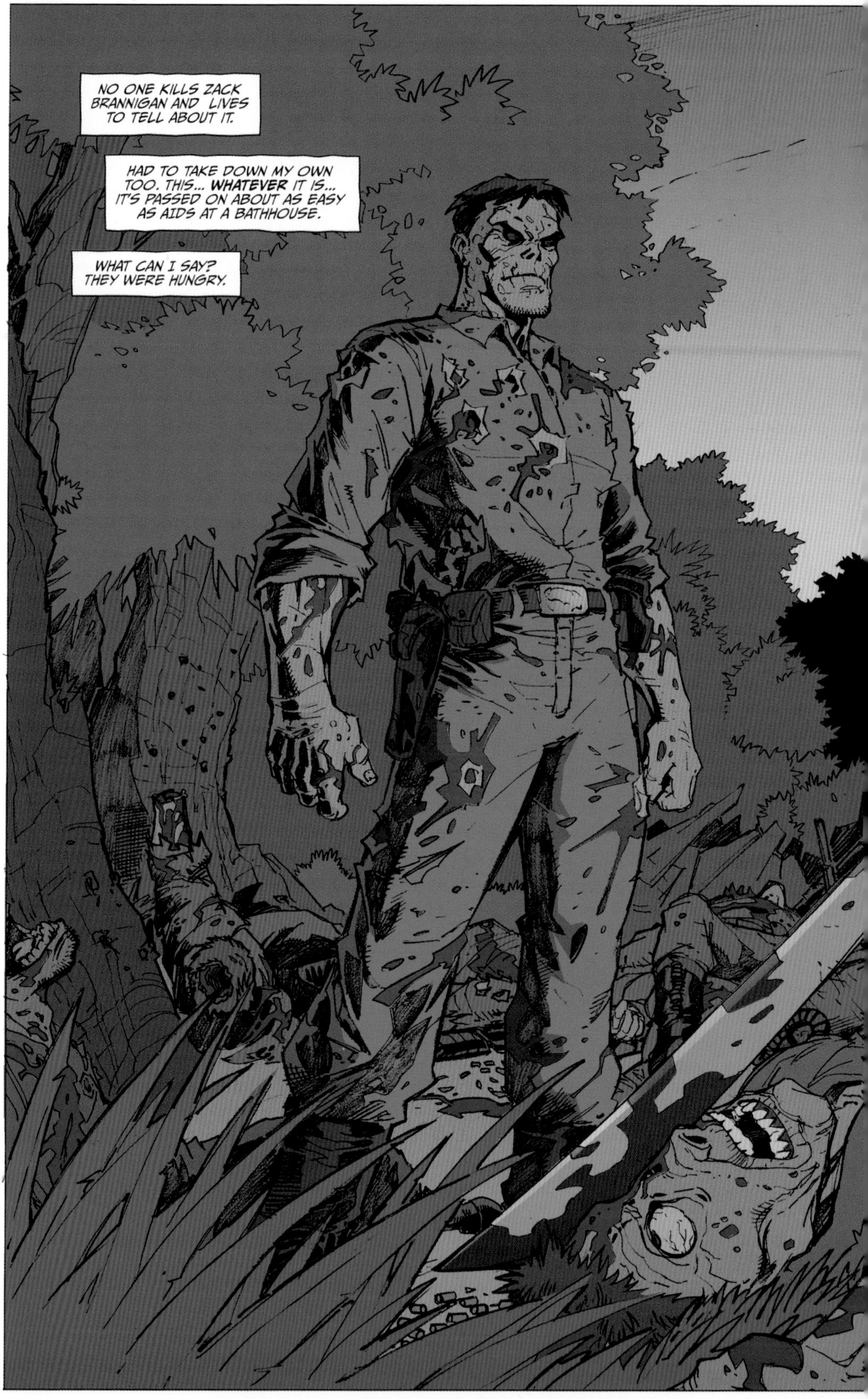
NO ONE KILLS ZACK BRANNIGAN AND LIVES TO TELL ABOUT IT.
HAD TO TAKE DOWN MY OWN TOO. THIS... **WHATEVER** IT IS... IT'S PASSED ON ABOUT AS EASY AS AIDS AT A BATHHOUSE.
WHAT CAN I SAY? THEY WERE HUNGRY.

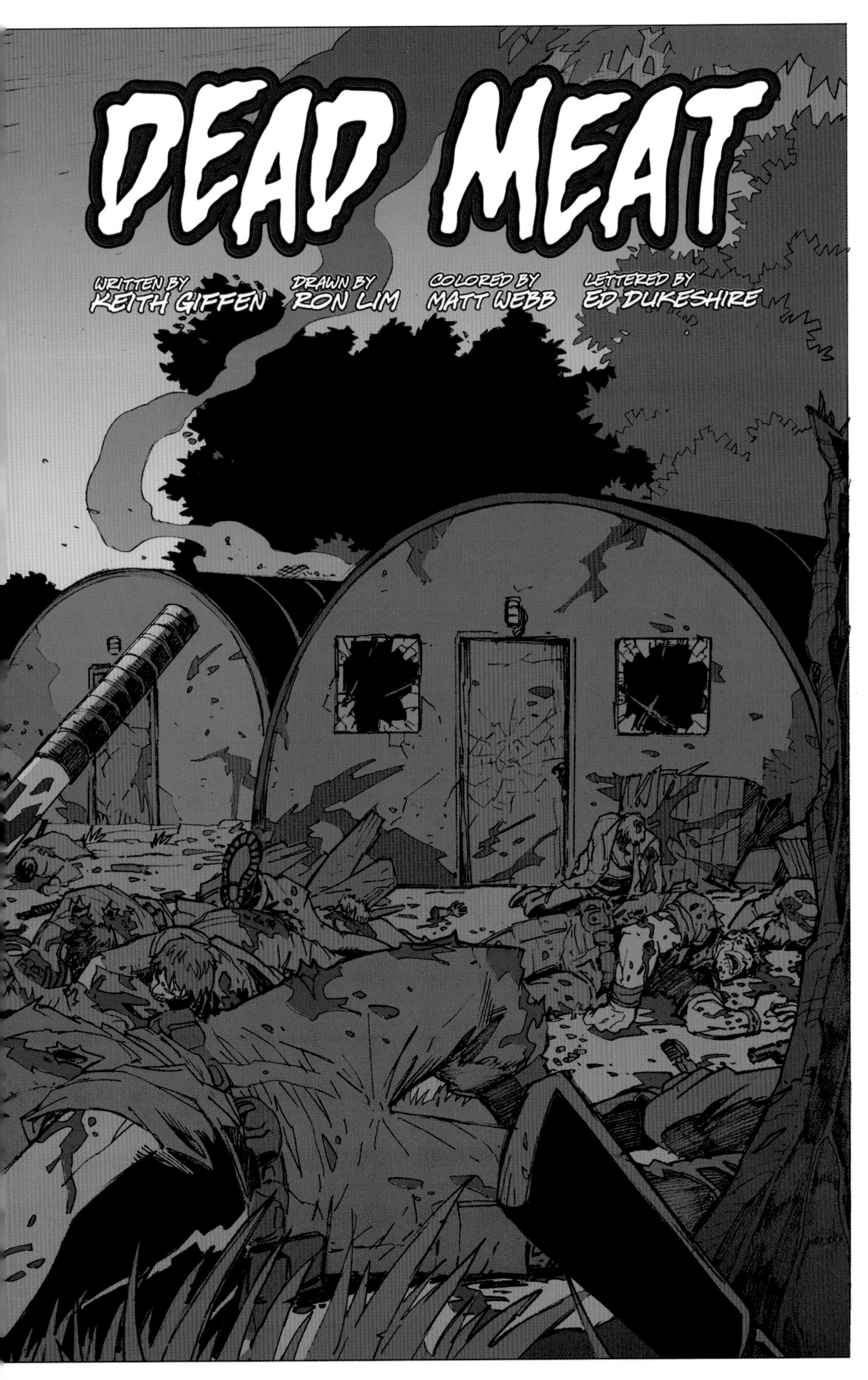
DEAD MEAT
WRITTEN BY KEITH GIFFEN
DRAWN BY RON LIM
COLORED BY MATT WEBB
LETTERED BY ED DUKESHIRE

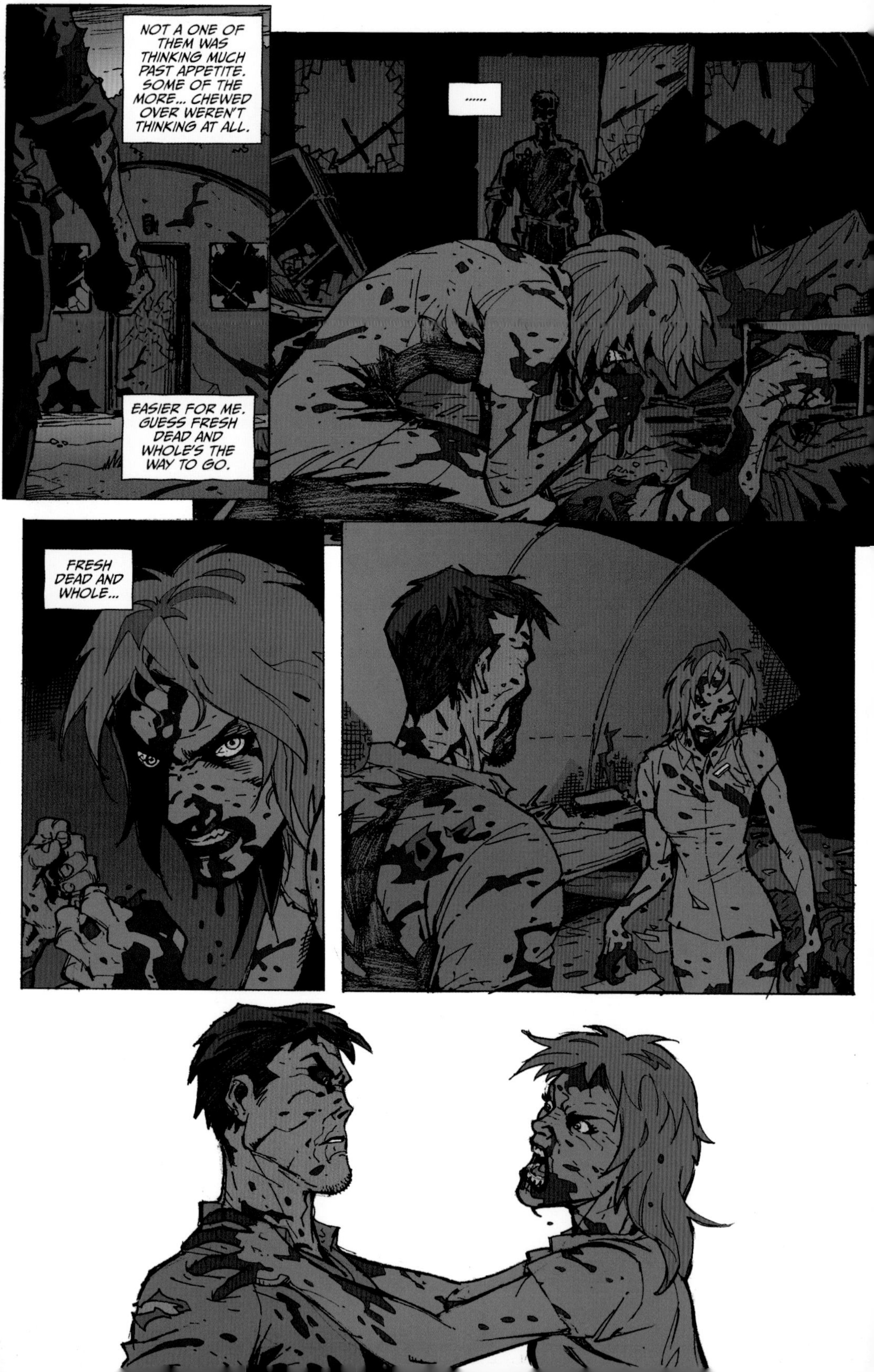
NOT A ONE OF THEM WAS THINKING MUCH PAST APPETITE. SOME OF THE MORE... CHEWED OVER WEREN'T THINKING AT ALL.
......
EASIER FOR ME. GUESS FRESH DEAD AND WHOLE'S THE WAY TO GO.
FRESH DEAD AND WHOLE...

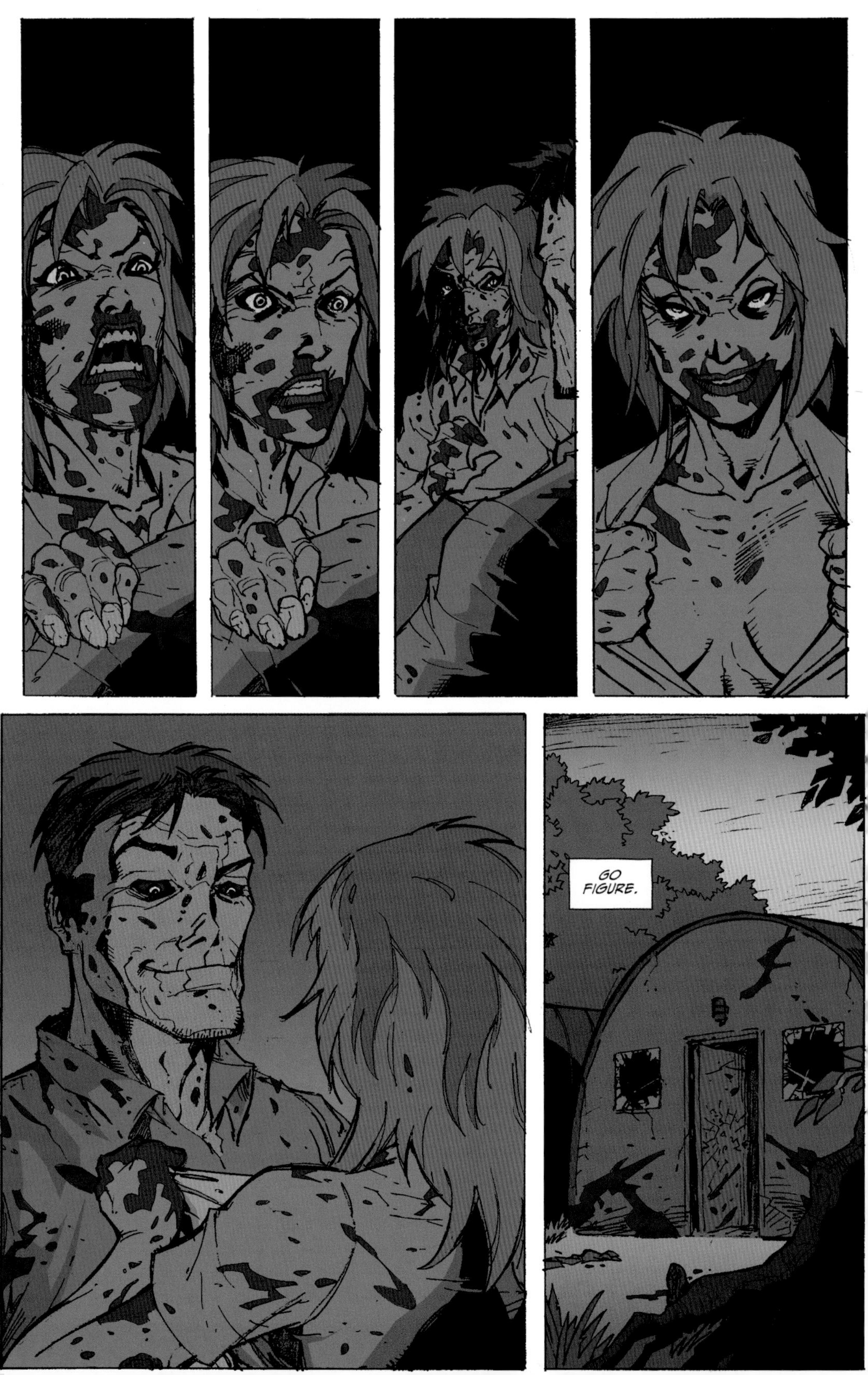
GO FIGURE.

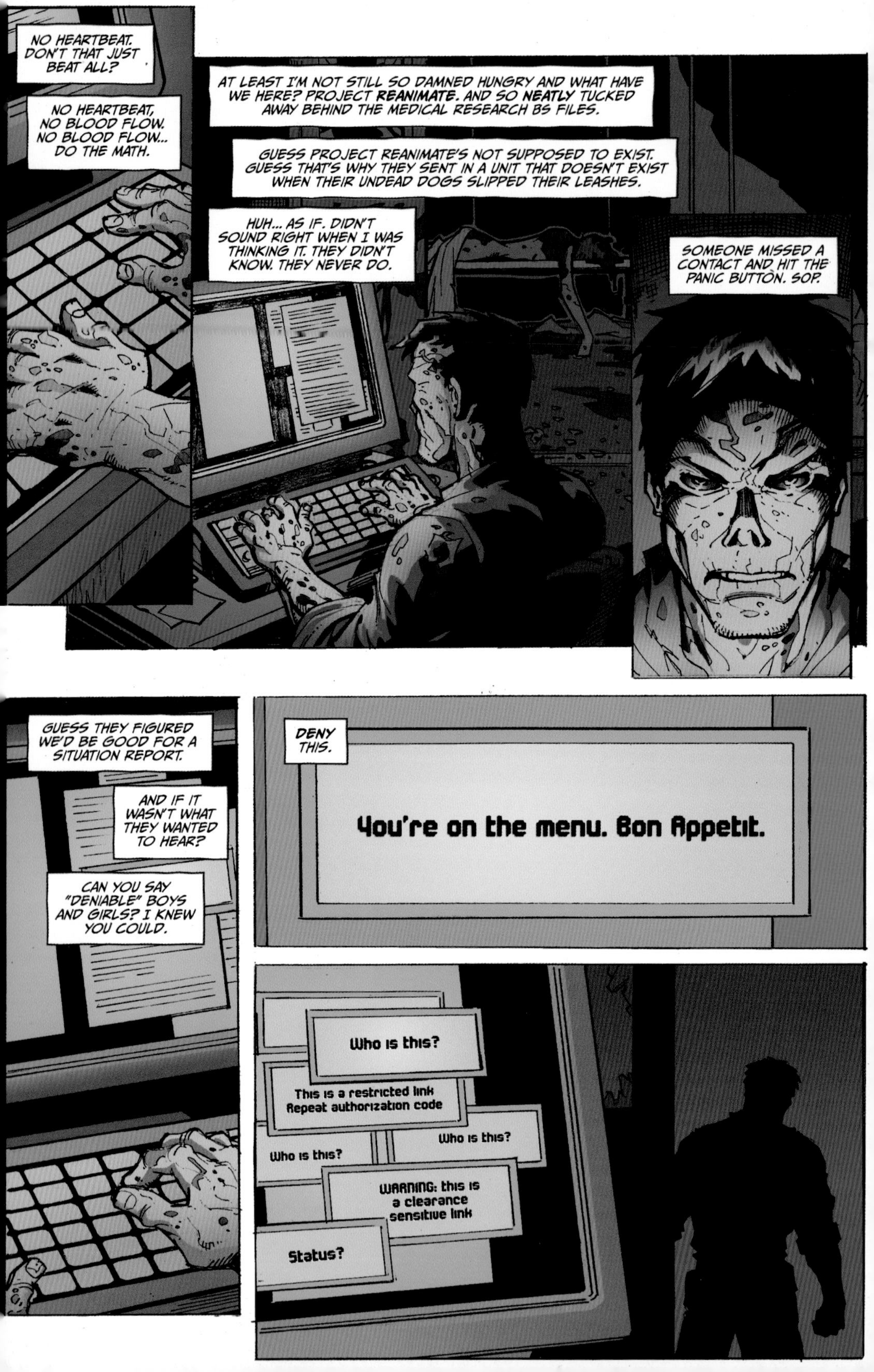
NO HEARTBEAT. DON'T THAT JUST BEAT ALL?
NO HEARTBEAT, NO BLOOD FLOW. NO BLOOD FLOW... DO THE MATH.
AT LEAST I'M NOT STILL SO DAMNED HUNGRY AND WHAT HAVE WE HERE? PROJECT **REANIMATE.** AND SO **NEATLY** TUCKED AWAY BEHIND THE MEDICAL RESEARCH BS FILES.
GUESS PROJECT REANIMATE'S NOT SUPPOSED TO EXIST. GUESS THAT'S WHY THEY SENT IN A UNIT THAT DOESN'T EXIST WHEN THEIR UNDEAD DOGS SLIPPED THEIR LEASHES.
HUH... AS IF. DIDN'T SOUND RIGHT WHEN I WAS THINKING IT. THEY DIDN'T KNOW. THEY NEVER DO.
SOMEONE MISSED A CONTACT AND HIT THE PANIC BUTTON. SOP.
GUESS THEY FIGURED WE'D BE GOOD FOR A SITUATION REPORT.
AND IF IT WASN'T WHAT THEY WANTED TO HEAR?
CAN YOU SAY "DENIABLE" BOYS AND GIRLS? I KNEW YOU COULD.
DENY THIS.
You're on the menu. Bon Appetit.
Who is this?
This is a restricted link Repeat authorization code
Who is this?
Who is this?
WARNING: this is a clearance sensitive link
Status?

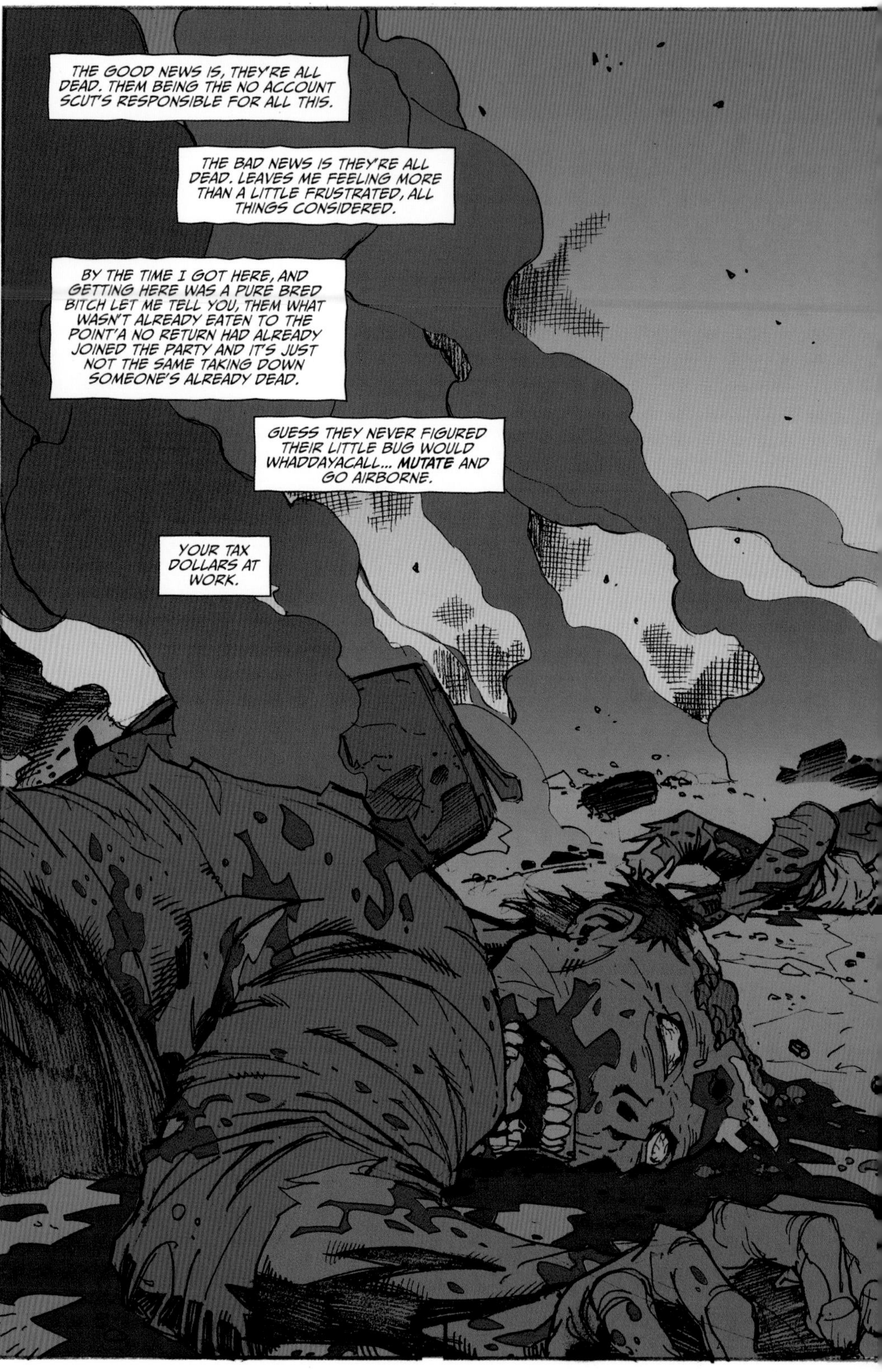
THE GOOD NEWS IS, THEY'RE ALL DEAD. THEM BEING THE NO ACCOUNT SCUT'S RESPONSIBLE FOR ALL THIS.
THE BAD NEWS IS THEY'RE ALL DEAD. LEAVES ME FEELING MORE THAN A LITTLE FRUSTRATED, ALL THINGS CONSIDERED.
BY THE TIME I GOT HERE, AND GETTING HERE WAS A PURE BRED BITCH LET ME TELL YOU, THEM WHAT WASN'T ALREADY EATEN TO THE POINT'A NO RETURN HAD ALREADY JOINED THE PARTY AND IT'S JUST NOT THE SAME TAKING DOWN SOMEONE'S ALREADY DEAD.
GUESS THEY NEVER FIGURED THEIR LITTLE BUG WOULD WHADDAYACALL... **MUTATE** AND GO AIRBORNE.
YOUR TAX DOLLARS AT WORK.

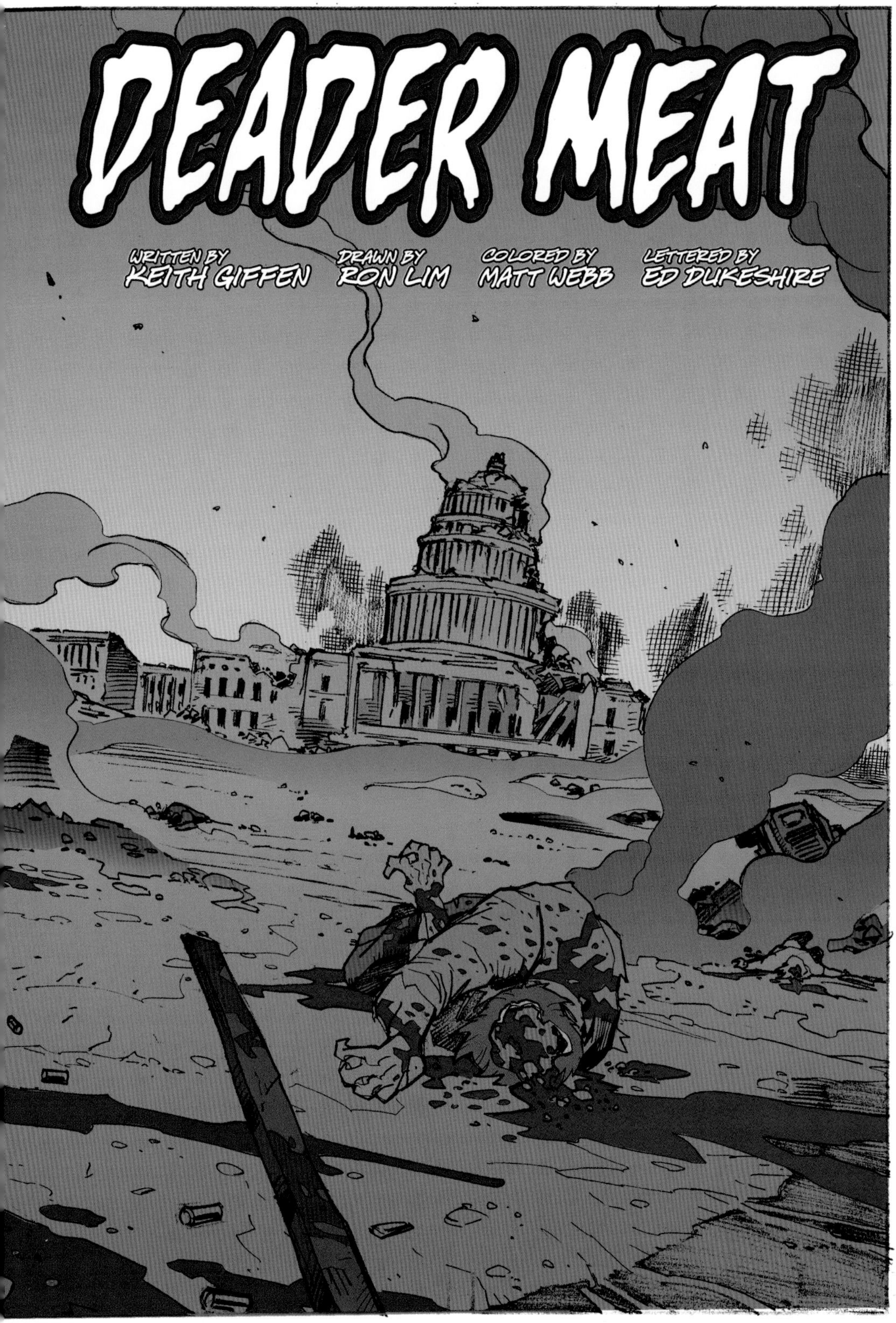
DEADER MEAT
WRITTEN BY KEITH GIFFEN
DRAWN BY RON LIM
COLORED BY MATT WEBB
LETTERED BY ED DUKESHIRE

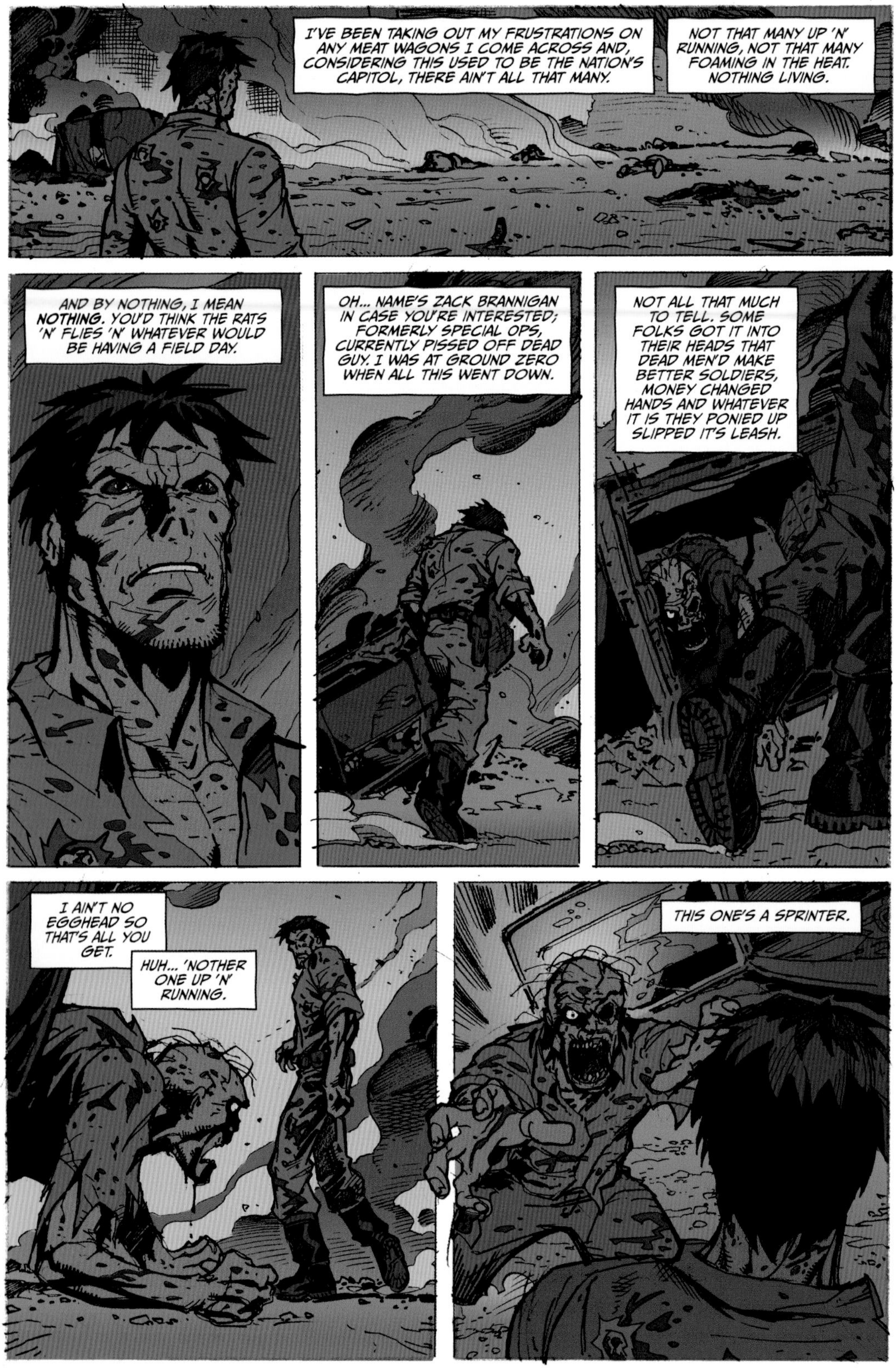
I'VE BEEN TAKING OUT MY FRUSTRATIONS ON ANY MEAT WAGONS I COME ACROSS AND, CONSIDERING THIS USED TO BE THE NATION'S CAPITOL, THERE AIN'T ALL THAT MANY.
NOT THAT MANY UP 'N' RUNNING, NOT THAT MANY FOAMING IN THE HEAT. NOTHING LIVING.
AND BY NOTHING, I MEAN **NOTHING**. YOU'D THINK THE RATS 'N' FLIES 'N' WHATEVER WOULD BE HAVING A FIELD DAY.
OH... NAME'S ZACK BRANNIGAN IN CASE YOU'RE INTERESTED; FORMERLY SPECIAL OPS, CURRENTLY PISSED OFF DEAD GUY. I WAS AT GROUND ZERO WHEN ALL THIS WENT DOWN.
NOT ALL THAT MUCH TO TELL. SOME FOLKS GOT IT INTO THEIR HEADS THAT DEAD MEN'D MAKE BETTER SOLDIERS, MONEY CHANGED HANDS AND WHATEVER IT IS THEY PONIED UP SLIPPED IT'S LEASH.
I AIN'T NO EGGHEAD SO THAT'S ALL YOU GET.
HUH... 'NOTHER ONE UP 'N' RUNNING.
THIS ONE'S A SPRINTER.

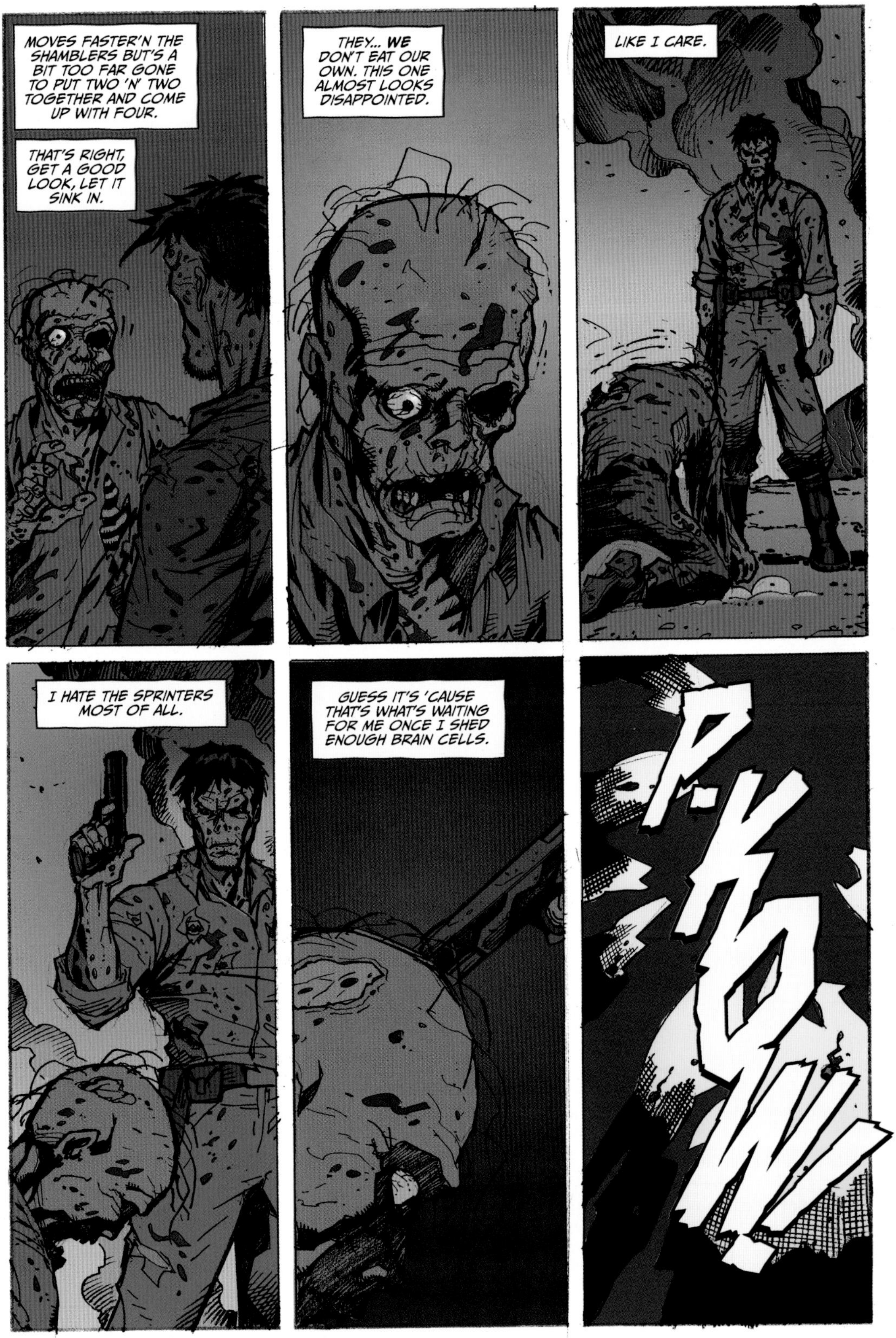
MOVES FASTER'N THE SHAMBLERS BUT'S A BIT TOO FAR GONE TO PUT TWO 'N' TWO TOGETHER AND COME UP WITH FOUR.
THAT'S RIGHT, GET A GOOD LOOK, LET IT SINK IN.
THEY... WE DON'T EAT OUR OWN. THIS ONE ALMOST LOOKS DISAPPOINTED.
LIKE I CARE.
I HATE THE SPRINTERS MOST OF ALL.
GUESS IT'S 'CAUSE THAT'S WHAT'S WAITING FOR ME ONCE I SHED ENOUGH BRAIN CELLS.
P-KOW!

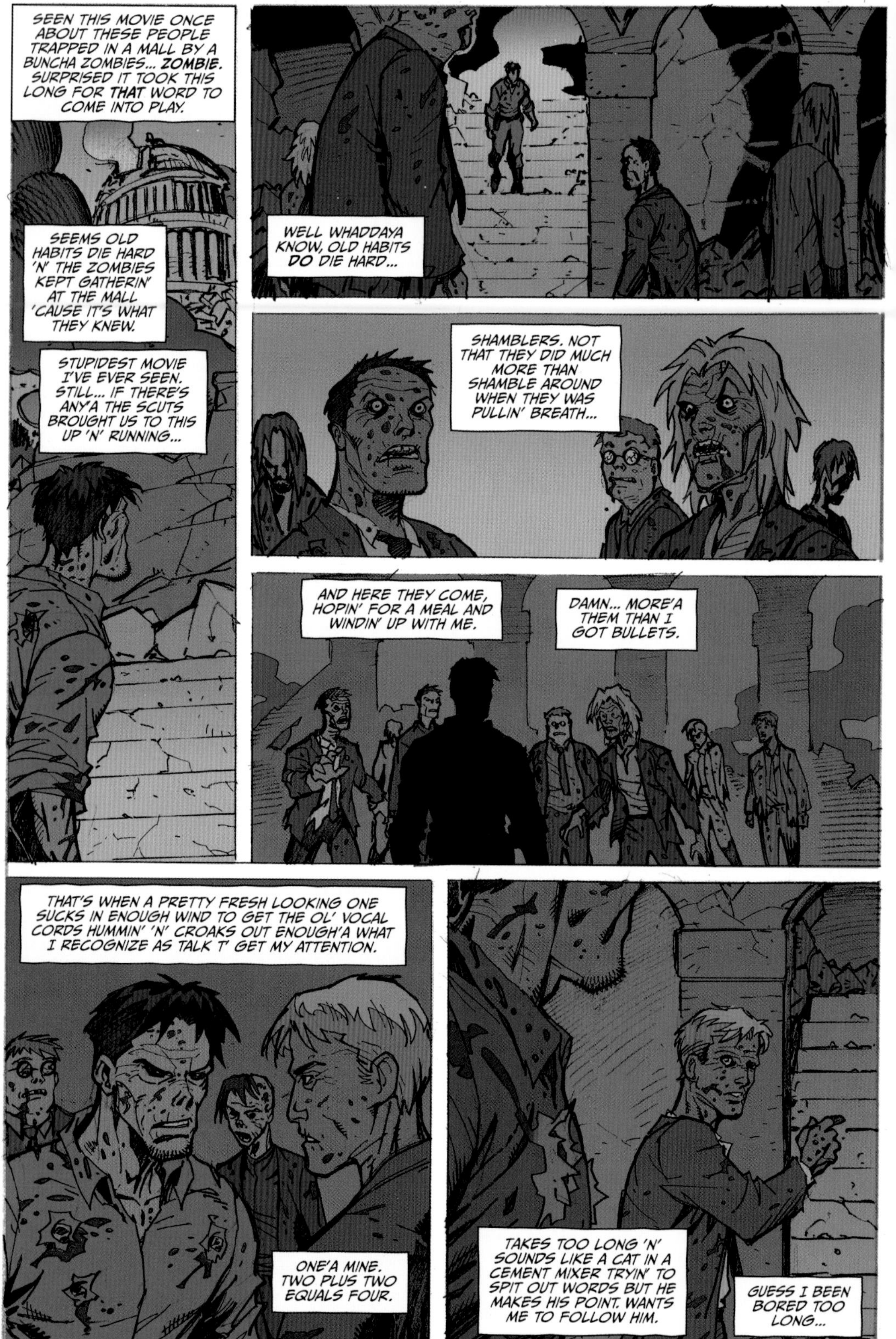
SEEN THIS MOVIE ONCE ABOUT THESE PEOPLE TRAPPED IN A MALL BY A BUNCHA ZOMBIES... ZOMBIE. SURPRISED IT TOOK THIS LONG FOR THAT WORD TO COME INTO PLAY.
SEEMS OLD HABITS DIE HARD 'N' THE ZOMBIES KEPT GATHERIN' AT THE MALL 'CAUSE IT'S WHAT THEY KNEW.
STUPIDEST MOVIE I'VE EVER SEEN. STILL... IF THERE'S ANY'A THE SCUTS BROUGHT US TO THIS UP 'N' RUNNING...
WELL WHADDAYA KNOW, OLD HABITS DO DIE HARD...
SHAMBLERS. NOT THAT THEY DID MUCH MORE THAN SHAMBLE AROUND WHEN THEY WAS PULLIN' BREATH...
AND HERE THEY COME, HOPIN' FOR A MEAL AND WINDIN' UP WITH ME.
DAMN... MORE'A THEM THAN I GOT BULLETS.
THAT'S WHEN A PRETTY FRESH LOOKING ONE SUCKS IN ENOUGH WIND TO GET THE OL' VOCAL CORDS HUMMIN' 'N' CROAKS OUT ENOUGH'A WHAT I RECOGNIZE AS TALK T' GET MY ATTENTION.
ONE'A MINE. TWO PLUS TWO EQUALS FOUR.
TAKES TOO LONG 'N' SOUNDS LIKE A CAT IN A CEMENT MIXER TRYIN' TO SPIT OUT WORDS BUT HE MAKES HIS POINT. WANTS ME TO FOLLOW HIM.
GUESS I BEEN BORED TOO LONG...

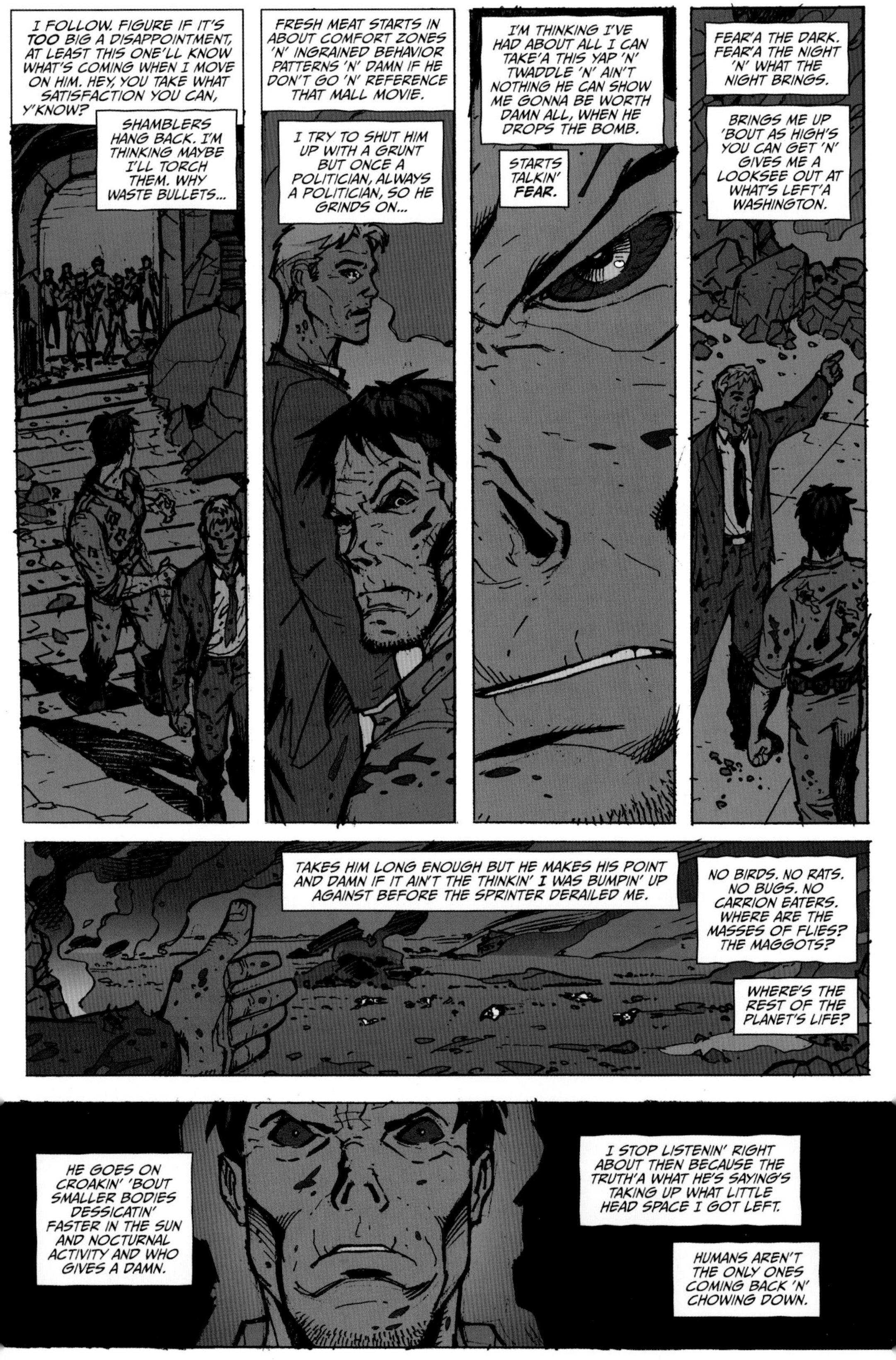
I FOLLOW. FIGURE IF IT'S TOO BIG A DISAPPOINTMENT, AT LEAST THIS ONE'LL KNOW WHAT'S COMING WHEN I MOVE ON HIM. HEY, YOU TAKE WHAT SATISFACTION YOU CAN, Y'KNOW?
SHAMBLERS HANG BACK. I'M THINKING MAYBE I'LL TORCH THEM. WHY WASTE BULLETS...
FRESH MEAT STARTS IN ABOUT COMFORT ZONES 'N' INGRAINED BEHAVIOR PATTERNS 'N' DAMN IF HE DON'T GO 'N' REFERENCE THAT MALL MOVIE.
I TRY TO SHUT HIM UP WITH A GRUNT BUT ONCE A POLITICIAN, ALWAYS A POLITICIAN, SO HE GRINDS ON...
I'M THINKING I'VE HAD ABOUT ALL I CAN TAKE'A THIS YAP 'N' TWADDLE 'N' AIN'T NOTHING HE CAN SHOW ME GONNA BE WORTH DAMN ALL, WHEN HE DROPS THE BOMB.
STARTS TALKIN' FEAR.
FEAR'A THE DARK. FEAR'A THE NIGHT 'N' WHAT THE NIGHT BRINGS.
BRINGS ME UP 'BOUT AS HIGH'S YOU CAN GET 'N' GIVES ME A LOOKSEE OUT AT WHAT'S LEFT'A WASHINGTON.
TAKES HIM LONG ENOUGH BUT HE MAKES HIS POINT AND DAMN IF IT AIN'T THE THINKIN' I WAS BUMPIN' UP AGAINST BEFORE THE SPRINTER DERAILED ME.
NO BIRDS. NO RATS. NO BUGS. NO CARRION EATERS. WHERE ARE THE MASSES OF FLIES? THE MAGGOTS?
WHERE'S THE REST OF THE PLANET'S LIFE?
HE GOES ON CROAKIN' 'BOUT SMALLER BODIES DESSICATIN' FASTER IN THE SUN AND NOCTURNAL ACTIVITY AND WHO GIVES A DAMN.
I STOP LISTENIN' RIGHT ABOUT THEN BECAUSE THE TRUTH'A WHAT HE'S SAYING'S TAKING UP WHAT LITTLE HEAD SPACE I GOT LEFT.
HUMANS AREN'T THE ONLY ONES COMING BACK 'N' CHOWING DOWN.

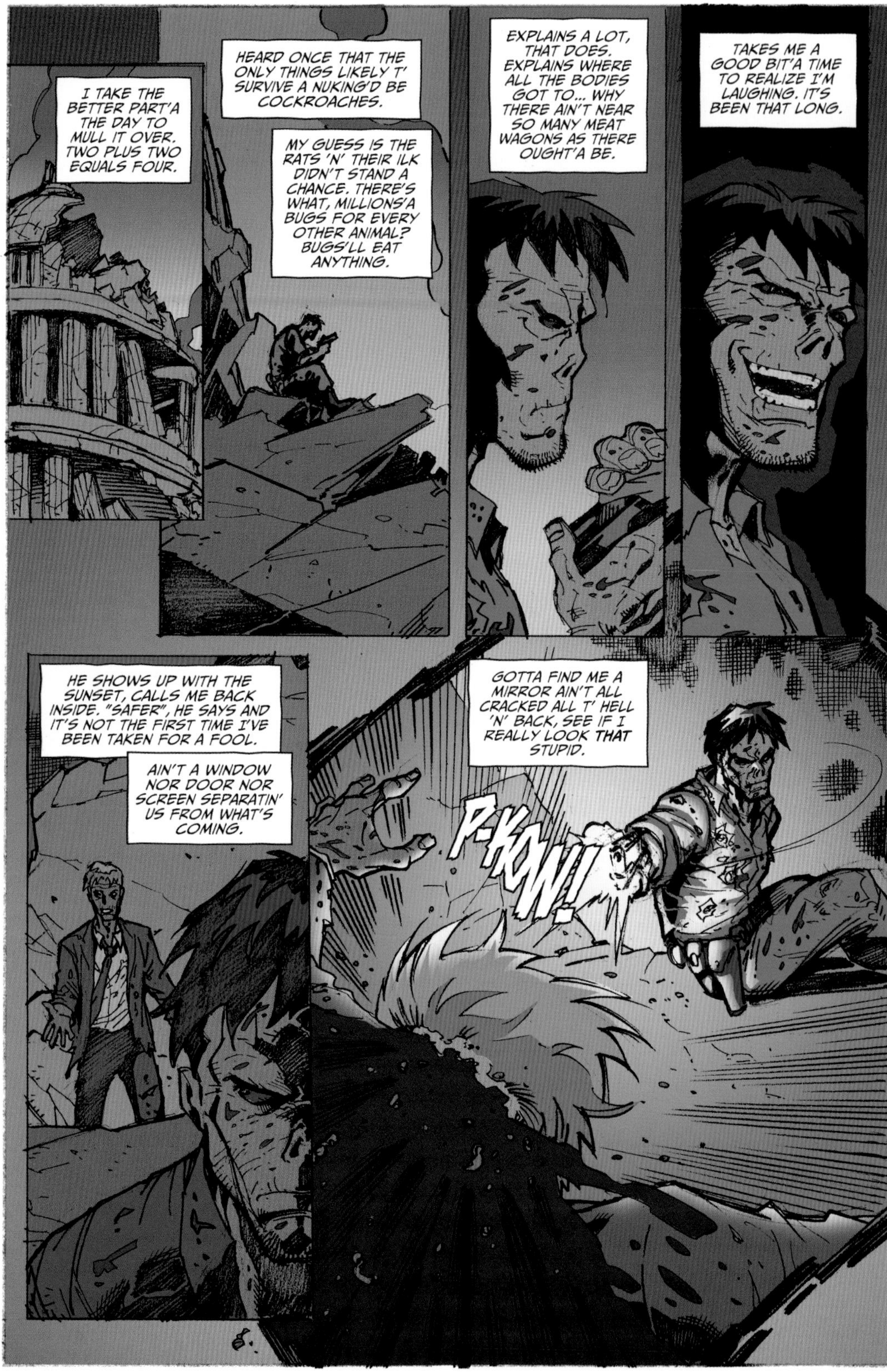
I TAKE THE BETTER PART'A THE DAY TO MULL IT OVER. TWO PLUS TWO EQUALS FOUR.
HEARD ONCE THAT THE ONLY THINGS LIKELY T' SURVIVE A NUKING'D BE COCKROACHES.
MY GUESS IS THE RATS 'N' THEIR ILK DIDN'T STAND A CHANCE. THERE'S WHAT, MILLIONS'A BUGS FOR EVERY OTHER ANIMAL? BUGS'LL EAT ANYTHING.
EXPLAINS A LOT, THAT DOES. EXPLAINS WHERE ALL THE BODIES GOT TO... WHY THERE AIN'T NEAR SO MANY MEAT WAGONS AS THERE OUGHT'A BE.
TAKES ME A GOOD BIT'A TIME TO REALIZE I'M LAUGHING. IT'S BEEN THAT LONG.
HE SHOWS UP WITH THE SUNSET, CALLS ME BACK INSIDE. "SAFER", HE SAYS AND IT'S NOT THE FIRST TIME I'VE BEEN TAKEN FOR A FOOL.
AIN'T A WINDOW NOR DOOR NOR SCREEN SEPARATIN' US FROM WHAT'S COMING.
GOTTA FIND ME A MIRROR AIN'T ALL CRACKED ALL T' HELL 'N' BACK, SEE IF I REALLY LOOK THAT STUPID.
P-KOW!!

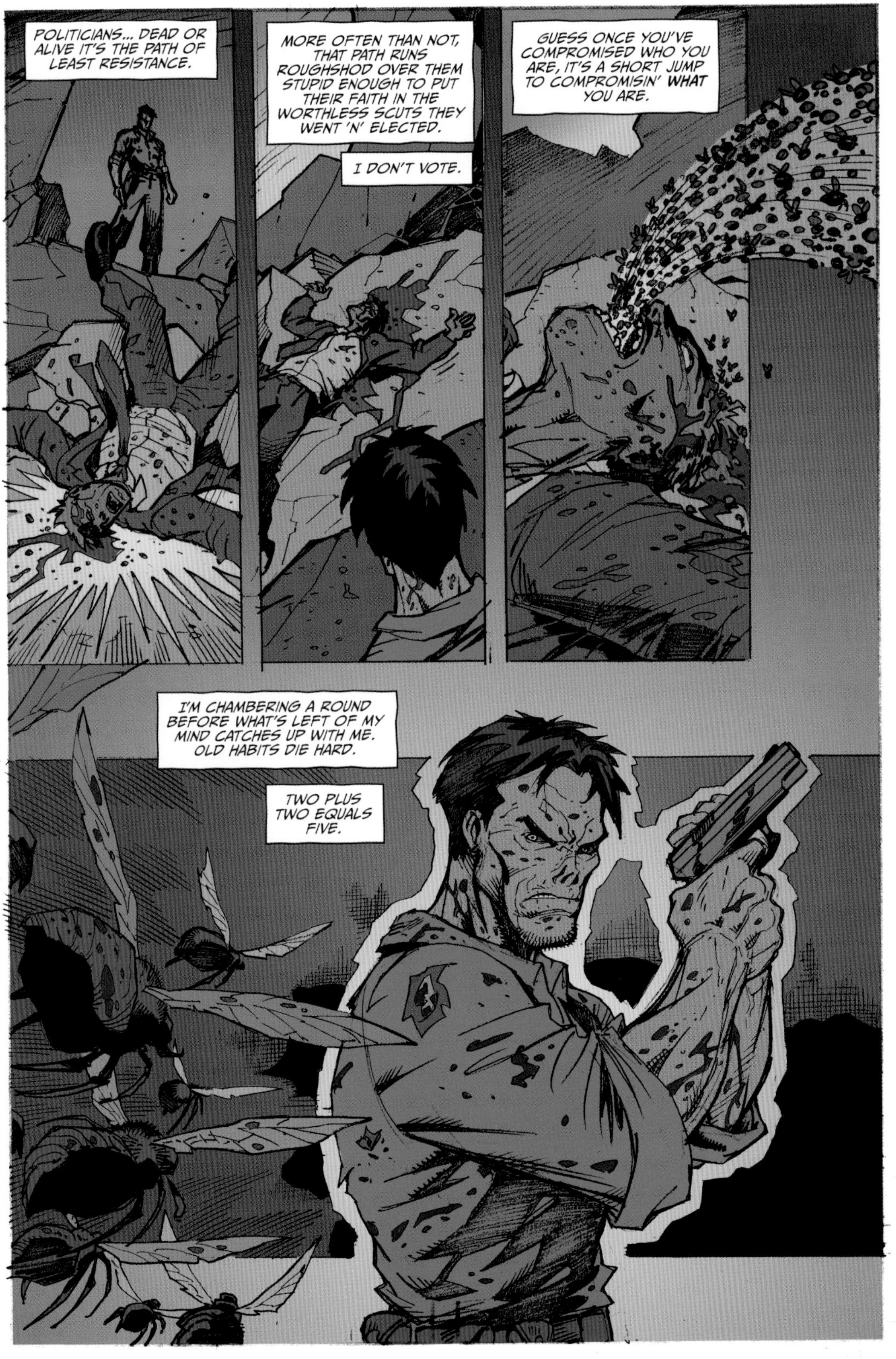
POLITICIANS... DEAD OR ALIVE IT'S THE PATH OF LEAST RESISTANCE.
MORE OFTEN THAN NOT, THAT PATH RUNS ROUGHSHOD OVER THEM STUPID ENOUGH TO PUT THEIR FAITH IN THE WORTHLESS SCUTS THEY WENT 'N' ELECTED.
I DON'T VOTE.
GUESS ONCE YOU'VE COMPROMISED WHO YOU ARE, IT'S A SHORT JUMP TO COMPROMISIN' WHAT YOU ARE.
I'M CHAMBERING A ROUND BEFORE WHAT'S LEFT OF MY MIND CATCHES UP WITH ME. OLD HABITS DIE HARD.
TWO PLUS TWO EQUALS FIVE.

AND FINALLY...

DEADEST MEAT

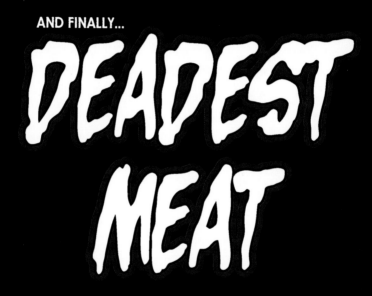

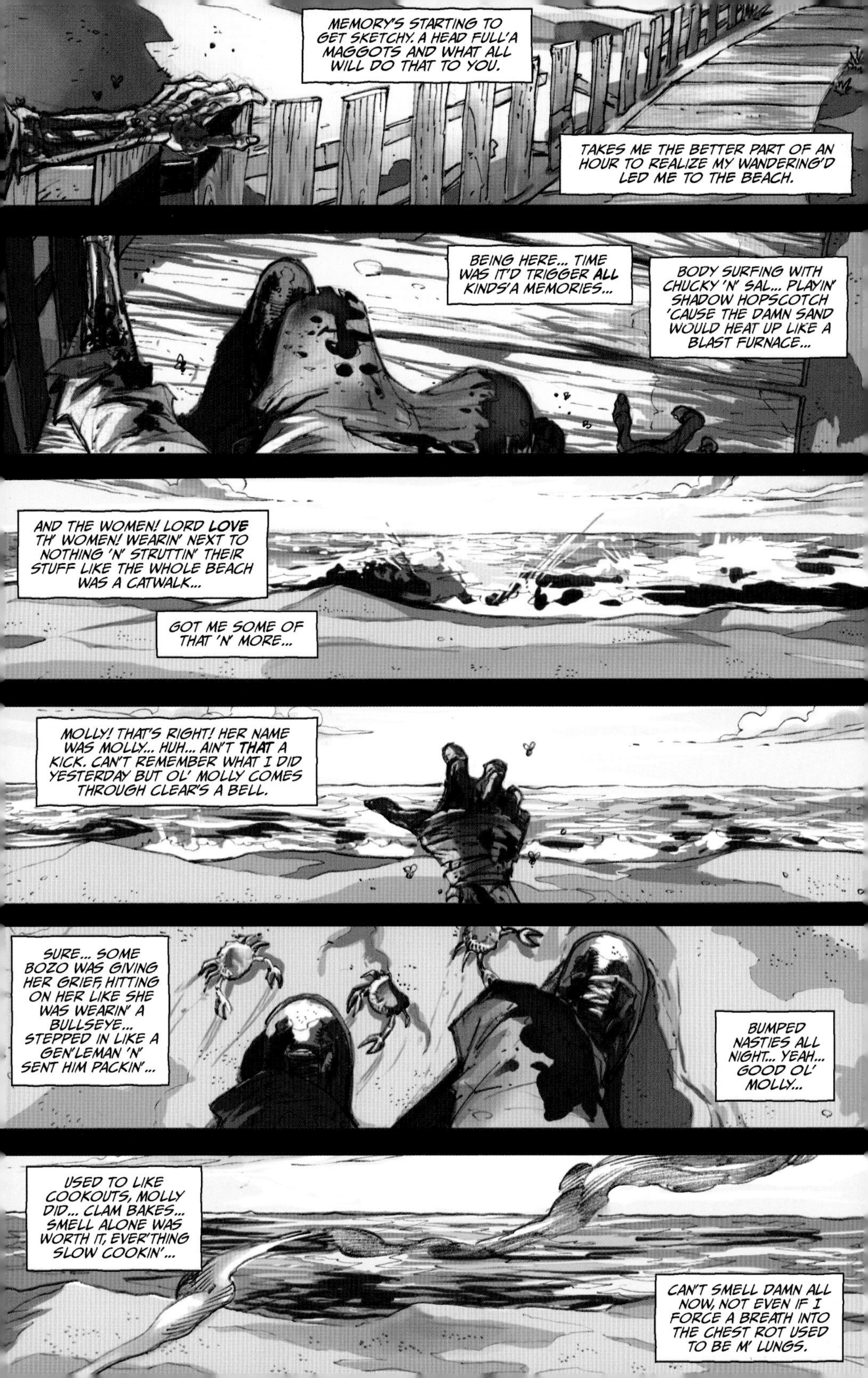
MEMORY'S STARTING TO GET SKETCHY. A HEAD FULL'A MAGGOTS AND WHAT ALL WILL DO THAT TO YOU.
TAKES ME THE BETTER PART OF AN HOUR TO REALIZE MY WANDERING'D LED ME TO THE BEACH.
BEING HERE... TIME WAS IT'D TRIGGER ALL KINDS'A MEMORIES...
BODY SURFING WITH CHUCKY 'N' SAL... PLAYIN' SHADOW HOPSCOTCH 'CAUSE THE DAMN SAND WOULD HEAT UP LIKE A BLAST FURNACE...
AND THE WOMEN! LORD LOVE TH' WOMEN! WEARIN' NEXT TO NOTHING 'N' STRUTTIN' THEIR STUFF LIKE THE WHOLE BEACH WAS A CATWALK...
GOT ME SOME OF THAT 'N' MORE...
MOLLY! THAT'S RIGHT! HER NAME WAS MOLLY... HUH... AIN'T THAT A KICK. CAN'T REMEMBER WHAT I DID YESTERDAY BUT OL' MOLLY COMES THROUGH CLEAR'S A BELL.
SURE... SOME BOZO WAS GIVING HER GRIEF, HITTING ON HER LIKE SHE WAS WEARIN' A BULLSEYE... STEPPED IN LIKE A GEN'LEMAN 'N' SENT HIM PACKIN'...
BUMPED NASTIES ALL NIGHT... YEAH... GOOD OL' MOLLY...
USED TO LIKE COOKOUTS, MOLLY DID... CLAM BAKES... SMELL ALONE WAS WORTH IT, EVER'THING SLOW COOKIN'...
CAN'T SMELL DAMN ALL NOW, NOT EVEN IF I FORCE A BREATH INTO THE CHEST ROT USED TO BE M' LUNGS.

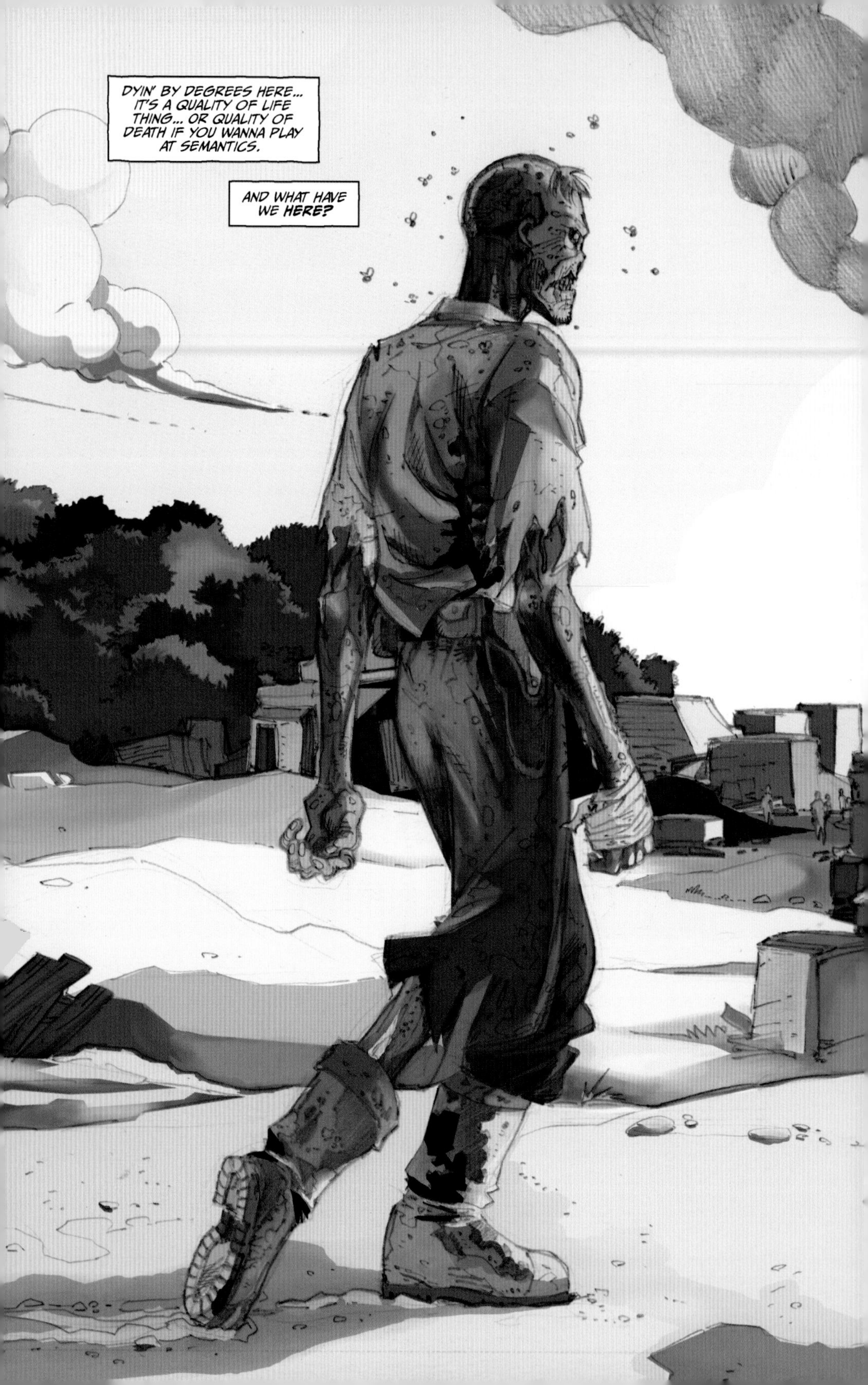
DYIN' BY DEGREES HERE... IT'S A QUALITY OF LIFE THING... OR QUALITY OF DEATH IF YOU WANNA PLAY AT SEMANTICS.
AND WHAT HAVE WE HERE?

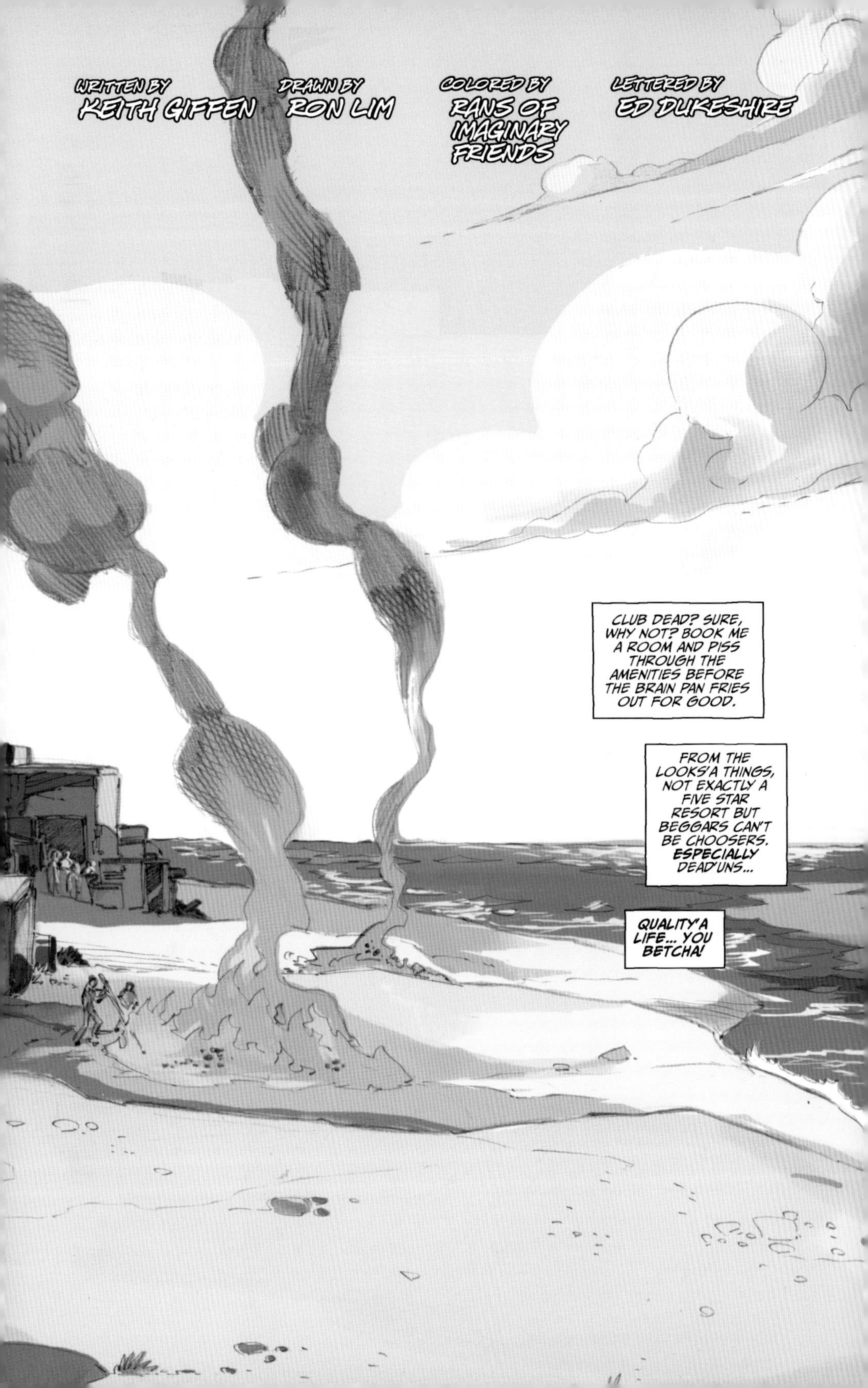
WRITTEN BY
KEITH GIFFEN
DRAWN BY
RON LIM
COLORED BY
RANS OF IMAGINARY FRIENDS
LETTERED BY
ED DUKESHIRE
CLUB DEAD? SURE, WHY NOT? BOOK ME A ROOM AND PISS THROUGH THE AMENITIES BEFORE THE BRAIN PAN FRIES OUT FOR GOOD.
FROM THE LOOKS'A THINGS, NOT EXACTLY A FIVE STAR RESORT BUT BEGGARS CAN'T BE CHOOSERS. ESPECIALLY DEAD'UNS...
QUALITY'A LIFE... YOU BETCHA!

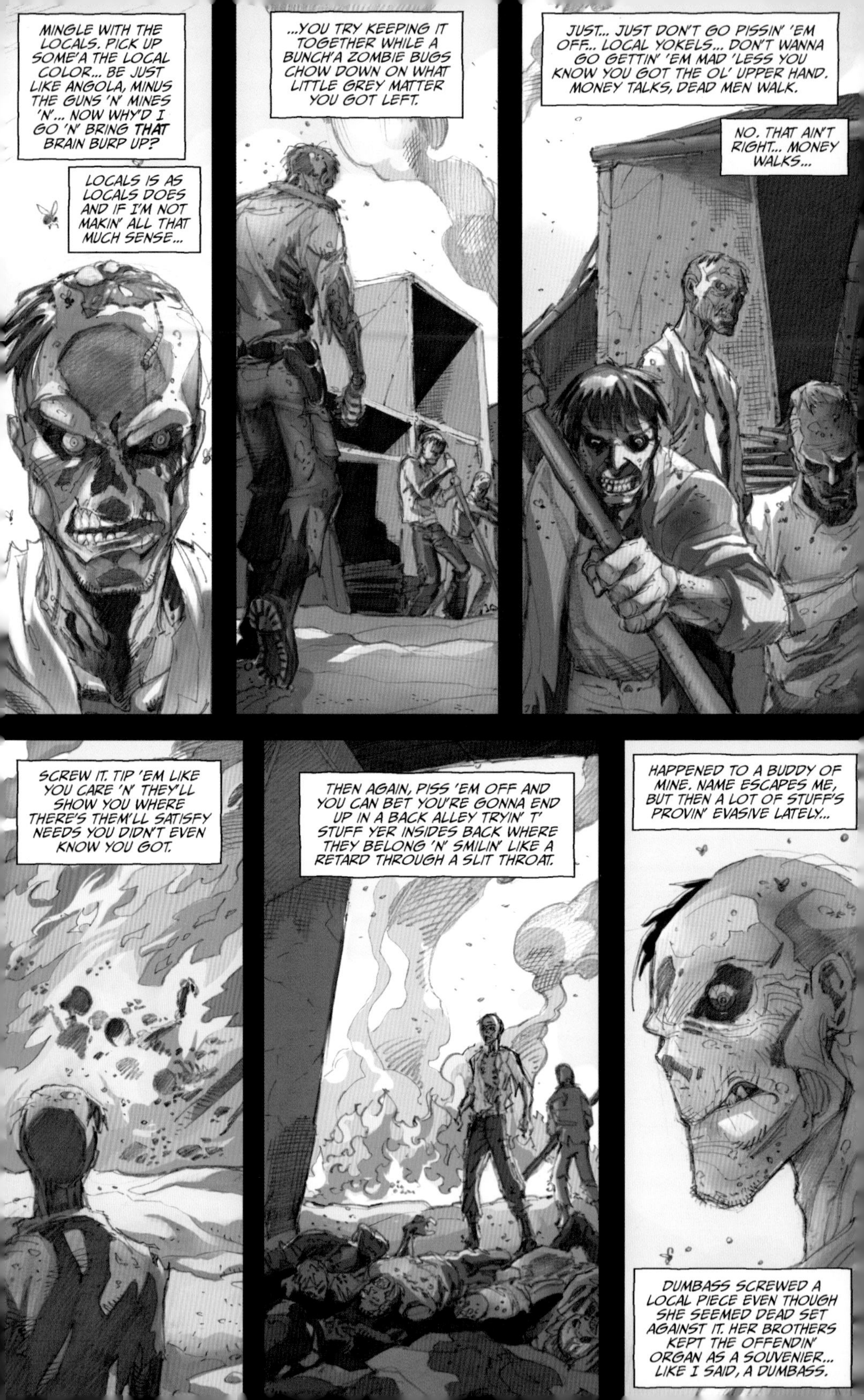
MINGLE WITH THE LOCALS. PICK UP SOME'A THE LOCAL COLOR... BE JUST LIKE ANGOLA, MINUS THE GUNS 'N' MINES 'N'... NOW WHY'D I GO 'N' BRING THAT BRAIN BURP UP?
LOCALS IS AS LOCALS DOES AND IF I'M NOT MAKIN' ALL THAT MUCH SENSE...
...YOU TRY KEEPING IT TOGETHER WHILE A BUNCH'A ZOMBIE BUGS CHOW DOWN ON WHAT LITTLE GREY MATTER YOU GOT LEFT.
JUST... JUST DON'T GO PISSIN' 'EM OFF... LOCAL YOKELS... DON'T WANNA GO GETTIN' 'EM MAD 'LESS YOU KNOW YOU GOT THE OL' UPPER HAND. MONEY TALKS, DEAD MEN WALK.
NO. THAT AIN'T RIGHT... MONEY WALKS...
SCREW IT. TIP 'EM LIKE YOU CARE 'N' THEY'LL SHOW YOU WHERE THERE'S THEM'LL SATISFY NEEDS YOU DIDN'T EVEN KNOW YOU GOT.
THEN AGAIN, PISS 'EM OFF AND YOU CAN BET YOU'RE GONNA END UP IN A BACK ALLEY TRYIN' T' STUFF YER INSIDES BACK WHERE THEY BELONG 'N' SMILIN' LIKE A RETARD THROUGH A SLIT THROAT.
HAPPENED TO A BUDDY OF MINE. NAME ESCAPES ME, BUT THEN A LOT OF STUFF'S PROVIN' EVASIVE LATELY...
DUMBASS SCREWED A LOCAL PIECE EVEN THOUGH SHE SEEMED DEAD SET AGAINST IT. HER BROTHERS KEPT THE OFFENDIN' ORGAN AS A SOUVENIER... LIKE I SAID, A DUMBASS.

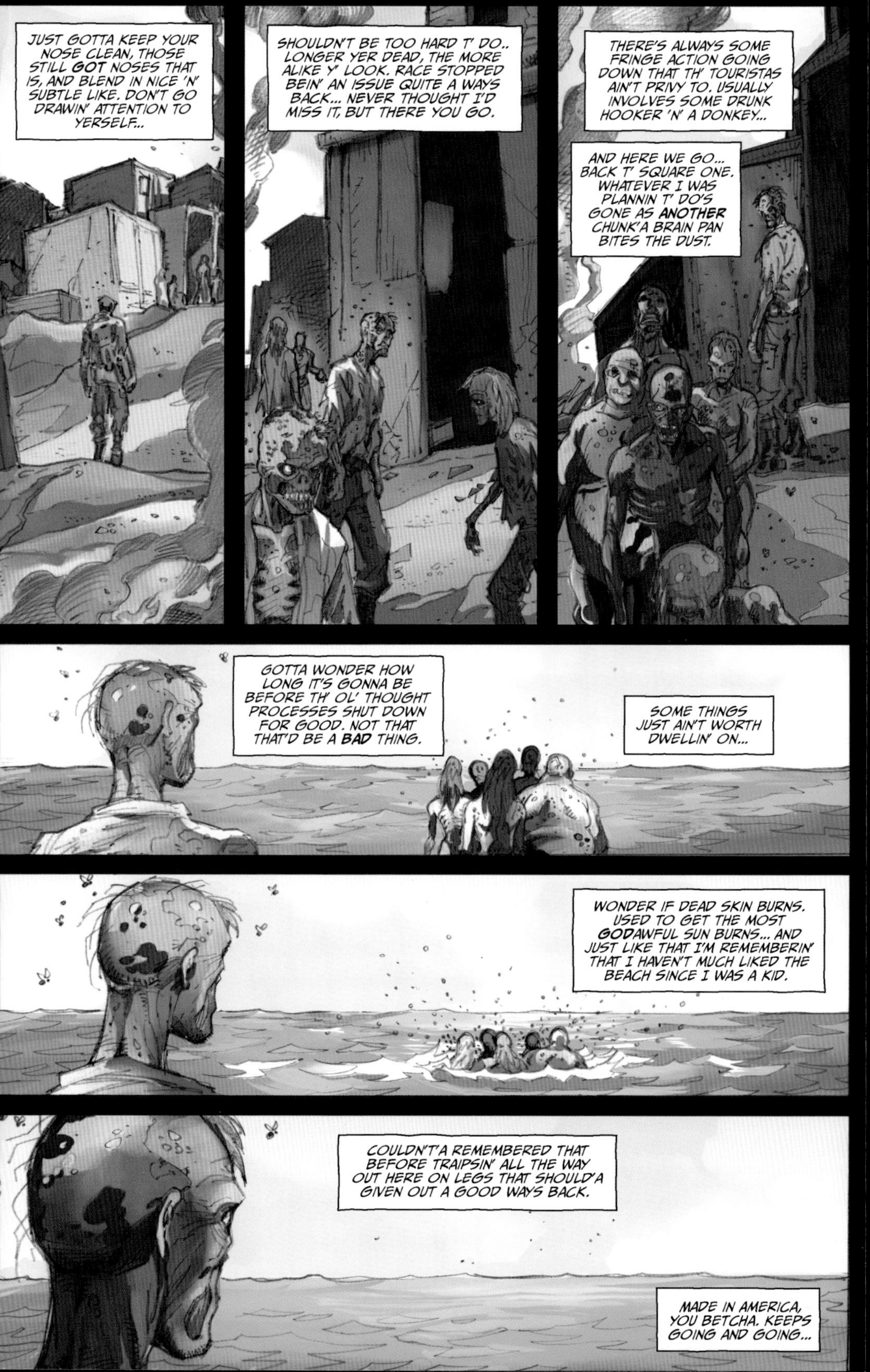
JUST GOTTA KEEP YOUR NOSE CLEAN, THOSE STILL GOT NOSES THAT IS, AND BLEND IN NICE 'N' SUBTLE LIKE. DON'T GO DRAWIN' ATTENTION TO YERSELF...
SHOULDN'T BE TOO HARD T' DO.. LONGER YER DEAD, THE MORE ALIKE Y' LOOK. RACE STOPPED BEIN' AN ISSUE QUITE A WAYS BACK... NEVER THOUGHT I'D MISS IT, BUT THERE YOU GO.
THERE'S ALWAYS SOME FRINGE ACTION GOING DOWN THAT TH' TOURISTAS AIN'T PRIVY TO. USUALLY INVOLVES SOME DRUNK HOOKER 'N' A DONKEY...
AND HERE WE GO... BACK T' SQUARE ONE. WHATEVER I WAS PLANNIN T' DO'S GONE AS ANOTHER CHUNK'A BRAIN PAN BITES THE DUST.
GOTTA WONDER HOW LONG IT'S GONNA BE BEFORE TH' OL' THOUGHT PROCESSES SHUT DOWN FOR GOOD. NOT THAT THAT'D BE A BAD THING.
SOME THINGS JUST AIN'T WORTH DWELLIN' ON...
WONDER IF DEAD SKIN BURNS. USED TO GET THE MOST GODAWFUL SUN BURNS... AND JUST LIKE THAT I'M REMEMBERIN' THAT I HAVEN'T MUCH LIKED THE BEACH SINCE I WAS A KID.
COULDN'T'A REMEMBERED THAT BEFORE TRAIPSIN' ALL THE WAY OUT HERE ON LEGS THAT SHOULD'A GIVEN OUT A GOOD WAYS BACK.
MADE IN AMERICA, YOU BETCHA. KEEPS GOING AND GOING...

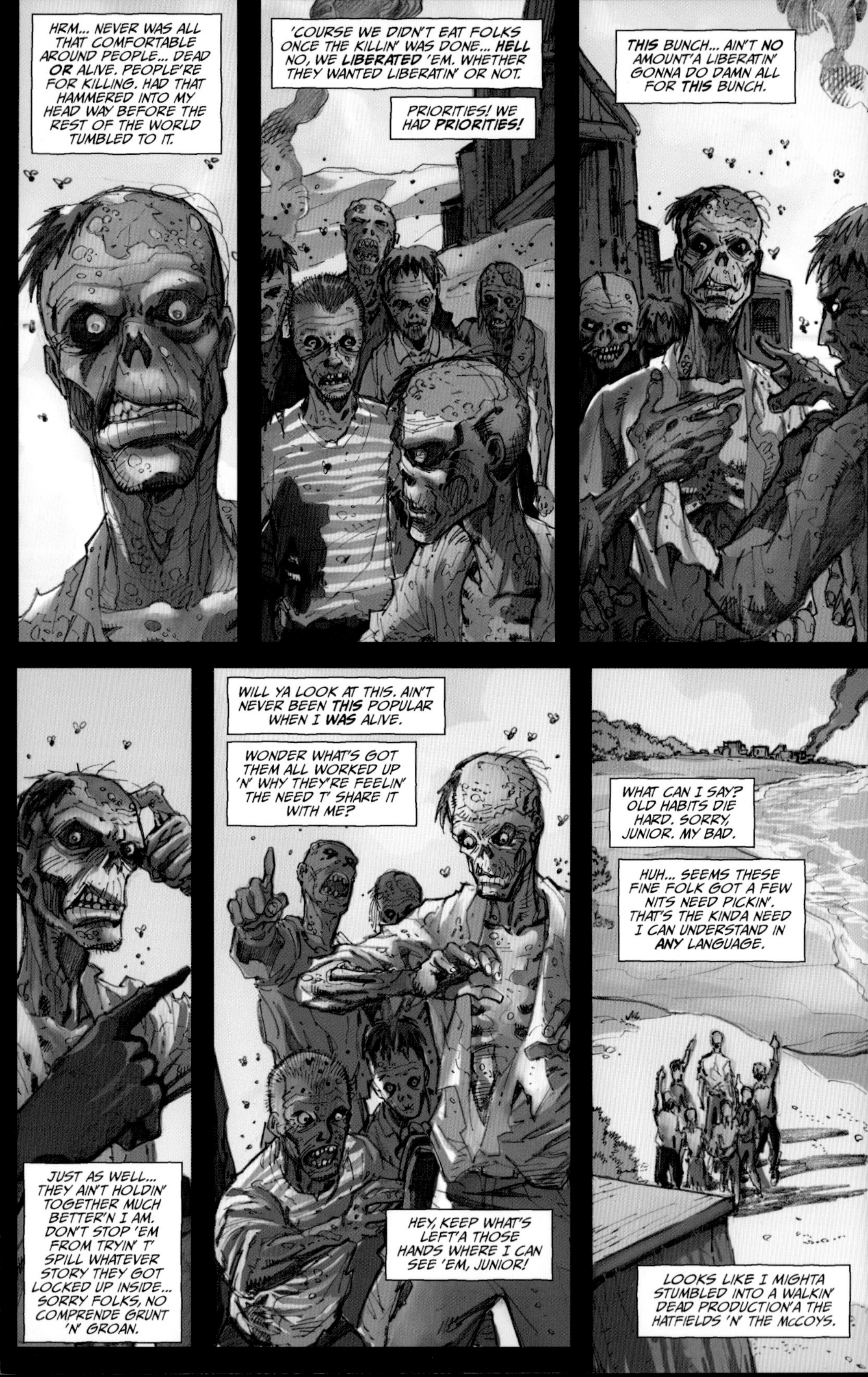
HRM... NEVER WAS ALL THAT COMFORTABLE AROUND PEOPLE... DEAD OR ALIVE. PEOPLE'RE FOR KILLING. HAD THAT HAMMERED INTO MY HEAD WAY BEFORE THE REST OF THE WORLD TUMBLED TO IT.
'COURSE WE DIDN'T EAT FOLKS ONCE THE KILLIN' WAS DONE... HELL NO, WE LIBERATED 'EM. WHETHER THEY WANTED LIBERATIN' OR NOT.
PRIORITIES! WE HAD PRIORITIES!
THIS BUNCH... AIN'T NO AMOUNT'A LIBERATIN' GONNA DO DAMN ALL FOR THIS BUNCH.
JUST AS WELL... THEY AIN'T HOLDIN' TOGETHER MUCH BETTER'N I AM. DON'T STOP 'EM FROM TRYIN' T' SPILL WHATEVER STORY THEY GOT LOCKED UP INSIDE... SORRY FOLKS, NO COMPRENDE GRUNT 'N' GROAN.
WILL YA LOOK AT THIS. AIN'T NEVER BEEN THIS POPULAR WHEN I WAS ALIVE.
WONDER WHAT'S GOT THEM ALL WORKED UP 'N' WHY THEY'RE FEELIN' THE NEED T' SHARE IT WITH ME?
HEY, KEEP WHAT'S LEFT'A THOSE HANDS WHERE I CAN SEE 'EM, JUNIOR!
WHAT CAN I SAY? OLD HABITS DIE HARD. SORRY, JUNIOR. MY BAD.
HUH... SEEMS THESE FINE FOLK GOT A FEW NITS NEED PICKIN'. THAT'S THE KINDA NEED I CAN UNDERSTAND IN ANY LANGUAGE.
LOOKS LIKE I MIGHTA STUMBLED INTO A WALKIN' DEAD PRODUCTION'A THE HATFIELDS 'N' THE McCOYS.

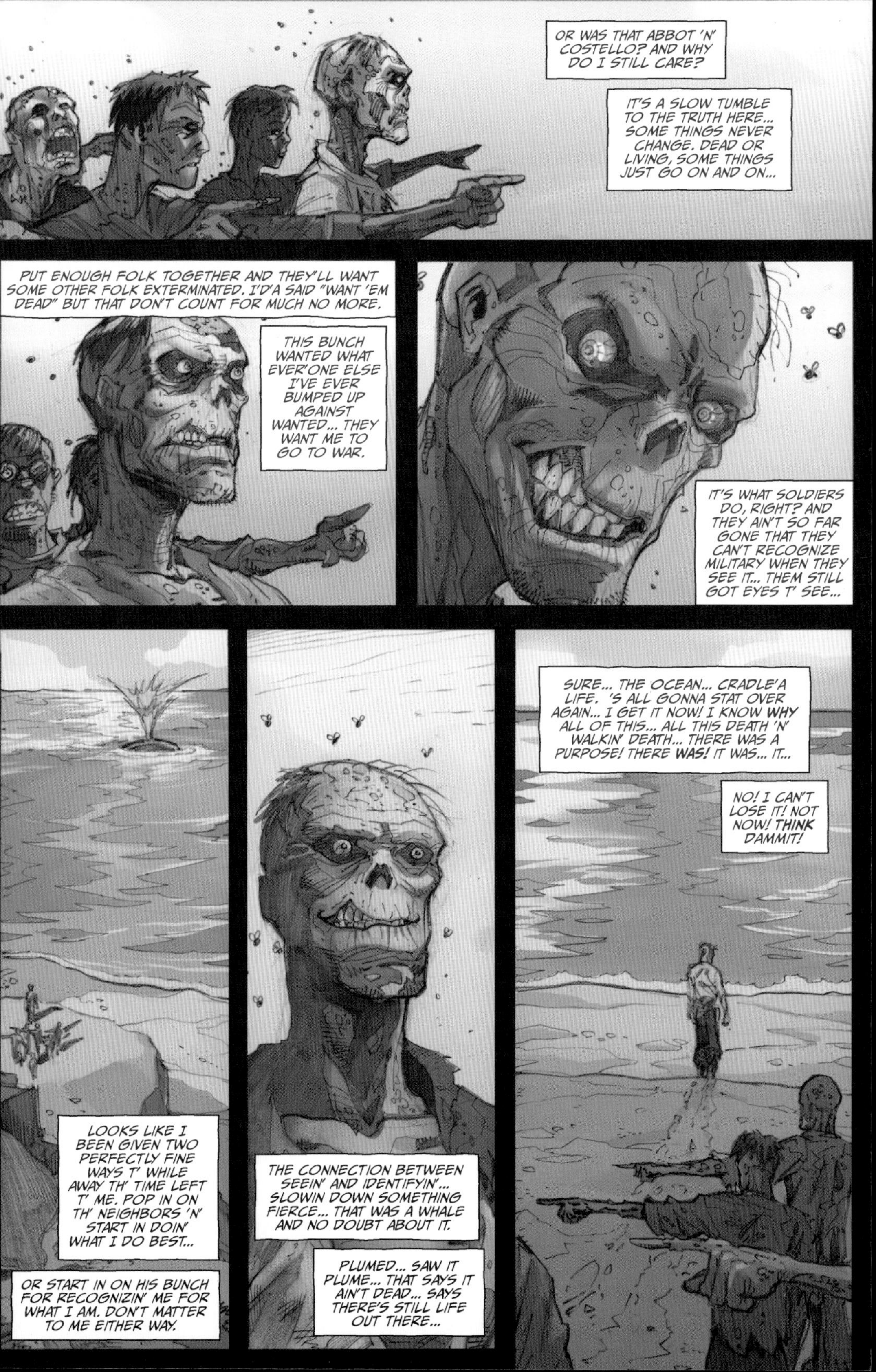
OR WAS THAT ABBOT 'N' COSTELLO? AND WHY DO I STILL CARE?
IT'S A SLOW TUMBLE TO THE TRUTH HERE... SOME THINGS NEVER CHANGE. DEAD OR LIVING, SOME THINGS JUST GO ON AND ON...
PUT ENOUGH FOLK TOGETHER AND THEY'LL WANT SOME OTHER FOLK EXTERMINATED. I'D'A SAID "WANT 'EM DEAD" BUT THAT DON'T COUNT FOR MUCH NO MORE.
THIS BUNCH WANTED WHAT EVER'ONE ELSE I'VE EVER BUMPED UP AGAINST WANTED... THEY WANT ME TO GO TO WAR.
IT'S WHAT SOLDIERS DO, RIGHT? AND THEY AIN'T SO FAR GONE THAT THEY CAN'T RECOGNIZE MILITARY WHEN THEY SEE IT... THEM STILL GOT EYES T' SEE...
LOOKS LIKE I BEEN GIVEN TWO PERFECTLY FINE WAYS T' WHILE AWAY TH' TIME LEFT T' ME. POP IN ON TH' NEIGHBORS 'N' START IN DOIN' WHAT I DO BEST...
OR START IN ON HIS BUNCH FOR RECOGNIZIN' ME FOR WHAT I AM. DON'T MATTER TO ME EITHER WAY.
THE CONNECTION BETWEEN SEEIN' AND IDENTIFYIN'... SLOWIN DOWN SOMETHING FIERCE... THAT WAS A WHALE AND NO DOUBT ABOUT IT.
PLUMED... SAW IT PLUME... THAT SAYS IT AIN'T DEAD... SAYS THERE'S STILL LIFE OUT THERE...
SURE... THE OCEAN... CRADLE'A LIFE. 'S ALL GONNA STAT OVER AGAIN... I GET IT NOW! I KNOW WHY ALL OF THIS... ALL THIS DEATH 'N' WALKIN' DEATH... THERE WAS A PURPOSE! THERE WAS! IT WAS... IT...
NO! I CAN'T LOSE IT! NOT NOW! THINK DAMMIT!

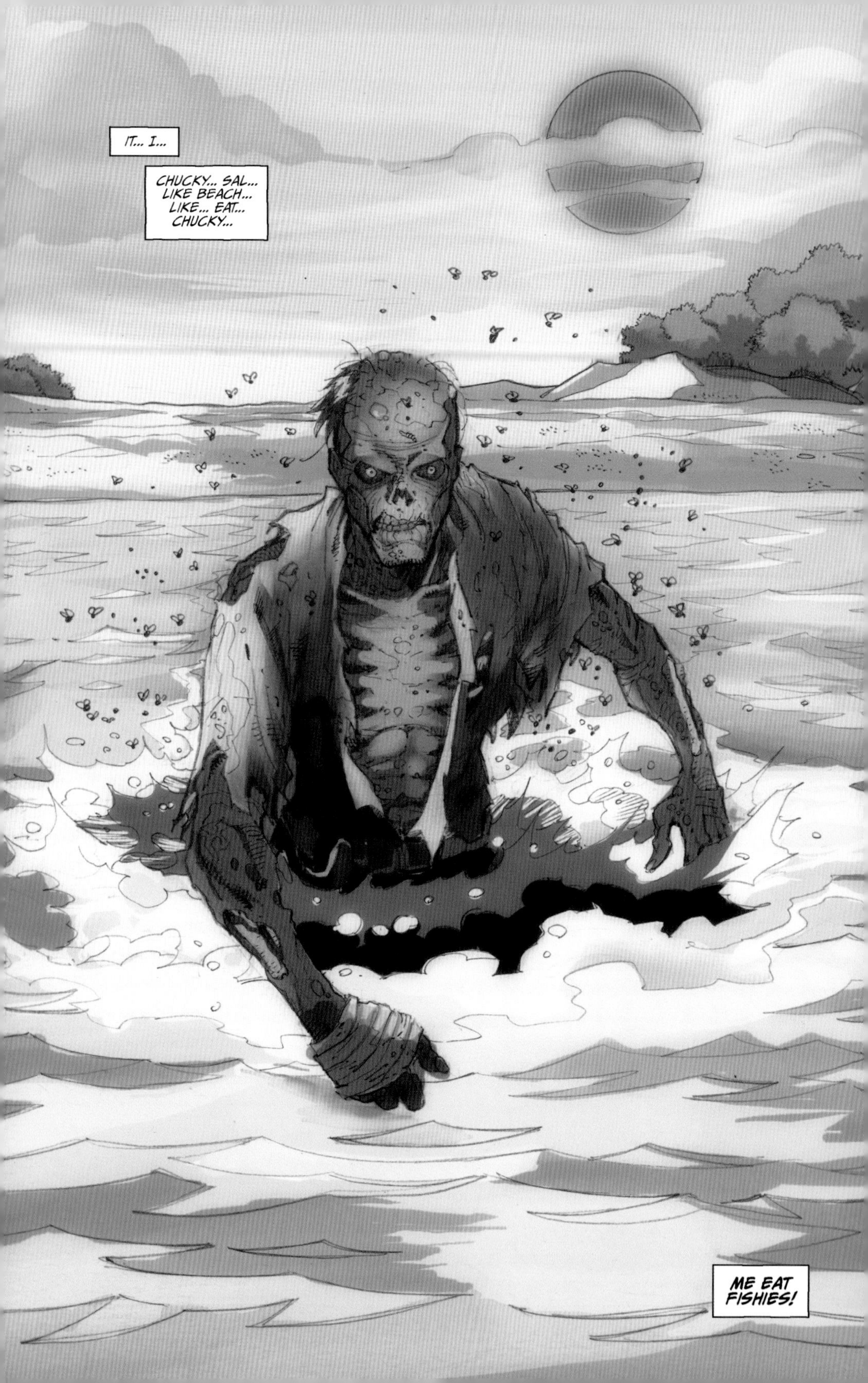
IT... I...
CHUCKY... SAL... LIKE BEACH... LIKE... EAT... CHUCKY...
ME EAT FISHIES!

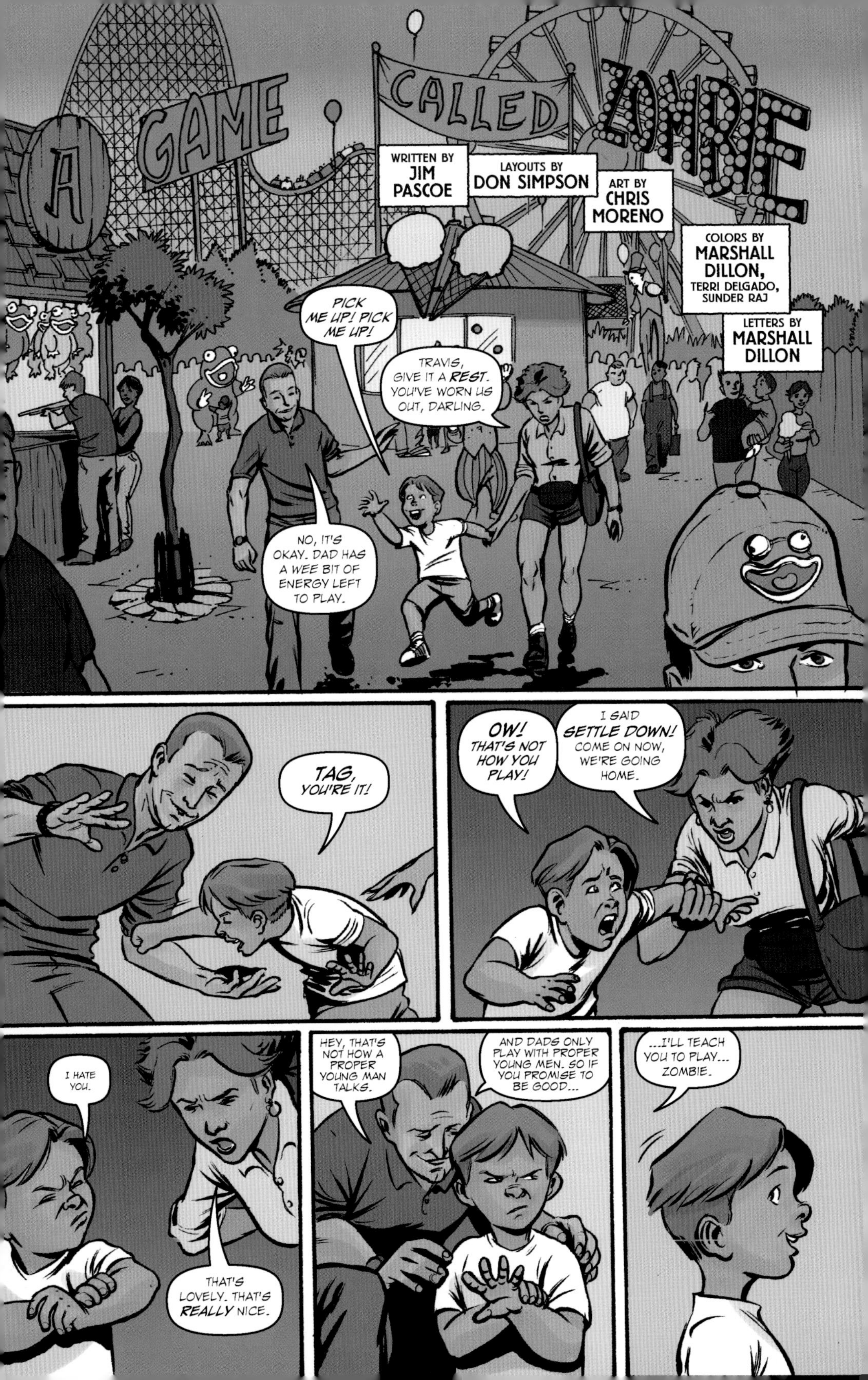
A GAME CALLED ZOMBIE
WRITTEN BY JIM PASCOE
LAYOUTS BY DON SIMPSON
ART BY CHRIS MORENO
COLORS BY MARSHALL DILLON, TERRI DELGADO, SUNDER RAJ
LETTERS BY MARSHALL DILLON
PICK ME UP! PICK ME UP!
TRAVIS, GIVE IT A REST. YOU'VE WORN US OUT, DARLING.
NO, IT'S OKAY. DAD HAS A WEE BIT OF ENERGY LEFT TO PLAY.
TAG, YOU'RE IT!
OW! THAT'S NOT HOW YOU PLAY!
I SAID SETTLE DOWN! COME ON NOW, WE'RE GOING HOME.
I HATE YOU.
THAT'S LOVELY. THAT'S REALLY NICE.
HEY, THAT'S NOT HOW A PROPER YOUNG MAN TALKS.
AND DADS ONLY PLAY WITH PROPER YOUNG MEN. SO IF YOU PROMISE TO BE GOOD...
...I'LL TEACH YOU TO PLAY... ZOMBIE.

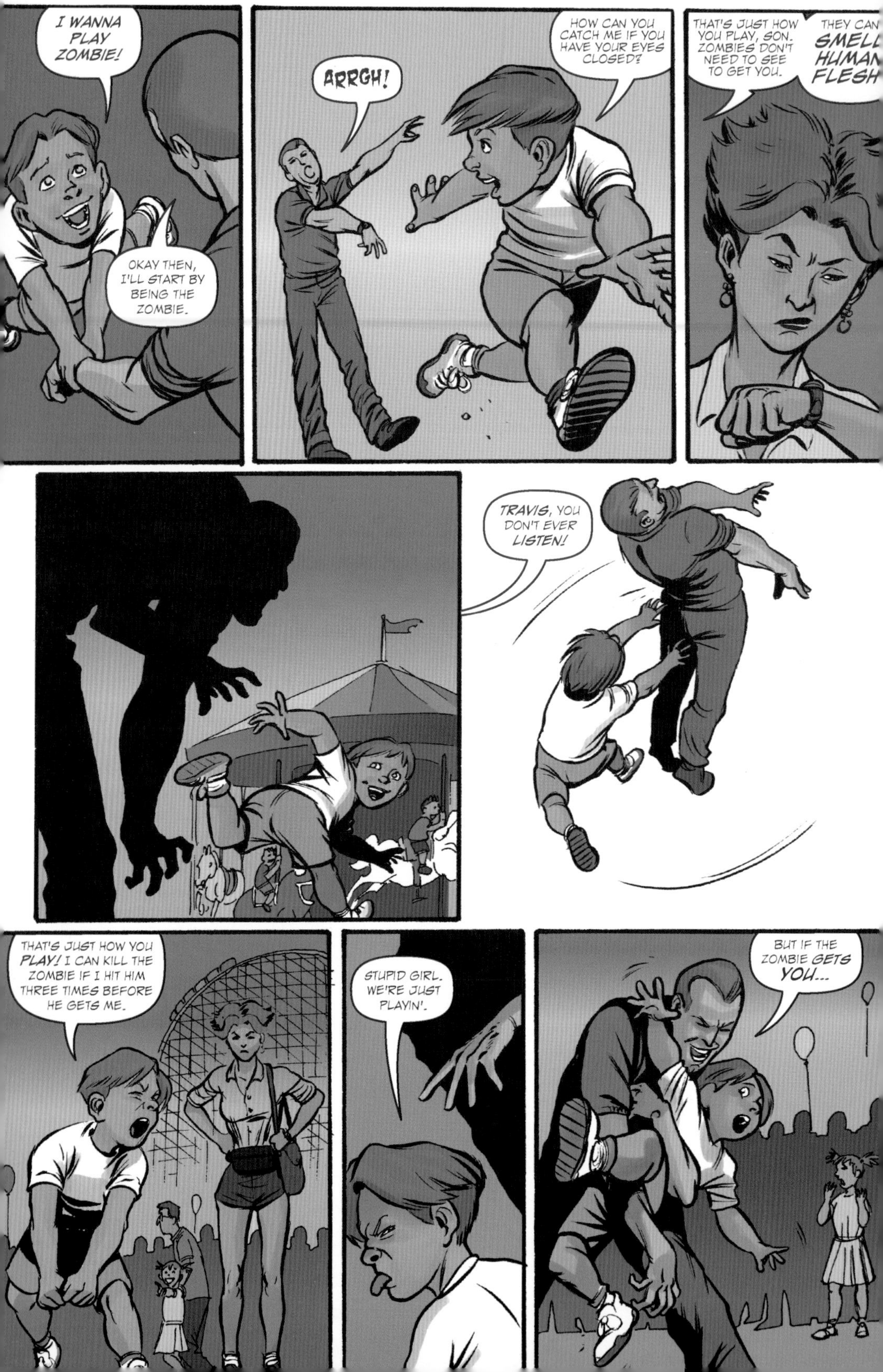
I WANNA PLAY ZOMBIE!
OKAY THEN, I'LL START BY BEING THE ZOMBIE.
ARRGH!
HOW CAN YOU CATCH ME IF YOU HAVE YOUR EYES CLOSED?
THAT'S JUST HOW YOU PLAY, SON. ZOMBIES DON'T NEED TO SEE TO GET YOU.
THEY CAN SMELL HUMAN FLESH
TRAVIS, YOU DON'T EVER LISTEN!
THAT'S JUST HOW YOU PLAY! I CAN KILL THE ZOMBIE IF I HIT HIM THREE TIMES BEFORE HE GETS ME.
STUPID GIRL. WE'RE JUST PLAYIN'.
BUT IF THE ZOMBIE GETS YOU...

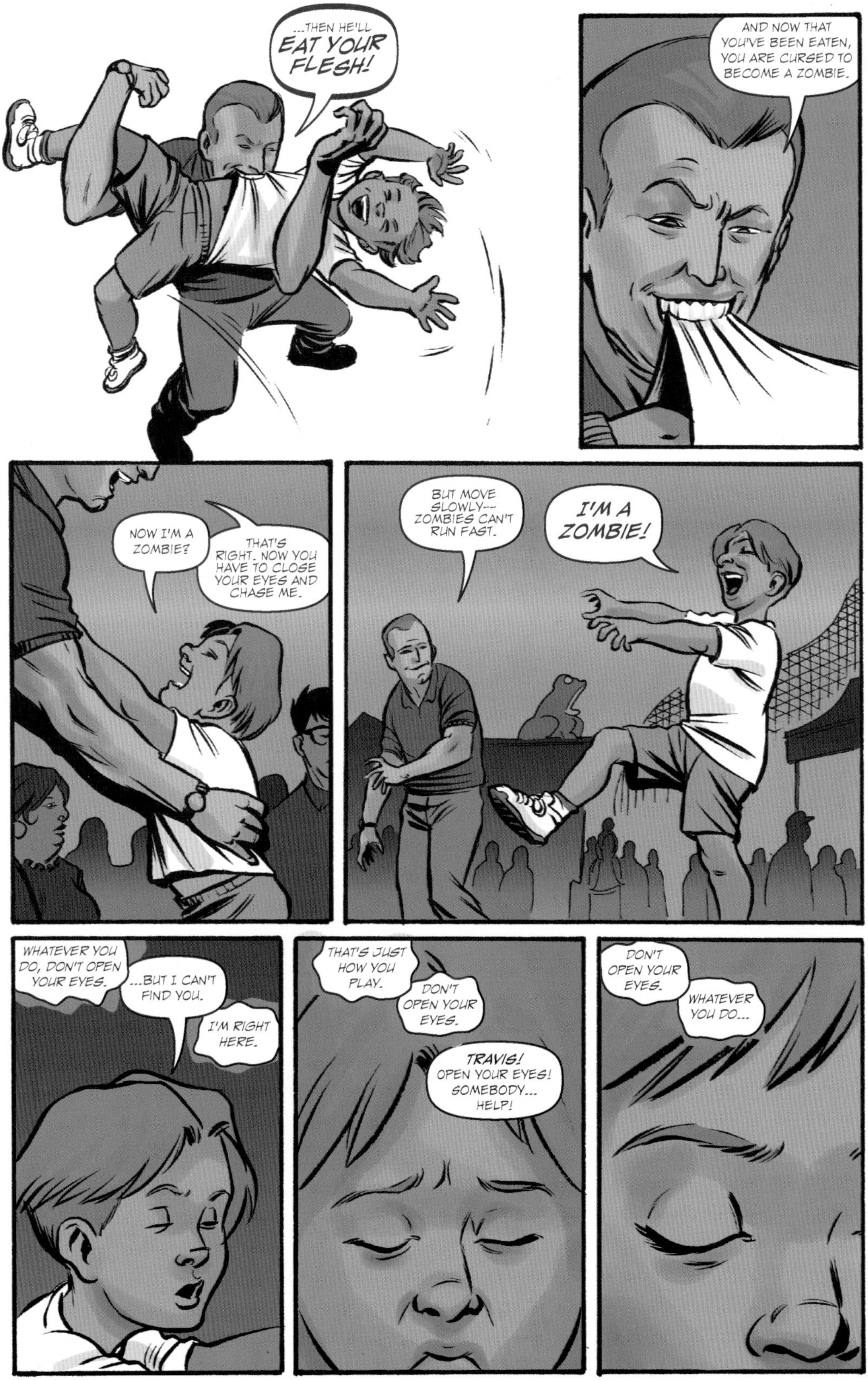
...THEN HE'LL EAT YOUR FLESH!
AND NOW THAT YOU'VE BEEN EATEN, YOU ARE CURSED TO BECOME A ZOMBIE.
NOW I'M A ZOMBIE?
THAT'S RIGHT. NOW YOU HAVE TO CLOSE YOUR EYES AND CHASE ME.
BUT MOVE SLOWLY-- ZOMBIES CAN'T RUN FAST.
I'M A ZOMBIE!
WHATEVER YOU DO, DON'T OPEN YOUR EYES.
...BUT I CAN'T FIND YOU.
I'M RIGHT HERE.
THAT'S JUST HOW YOU PLAY.
DON'T OPEN YOUR EYES.
TRAVIS! OPEN YOUR EYES! SOMEBODY... HELP!
DON'T OPEN YOUR EYES.
WHATEVER YOU DO...

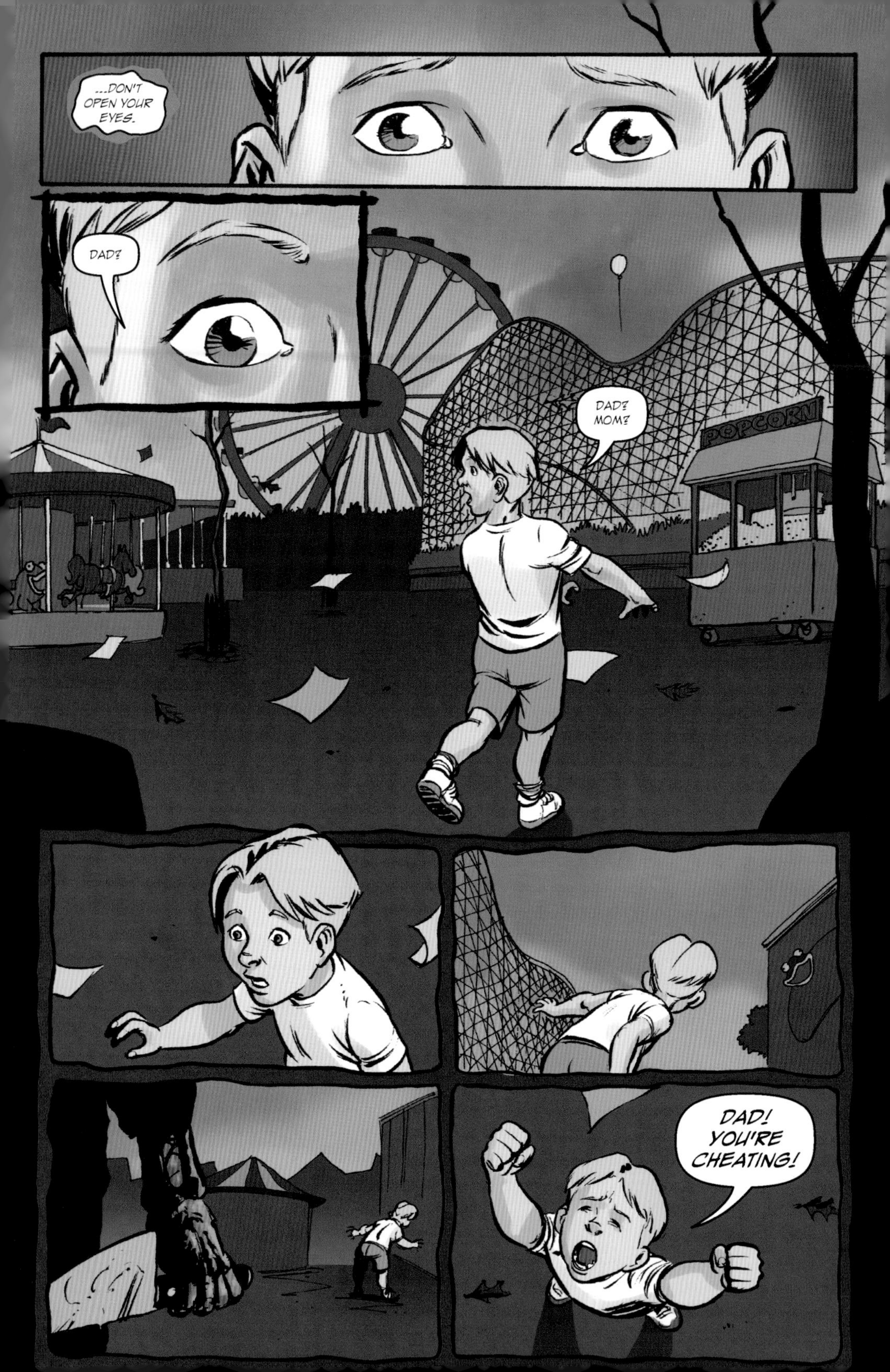
...DON'T OPEN YOUR EYES.
DAD?
DAD? MOM?
POPCORN
DAD! YOU'RE CHEATING!

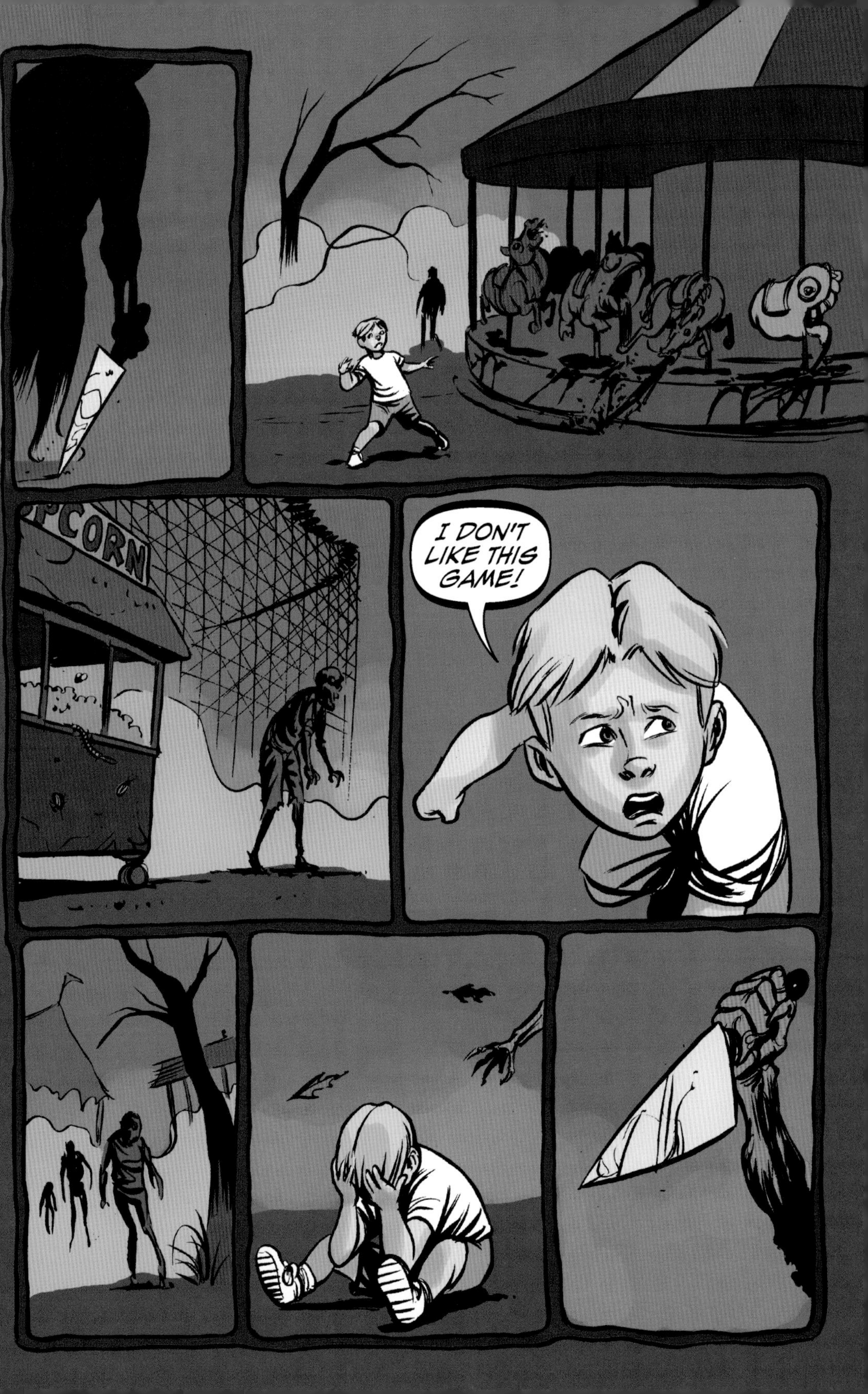
PCORN
I DON'T LIKE THIS GAME!

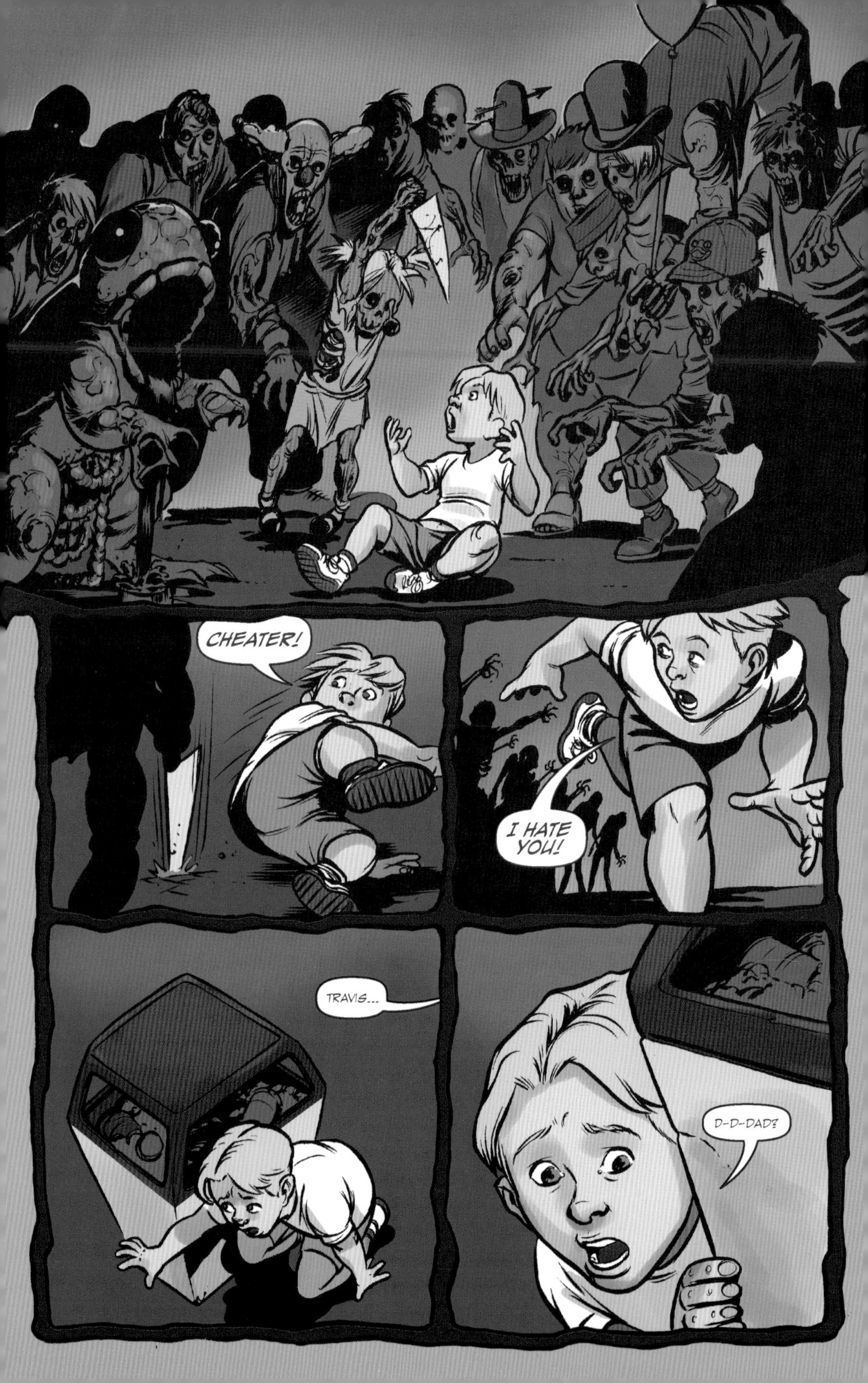
CHEATER!
I HATE YOU!
TRAVIS...
D-D-DAD?

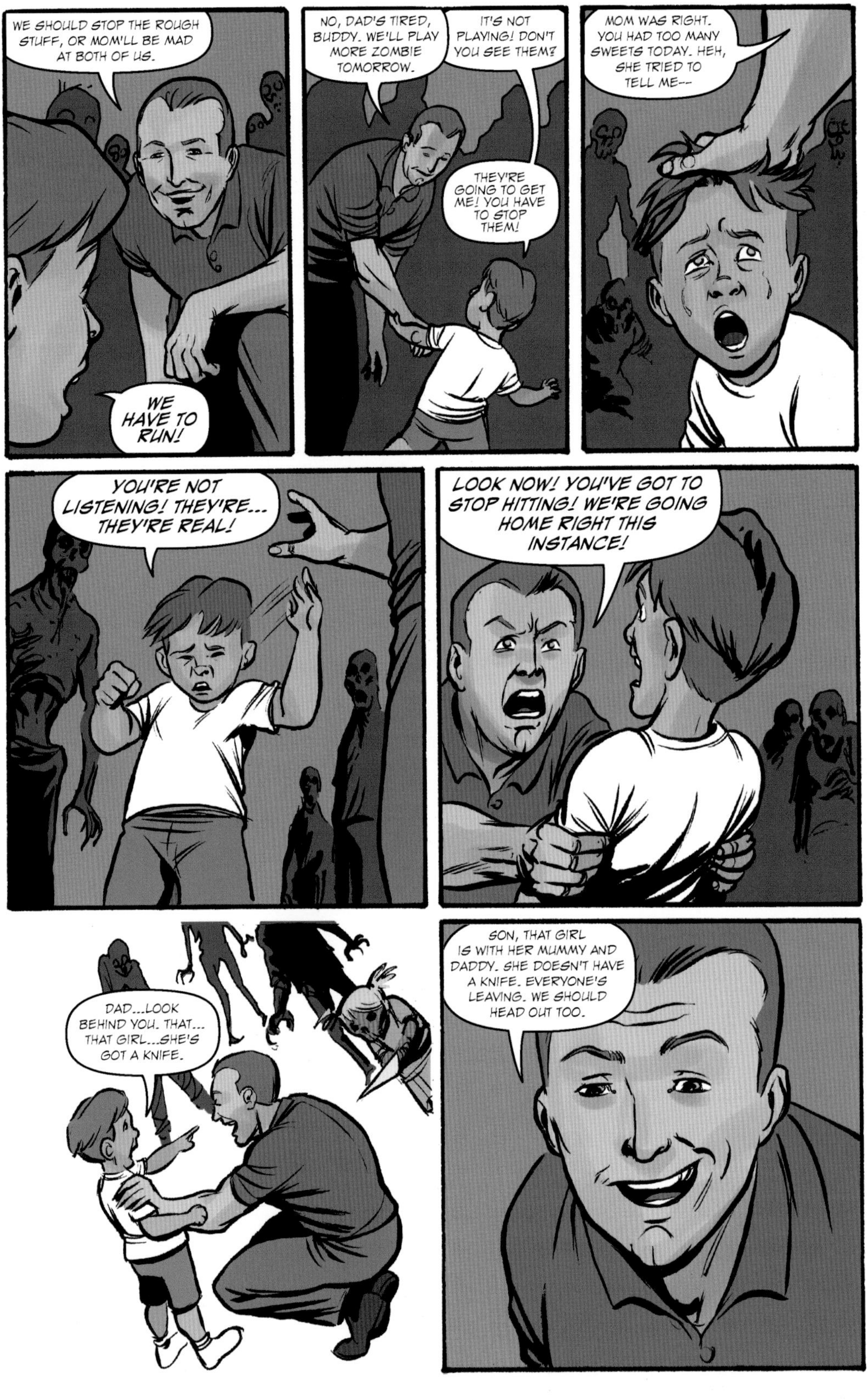
WE SHOULD STOP THE ROUGH STUFF, OR MOM'LL BE MAD AT BOTH OF US.
WE HAVE TO RUN!
NO, DAD'S TIRED, BUDDY. WE'LL PLAY MORE ZOMBIE TOMORROW.
IT'S NOT PLAYING! DON'T YOU SEE THEM?
THEY'RE GOING TO GET ME! YOU HAVE TO STOP THEM!
MOM WAS RIGHT. YOU HAD TOO MANY SWEETS TODAY. HEH, SHE TRIED TO TELL ME--
YOU'RE NOT LISTENING! THEY'RE... THEY'RE REAL!
LOOK NOW! YOU'VE GOT TO STOP HITTING! WE'RE GOING HOME RIGHT THIS INSTANCE!
DAD...LOOK BEHIND YOU. THAT... THAT GIRL...SHE'S GOT A KNIFE.
SON, THAT GIRL IS WITH HER MUMMY AND DADDY. SHE DOESN'T HAVE A KNIFE. EVERYONE'S LEAVING. WE SHOULD HEAD OUT TOO.

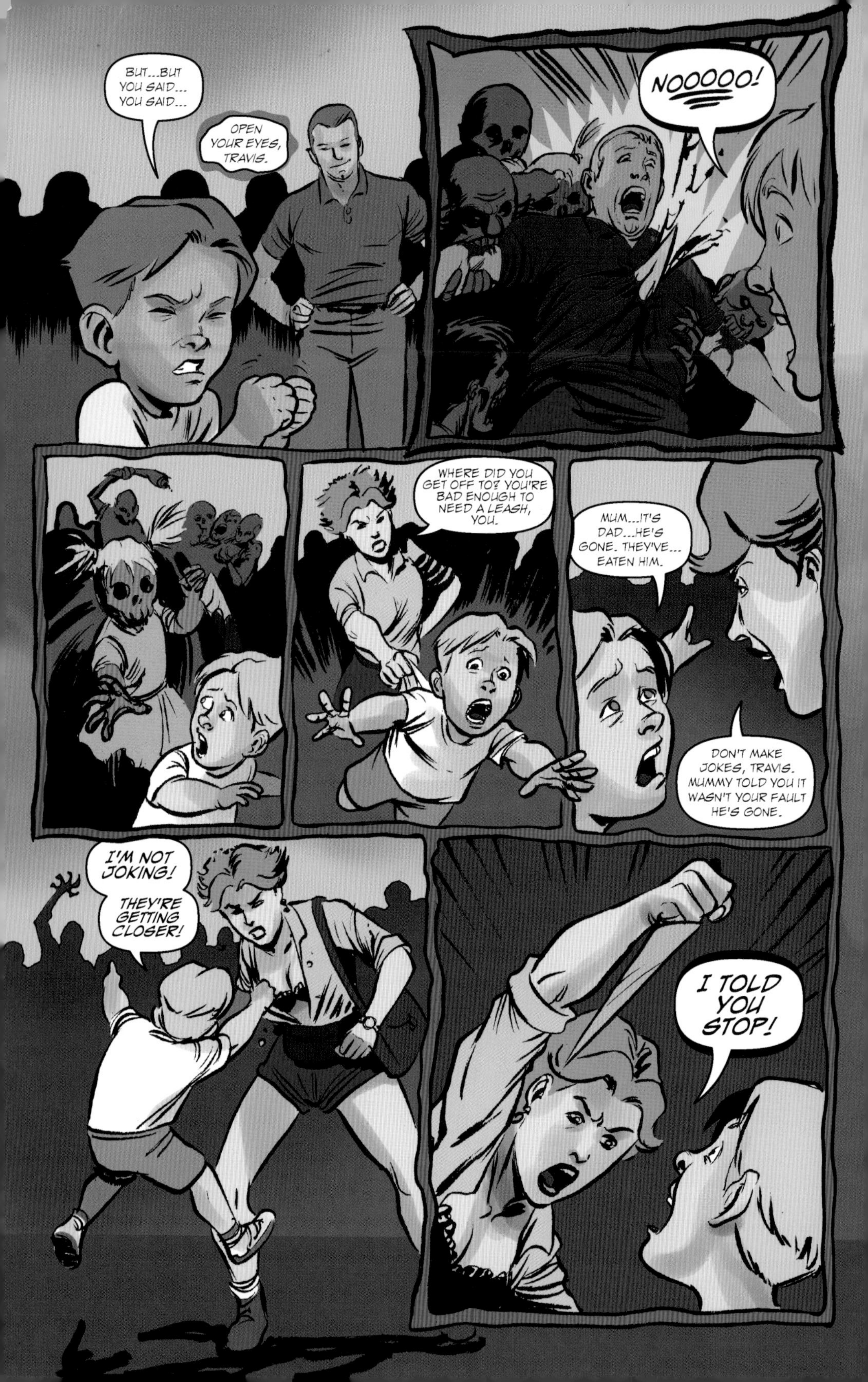
BUT...BUT YOU SAID... YOU SAID...
OPEN YOUR EYES, TRAVIS.
NOOOOO!
WHERE DID YOU GET OFF TO? YOU'RE BAD ENOUGH TO NEED A LEASH, YOU.
MUM...IT'S DAD...HE'S GONE. THEY'VE... EATEN HIM.
DON'T MAKE JOKES, TRAVIS. MUMMY TOLD YOU IT WASN'T YOUR FAULT HE'S GONE.
I'M NOT JOKING!
THEY'RE GETTING CLOSER!
I TOLD YOU STOP!

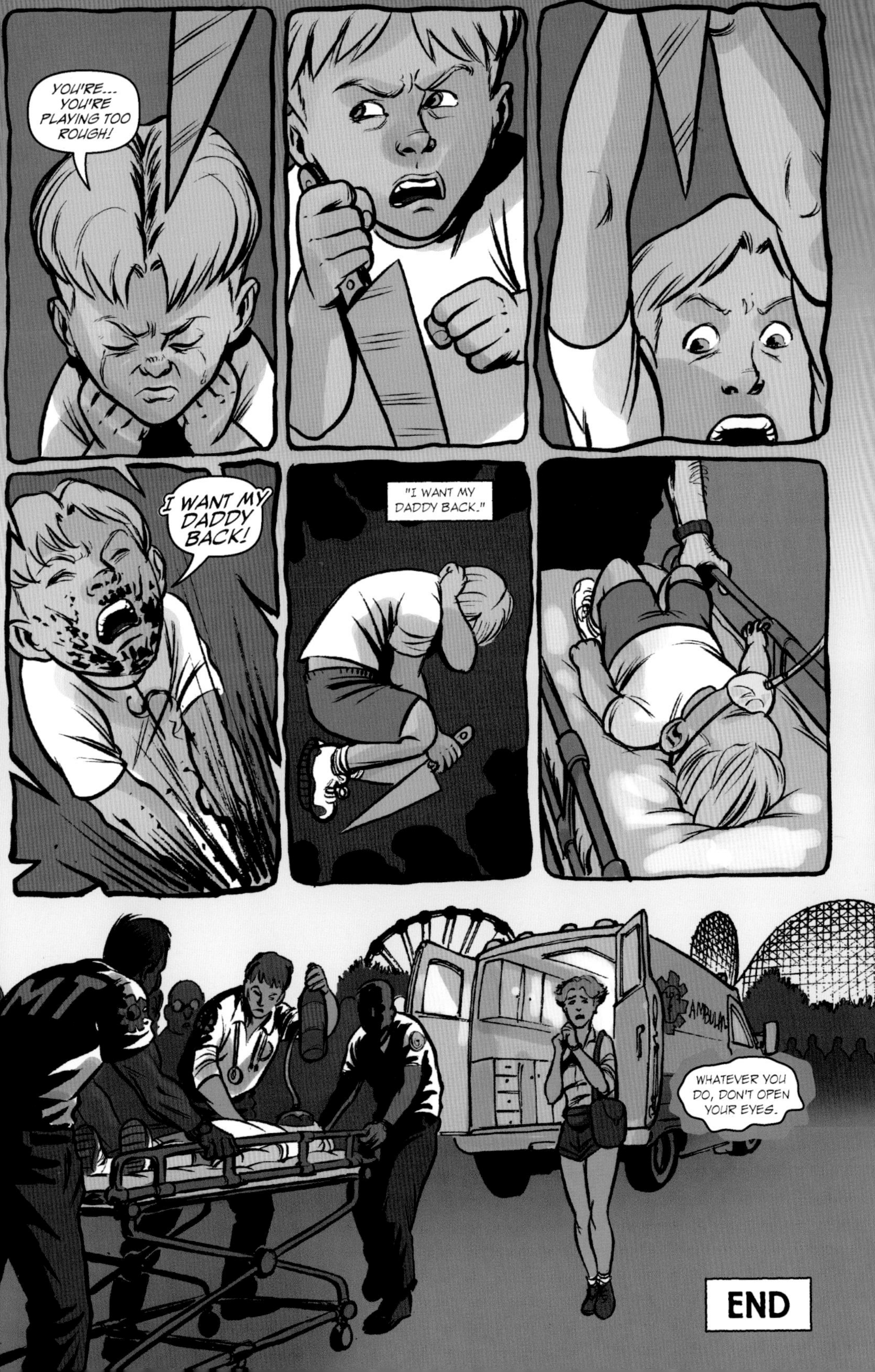
YOU'RE... YOU'RE PLAYING TOO ROUGH!
I WANT MY DADDY BACK!
"I WANT MY DADDY BACK."
WHATEVER YOU DO, DON'T OPEN YOUR EYES.
END